writing to be read

KEN MACRORIE
Emeritus Professor of English
Western Michigan University

writing to be read

revised
third edition

BOYNTON/COOK PUBLISHERS, INC.
UPPER MONTCLAIR, NEW JERSEY 07043

Library of Congress Cataloging in Publication Data

Macrorie, Ken, 1918–
Writing to be read.

Bibliography: p.
Includes index.
1. English language–Composition and exercises.
I. Title.
PE1408.M3326 1984 808'.042 84-14922
ISBN 0-86709-133-9 (previously ISBN 0-8104-5979-5)

For information address Boynton/Cook Publishers, Inc.
52 Upper Montclair Plaza
Upper Montclair, NJ 07043

84 85 86 87 88 5 4 3 2 1

The author would like to thank the proprietors for permission to quote from copyrighted works, as follows:

RAY BRADBURY: from "Seeds of Three Stories," written for *On Writing, By Writers,* William W. West, Editor; copyright 1966 by Ginn and Company. Reprinted by permission of the publisher.

ANATOLE BROYARD: "The Obstetrics of the Soul," a review of *Death as a Fact of Life.* © 1973 by The New York Times Company. Reprinted by permission.

SAMUEL BUTLER: from *The Complete Works of Samuel Butler* and *The Notebooks of Samuel Butler,* published by Jonathan Cape Ltd. Reprinted by permission of the Executors of the Samuel Butler Estate.

TRUMAN CAPOTE: from *Writers at Work, The Paris Review Interviews,* edited by Malcolm Cowley. Copyright © 1957, 1958, by The Paris Review, Inc. Reprinted by permission of The Viking Press, Inc.

STUART CHASE: from "Writing Nonfiction," written for *On Writing, By Writers,* William W. West, Editor; copyright 1966 by Ginn and Company. Reprinted by permission of the publisher.

JOHN CIARDI: from "Work Habits of Writers," written for *On Writing, By Writers,* William W. West, Editor; copyright 1966 by Ginn and Company. Reprinted by permission of the publisher.

W. H. COHEN: translations of two Haiku poems by Issa and Oemaru from *To Walk in Seasons,* compiled and edited by W. H. Cohen, published by Charles E. Tuttle Publishing Co., Inc., Tokyo. Reprinted by permission.

SIDNEY COX: from *Indirections for Those Who Want to Write.* Reprinted with permission of the publisher. Published by Alfred A. Knopf, Inc. Copyright © 1947 by Alfred A. Knopf, Inc.

T. S. ELIOT: from *Writers at Work, The Paris Review Interviews,* Second Series, Copyright © 1963 by The Paris Review, Inc. All rights reserved. Reprinted by permission of The Viking Press, Inc.

MICHIHIKO HACHIYA: from *Hiroshima Diary,* published by the University of North Carolina Press, reprinted by permission of The University of North Carolina Press.

JAMES D. HART: from *Oxford Companion to American Literature,* Fourth Edition. Reprinted by permission of the publisher. Copyright 1965 by Oxford University Press.

ERNEST HEMINGWAY: from *Writers at Work, The Paris Review Interviews,* Second Series, Copyright © 1963 by The Paris Review, Inc. All rights reserved. Reprinted by permission of The Viking Press, Inc.

DOROTHY LAMBERT: "What Is a Journal?" an unpublished MS substantially the same as "Keeping a Journal," published in the *English Journal,* February, 1967, reprinted with the permission of the National Council of Teachers of English and Dorothy Lambert.

ALAN LEVY, BERNARD KRISHER, AND JAMES COX: from *Draftee's Confidential Guide,* published by New American Library, Signet Books. Published by Indiana University Press. Reprinted by permission of Indiana University Press.

ROBERT LIPSYTE: "Mets Beat Giants 8–6 on Swoboda's Homer in 9th," © 1966 by The New York Times Company. Reprinted by permission.

MARIANNE MOORE: from *Writers at Work, The Paris Review Interviews,* Second Series, Copyright © 1963 by The Paris Review, Inc. Reprinted by permission of The Viking Press, Inc.

ANNA QUINDLEN: "About New York," May 27, 1982. Copyright © 1982 by The New York Times Company. Reprinted by permission.

MIKE RECHT: "Mets Shock Giants with Swoboda's Pinch Homer," reprinted with permission of The Associated Press.

G. B. SHAW: from *The Quintessence of Ibsenism,* published by Constable & Co., Ltd., permission of The Public Trustee and The Society of Authors.

JEAN SHEPHERD: "A Midtown Stroll After Midnight," by Jean Shepherd. Reprinted from *The New York Guidebook* edited by John A. Kouwenhoven, Copyright © 1964 by John A. Kouwenhoven and used by permission of the publisher, Dell Publishing Co., Inc.

WALLACE STEVENS: from *Opus Posthumous,* reprinted with permission of the publisher. Copyright 1957. Published by Alfred A. Knopf, Inc.

CHRISTOPHER ST. JOHN: from *Ellen Terry and Bernard Shaw: A Correspondence,* edited by Christopher St. John, published by Constable & Co., Ltd., by permission of The Public Trustee and The Society of Authors.

MAY SWENSON: "The Centaur" (Copyright © 1956 May Swenson) is reprinted with the permission of Charles Scribner's Sons from *To Mix with Time* by May Swenson.

JAMES THURBER: from *Writers at Work, The Paris Review Interviews,* edited by Malcolm Cowley. Copyright © 1957, 1958 by The Paris Review, Inc. Reprinted by permission of The Viking Press, Inc.

WILLIAM CARLOS WILLIAMS: "Poem" from *The Collected Earlier Poems of William Carlos Williams.* Copyright © 1938, 1951 by William Carlos Williams. Reprinted by permission of New Directions Publishing Corporation. "The Dance" from *The Collected Later Poems of William Carlos Williams.* Copyright 1944 by William Carlos Williams.

preface

Most of the student writings
in this book are alive.

They tell truths that are
surprising and memorable.

I can't think of two more shocking statements to be made in a textbook on writing. Out of hundreds of texts I've examined in the last twenty-five years, I've seen no others which present a solid body of good writing done by persons who followed the program in the books.

Yet all such books are supposed to improve the writing of their users. Improve it! Most of the phony, pretentious, dead sentences "composed" in "English" courses do not need improvement, but embalming.

Since writing the first edition of this book I have talked with hundreds of teachers around the country who are ashamed that American taxpayers pay money to support the teaching of writing which no one wants to read. The publication of *Writing to Be Read* was one of several indications that these individuals were not alone in their feeling. Conversations and correspondence with them have shown me that fundamental in the making of writers is not a knowledge of this or that grammatical point, a strategy of style, or a strong desire to write, but fully carrying out the act of writing to be read by real persons who respond.

New material in this third edition helps put that act into process for students and teachers: an Introduction about the powerful effects of reading aloud what one writes, a replacement for Chapter 21, now called " 'Tell Me Something' Interviews," and, in Chapter 17, new assignments that carry writers through comparison and contrast in ways that produce genuine analysis.

Most of the examples of good writing cited in this book are the work of students who have followed part of the program it embodies. Some wrote in my classes; many wrote in the classes of John Bennett of

Central High School, Kalamazoo, Michigan, who for six years published with me a broadsheet of our students' writing.

Here I wish to thank all teachers around the country who have sent me writing by their students—so much that I have occasionally lost the source of a writing used in this book. Luckily none was copyrighted, so I have committed no low crimes or misdemeanors; but I apologize to anyone not properly thanked.

I will not repeat my thanks to all those named in the first edition of this book, but simply speak my gratefulness this time to Sister Marie Tucker of St. Teresa's Academy (Kansas City, Missouri); James Gardner of Manchester Community College (Connecticut); Mary Ann Gates of Hickman High School (Columbia, Missouri); James Giachino, formerly of Berkshire Community College (Pittsfield, Massachusetts); Marjorie Donker of Western Washington State College; Will Brenner of East Grand Rapids High School (Michigan); Mindy Stiles, practice teaching at South Junior High School (Kalamazoo, Michigan); Patrick Morey, whose address I cannot locate; Lynne Alvine, of Parry McCluer High School in Buena Vista, Virginia, whose students provided most of the interviews for Chapter 21; and my editor, Robert Boynton, whose contributions as a publisher to the teaching of English are without parallel.

The notion of free writing, so fundamental to the program presented here, comes from a suggestion to persons who want to become professional writers made by Dorothea Brande in *Becoming a Writer* (Harcourt, Brace, 1934).

K.M.

Santa Fe, NM

contents

Preface

Introduction 1

1 The Language in You 9

2 Writing Freely 14

Telling truths, 14
Writing freely without focus, 17
Writing freely with focus, 20

3 What Is Good Writing? 25

4 Tightening 34

5 Deceiving Oneself 41

6 People Talking 52

7 Fabulous Realities 60

8 Writing Case Histories 67

9 Repeating 75

Weak and strong repetition, 75
Parallel construction, 80

10 The Helping Circle 84

11 Remembering Childhood 95

Achieving distance, 95
Beginnings and endings, 104

12 Sharpening 109

13 Creating Form 119

Patterns, 119
The hook, 125

14 Playing with Words 127

15 Your Subject Choosing You 140

16 Keeping a Journal 155

17 Writing Secondhand 168

Showing why a writing affects you, 172

18 Controlling Sound 185

19 Writing Reports 195

The live core, 195
The alternating current, 207

20 Writing Poems 214

21 "Tell Me Something" Interviews 230

22 The Order of Words 244

23 Observing Conventions 253

Dialogue, 254
Semicolons, commas, periods, dashes, colons, 254
Signals for emphasis, 257
Numerals, 258
Titles, 259
Signaling possession, 259
Scholarly writing, 260
Borrowing words, 264

Suggestions to Teachers 266

List of Sources 277

Index 283

writing to be read

introduction

One summer, some of the brightest young teachers in America and I read *The Declaration of Independence,* a newspaper feature story, and a research report about writing. They moved us. We asked why.

Analyzing them, we found those pieces of writing strongest when most of their sentences seemed to have been spoken by an individual in the grip of feeling as well as in command of ideas and information.

At times, Thomas Jefferson was so moved in writing the *Declaration* that his sentences took on a *voice.* They seemed *alive.* Speaking of the King of England, he wrote:

> He has erected a multitude of New Offices, and sent hither swarms of Officers to harass our People, and eat out their substance . . .
>
> He has plundered our seas, ravaged our Coasts, burnt our towns, and destroyed the lives of our people.

An angry man is speaking there. You may say that the sentences—with their parallel structure, "plundered . . . ravaged . . . burnt . . . and destroyed"—are more formal than you hear in conversation. But that's not true, and the reverse is my point. If we study the conversation of people in the grip of emotion, we often find it full of parallel structure (as well as alliteration, assonance, and other "writing" devices.) "I can't stand it! You don't empty the wastebaskets, you don't do the dishes, you don't keep the house in order, and yet you want credit for staying home and being the housewife while I, the woman, earn the money for the groceries!" That's parallel structure also, and the words were not written in Congress, but spoken in the kitchen.

In that seminar at Bread Loaf Graduate School of English in Vermont, the second printed piece we looked at and listened to was a column by the *New York Times* writer Anna Quindlen about a receptionist in the RCA Building. The words of this newspaper story (March 27, 1982) captivated us also:

> Millie has a big book of what companies are on what floors in the 14 Rockefeller Center buildings for which she is responsible. She has pamphlets about tourist attractions and restaurants. But nearly all the information that anyone could ever want about the center and the city is "up here," as Millie likes to say, patting the rise of parti-colored light hair above her high forehead.

Part of the aliveness of Quindlen's column arises from what Millie says in her own words. The piece ends like this:

> Millie was 69 years old this week. "You can have my age, I don't give a hoot," she said. In exactly a year, she will reach retirement age. The question is who can replace her . . . "It will take somebody a while before they will have it all up here," she said, patting her hair again.

In our seminar we tried to pin down the characteristics of writings that delighted, informed, and moved us—whether they were done by professionals or us. We were reading both aloud regularly to each other. One of the characteristics of live writing was that the writers had something to say that had counted for them, and was still counting for them as they wrote. Another characteristic was that this caring about it, and often being moved by it, got into their words, which then took on rhythms that in turn moved us.

We found that even a research report could be live if the author believed strongly in its findings and their usefulness. Here are the opening lines to a Ford Foundation Research Report by Donald Graves (1978):

> People want to write. The desire to express is relentless. People want others to know what they hold to be truthful. They need the sense of authority that goes with authorship. They need to detach themselves from experience and examine it by writing.

When we recorded the effect of dozens of pieces of our own writing that were read aloud in the seminar, we concluded that live writing could arise not only when a piece was emotional, but also when it was what we call *philosophic.* For example:

> We hold these truths to be self-evident, that all men are created equal, that they are endowed by their Creator with certain unalienable rights, that among these are Life, Liberty and the pursuit of Happiness . . .

or factual:

> . . . Millie Ferrer, who greets much of the immediate world from behind a great black marble slab of a desk, as long as a city bus, at the entrance to the RCA Building in Rockefeller Center.

We found that live writing doesn't waste words and carries surprises, both in what it says and how it says it. No clichés. No tedious recounting of old stuff. New, strong comparisons.

I could go on for pages analyzing what makes that writing alive, but I think you can hear that above all it possesses a *voice,* and commands our attention the way a person speaking to us forcefully commands it.

READING ALOUD

In the seminar at Bread Loaf those teachers and I discovered what should have been obvious to us throughout our careers—that if the best writing has *voice,* we should deal with writing more as if it's a speaking act than we do. This was a truth we stumbled on more than worked out. One day when a teacher was reading aloud the writing of another so we could all help the writer improve it, I realized that his bad reading was killing the writing and its author. Why was the reader reading it badly? That teacher had undoubtedly read aloud many pieces of writing in front of classes. I noticed that as the director of the seminar, I usually read aloud the writings better than the others did. Why? We were all teachers in that room. Eventually I understood. When the teachers turned their writings into me, I read them outside class before they saw them. Then they read the writings cold, never having seen them before. And so they had to figure out the meaning and purpose of a paper phrase by phrase, sentence by sentence while reading aloud. Often, not knowing what was coming next, the reader would fail to give the words the right intonation and emphasis. But the papers I read aloud in class I had seen before, and understood what the authors were trying to say.

When we talk in ordinary conversation, we're in charge of our meaning and intention. So we just form the words in our mouths and throat, and they come out miraculously said just right for their meaning. We never say "I had the most exciting experience in my life today!" in a monotone. We never speak that sentence emphasizing the word *in*. We have learned to intone and emphasize words in ways that best express their meaning, and unless we're scared by our audience or physically ill, we do the job of "reading aloud" our speech just about perfectly. And we control all those human powers of expression—rhythm, emphasis, tone, pitch, pause, etc.—unconsciously. Before we speak the angry sentence, "I'm going, and you can stay here!" we don't say to ourselves, "Now which word should I emphasize most! Oh yes, the word *you*." We just launch into the sentence and hit *you* hard without thinking. When we feel condescending or sarcastic, we don't have to tell our voice to sound that way. It just does.

So in the seminar we found we all knew how to read aloud because we know how to speak aloud. We've already got that knowledge and ability. If the passage of printed or handwritten writing in front of us contains words we don't know or thoughts we can't understand, then we won't read it well. But otherwise we will. We soon found that out in this way:

1. Sitting in a circle, we wrote for ten minutes or maybe a half hour in class. Then all of us passed our papers several chairs to the right.
2. We agreed to try to read the papers aloud in a natural way, not as showoff actors. We promised to capitalize on our ability to speak sentences meaningfully, with all our years of acquired skill in phrasing, building rhythms, emphasizing, finding the right tone and pitch for particular sentences by thinking not of ourselves but of their meanings.
3. We took the paper we had been passed and walked away from the others to a spot where we could read it aloud to ourselves quietly in order to get its meaning and intention.
4. To the whole seminar, two people then read the papers they had been given. Then we split into groups of four and finished up reading aloud all the papers.
5. Later, I asked the teachers to read their own work aloud to themselves before they brought it to class. And if possible, to get someone else, relative or friend, to take the writer's paper and read it

aloud for meaning as we did in class, first with a rehearsal and then confronting the writer.

During both these read-alouds of the paper, the author caught weak repetitions, bad word choices, and grammatical errors. Automatically, voices and ears made these read-alouds into editing sessions. And beyond that, the responders' involuntary reactions to the flow of words, actions, and ideas in the writing became valuable to the writer.

When we read those papers aloud, we felt good because we knew we were doing justice to the writer's paper. We had presented it in a way that pleased the writer and made its full force felt by the listeners. We did that partly because we knew that our good reading of someone else's paper would probably bring forth a good reading of our own paper by another member of the seminar. We were putting ourselves in touch with all the powers human beings own as speaking animals.

. . .

The use of that strategy lifted the performance of the seminar members in many ways. It made us a group working for each other. We began to wonder why that simple act did so much for our writing. Here are some of the reasons we came up with:

—We learn language first by *talking* it out with our mothers. We call that basic code our "Mother Tongue." Our mothers never have any doubt that we will learn to speak that language, complex as it is, very quickly. Never any doubt—because they know learning to speak is our entrance into the human race. The task is often pleasant and full of rewards—like cookies, and hugs, and oohs and aahs from Mom and Dad.

—As young kids, most of us are entranced by parents or grandparents reading aloud or telling us fairy stories, animal stories, etc. Apparently the words take on a magic property because we see and hear someone we trust putting them into the air where we can grab them. We associate the stories with that person and the way she or he utters them. It's an event, that reading, a ceremony unlike the act we're forced to carry out later in school—reading *silently* and being tested on our ability to do so. In some schoolrooms we're even told never to whisper-mumble the words we're reading in books or to form our lips as if to make the sounds.

I think of the great speech therapist Charles Van Riper once telling me that often when people see a badly dressed person walking down a street talking to herself or himself, they conclude that the person is crazy. Yet we all talk to ourselves, he said, and should. Talking to ourselves helps us think, because we take ourselves into a conversation (between *I* and *me*) that enables us to consider more objectively what we have just thought. Or we play with the sounds of words, loll them on our tongues and savor them.

Walking through airports lately I've seen dozens of people in conversation at pay phones lining the corridors. Almost all of them gesture broadly with the hand that isn't holding the phone. They move back and forth on feet that seem wired to the meaning of what they're saying. The other day I drove several blocks behind a car in which the man driving was talking to a woman sitting on his right. All the while, he was gesturing broadly and brilliantly with his left hand, which he held extended out the window. I saw him wave away an idea, run his fingers through a dance that reminded me of a piano player's hand on a keyboard, and point his index finger back at his companion on the right. It was a performance that he couldn't resist giving. I believe there is an energy in our speaking words that we should take advantage of in writing, and we undoubtedly tap some of it when our writing carries a *voice*. Our intended meaning charges us up. Speaking and writing are performing arts.

—I say those things because writing is more like conversation than we realize. It's talking to others on paper—although they may be far away in space and time. There are differences between speech and writing. When we speak, we usually repeat words more than we do in writing. We back up, drop ideas, and then move forward again. We stammer more in speech than in writing. If we tape record our everyday conversation we're embarrassed by its sloppiness, but we shouldn't criticize ourselves severely because in conversation we're communicating partly by our expression and body language, which we can't utilize when writing. Still, with all those differences, our writing is, or should be, very much like speech.

—Most people do little reading aloud once their children are grown beyond fairy stories. And yet reading aloud does so much more than reading silently, for the text and for us. It makes us not only speaker, but listener, and we are used to listening to words for meaning more than we are to looking at them for meaning. We talk and listen constantly with others. Speaking is not simply something we often do socially, it's what makes us human beings. We touch and embrace people and dance or play games with them, but our central activity with others is conversing. At times many of us are poor listeners, but we catch a great deal from listening. We have to. It's one of our defenses in life, a survival technique. We must ever be listening to others because they may say something that makes a difference in our lives. There may be fire in the next room. Someone may be cheating us. We may miss the changed time for the party. So reading aloud a piece of writing, whether written by a friend, a published author, or ourselves, keeps us in touch with language in the way we most habitually deal with it.

—When we hear a sermon or lecture or read a textbook, we seldom feel the same urgency to get the meaning because it isn't aimed at us as known, particular individuals. That's why reading aloud most textbooks is a torture. But even doing that would help us get meaning, because it goes back to a basic element of conversing—listening.

—When we read aloud with understanding, sometimes we get more meaning than when we read silently with understanding. The writer seems to be talking to us. When we read our own writing aloud we're creating another voice—as if someone else is speaking to us, and we're back in the conversational mode, back in that ceremony of meaning.

It's much more of an effort to read aloud than to read silently. We must gear up to produce that column of air, we must take the time to voice the words. But the payoff is handsome. Those teachers at Bread Loaf and I are just beginning to realize how much making that effort counts in the making of meaning. Often we will learn so much more from a printed text, even when we're alone with it, if we will force ourselves to read it aloud.

THE USES OF READING ALOUD

Outside school we usually *speak* our intended meaning relatively clearly and quickly. That's because we're doing *free speaking.* That is, we're not worrying about our grammar or the level or appropriateness of our vocabulary. We're just putting some words into the air and expecting collaboration from listeners in making meaning out of them. Many writing teachers have found that *free writing,* as we miscall it, has enabled many people to write with a great deal more power than they achieve when they're trying to write school-language that will satisfy an English teacher.

Here are some truths I've only recently realized about myself:

1. When I'm proofreading my own writing, I find more errors when reading aloud than when reading silently.
2. When I flub a word in reading a writing aloud, often I find that this word was not well chosen, or the whole sentence in which it occurs is poorly constructed.
3. When I'm writing at my best, I hear the words I'm putting down on paper. They sound in my head.
4. When I'm reading a passage of someone else's writing—printed

or handwritten—that I like, I hear a voice in my head uttering the words aloud.

5. There are few things worse than having to sit and listen to another person read aloud badly something I've written that I like.

As the director of the seminar I've mentioned, I asked the teachers to soak themselves in reading aloud, to read everything aloud they could without being thought mentally ill. I suggested that in their world outside the classroom they read aloud advertisements in the newspaper, signs they passed by, words that struck their eye. In the seminar, I asked the teachers to read aloud announcements that I customarily read myself to the group. "Please read this aloud off in the corner to yourself, or mumble through it at your seat, and then read it aloud to all of us."

For a number of days running I read aloud to the group for five or ten minutes some piece of writing that I cared a great deal about. Before I did that, I read through the piece aloud on my own, thinking of meaning and the author's intention. I asked the teachers then to do the same thing in their rooms or in the student center on the Bread Loaf campus, and then come together in class in groups of four and read aloud a printed piece they cared about. I wanted all of them, shy or confident, to become at ease reading aloud to others. And they did.

In that seminar in every way we sounded writing. We enjoyed that, and became better readers and better writers. In that room, well-written words filled the air, and their rhythms and tones got in our ears, into our pores. It was like getting wet with sounded meaning.

But also in that seminar we came to realize that to be powerful, a writing has to be more than just alive in its sound. It has to have a core of fact or fiction, and some firm flesh, as you get in a Jonathan apple. It can't be a little old shriveled-up brown thing. It has to be a whole fresh apple, something you can bite into several times and that will stay with you after you've eaten it. What is there must be rounded and in some way complete.

School is all wrong. They ask you what you don't know, not what you know. When I took the test in sixth grade, "Where is Cape Fear?" I said I didn't know but that I could give the names of the Twelve Apostles and I did.

ROBERT MORLEY, BRITISH ACTOR

chapter 1 the language in you

THOUSANDS of persons in the United States believe they don't know how to write well. But look at what children do. A third-grade girl writes:

> **When mother fride my egg this morning it limbered out like corn surp. Then it got buggles. They went up, then went down, like breethen heavy.**

The writer surprised the reader with an original use of the verb *limber,* meaning to become supple or flexible. She compared the movement of the egg to the slow spreading of corn syrup in a pan. She invented her own term, *buggles* (playing on *bubbles*), and showed she knew what she was talking about. She compactly described the movement of a frying egg. This passage is not only fresh and surprising but precise and true. It puts the reader there, watching the egg and feeling its action through his own experience, "like breethen heavy."

At times all children make memorable statements in writing or speaking. But as they advance in school, their language turns ever duller and emptier. By the time they become seniors in high school, they are often submitting paragraphs to their teacher that sound like the one writtten by this boy:

> **I consider experience to be an important part in the process of learning. For example, in the case of an athlete, experience plays an important role. After each game, he tends to acquire more knowledge and proficiency, thereby making him a better athlete. An athlete could also gain more knowledge by studying up on the sport, but it is doubtful if he could participate for the first time in sport with study alone and without experience and still do an adequate job.**

The writer says nothing new—athletes learn by experience. And he doesn't put the reader there, watching a player bunt foul or tackle a tailback. A five-year-old boy at breakfast says, "The Rice Krispies are doing the dead man's float." He doesn't tell the reader anything new either, but he speaks originally. With the metaphor he puts the reader in the milk.

A second-grader told to quiet her feet in class said, "They're too Saturday to listen." She expected the listener to make the jump necessary to understand her metaphor. The boy writing about athletes expected nothing of his reader.

A sixth-grader wrote a letter to the custodian of a state park who had showed his class around:

> **Dear Mr. Lemmien,**
>
> **I liked the trailer ride and the dips got my stomach. Thank you for everything.**
>
> **Your Friend,**
> **David Booth**

David communicated a significant moment in five short words: "the dips got my stomach." The word *dips* gives the passage authority. The sentence is believable, unforgettable. None of the sentences in the writing about athletes carries as much meaning.

Young children don't always talk and write with such point and liveliness, but they do so often enough that their parents repeat their sayings and writings to other persons with delight. When these children grow up and become high school and college students, they seldom turn in writing that is memorable. Yet outside class, they often use language with power.

Entering the school cafeteria, a girl says that she can't see a clear table. Her friend answers:

> **I don't see one either. It's like looking for your best friend at the Rose Bowl on T.V.**

At times you have spoken and written skillfully. You can rediscover your tongue—if you've lost it—and bring your writing to life. One way is to take the pressure off for a while. In schoolrooms where students have been asked to write freely, they have written like this:

> **I like to go fishing. But I don't like to touch the soft, elongated, repulsive nightcrawlers. They wiggle and contract themselves. Then I can't grab the one I want. Of all the other things in this world I can't stand, baiting the hook is the worst. It's like giving a shot. Sometimes the hook won't go through the worm's wrinkled, slimy body. Then I have to wiggle and force it. That's like stepping on a cockroach and hearing the bones crack, or piercing a stubborn earlobe.**

GERTIE BAX

> **The wooden bars on the chair look like prison bars as they reflect on the floor from the light. I was in trouble once and getting into trouble makes a person feel bad that it happened and that it never should have happened but it did and there is no way around. I had to sit in a room for three hours waiting, hoping that my brother would be all right and hoping the other boy was too, although from those minutes on, I knew I hated him. Only a chair, a desk, and a man saying, "I'll be back in about a half hour," which really became three. I had to sweat it out walking back and forth in the room with nothing to look at but four lousy walls, I wanted to get out. I wanted them to come and get me out of there. Thoughts passed through my mind as I sat there in the only chair. Chairs can be made to look like different things when their shadow is lying on the floor. The chair over there in the corner looks like part of a ladder.**

> **The chair in the police station was uncomfortable and I couldn't sit in it. It was a cheap looking chair in a cheap looking room meant for people who are wrong.**
>
> (NAME WITHHELD)

A girl once told her teacher that she couldn't write any kind of paper because she had been raised in a Polish-speaking home and couldn't compose sentences in idiomatic English. Encouraged to write freely of what she cared about, she wrote this of her father:

> **The only difference between him and a lion is that a lion does not laugh. Upon meeting up with him, one most naturally will see the strict lines on his face and his mouth set just so. He may appear tough, but he also has the devil in him. His appearance is stirring. He looks like a foreign foreigner. His voice is low and scary. It really frightens my friends, even male ones. Sometimes when I call to say I may be home later, he answers the phone with a deep, husky, and broken "Haaallooo" and I feel I should apologize for calling.**
>
> (NAME WITHHELD)

Outside of class, and in the years of childhood, you and every other person have at times expressed yourself forcefully, with art. It's nonsense to say you can't do that again when you want to.

> *Man's maturity: to have regained the seriousness that he had as a child at play.*
>
> FRIEDRICH NIETZSCHE

COLLECTING ONE: Listen for what children say and look for what they write. Use a tape recorder if available. Write down five statements you think are memorable. Include the age of the child if possible and the situation in which he spoke or wrote. Ask your parents if they remember a phrase you spoke when you were young. Perhaps they preserved a bit of your writing. Record children's statements that are remarkable because they reveal freshness, accuracy, and invention in language. Do not record statements that are humorous only because the child speaks out of ignorance of the world or of language.

COLLECTING TWO: The language in that pretentious paragraph beginning "I consider experience" was once dubbed *Engfish* by a student. You see it in school work and government publications and business letters. "The area of disagreement which led to the outbreak of hostilities could be characterized as involving territorial questions relating to the possession and utilization of waterways." What the writer meant to say was "The war broke out over the ownership of the Suez Canal." Look for examples of Engfish. Collect three or more and bring them to class.

On a huge hill,
Cragged and steep, Truth stands, and he that will
Reach her, about must, and about must go . . .

JOHN DONNE

chapter 2 writing freely

TELLING TRUTHS

ALL GOOD writers speak in honest voices and tell the truth. For example, here is Eudora Welty in her novel *Delta Wedding* writing about India, a girl of nine, watching her Uncle George make up with his wife after a quarrel:

> Just now they kissed, with India coming up close on her toes to see if she could tell yet what there was about a kiss.

Asked what makes students write badly, Eudora Welty once said:

> The trouble with bad student writing is the trouble with all bad writing. It is not serious, and it does not tell the truth.

This is the first requirement for good writing: truth; not *the* truth (whoever knows surely what that is?), but some kind of truth—a connection between the things written about, the words used in the writing, and your real experience in the world you know well—whether in fact or dream or imagination.

Part of growing up is learning to tell lies, big and little, sophisticated and crude, conscious and unconscious. Good writers differ from bad ones in that they constantly try to shake the habit. They hold themselves to the highest standard of truth telling. Often they emulate children, who tell the truth so easily, partly because they don't sense how truth will shock their elders.

A seventh-grade boy once wrote:

> **I'd like to be a car. You get to go all over and get to go through mud puddles without getting yelled at . . . that's what I'd like to be.**

The style of this passage is not distinguished. *Get* is here not a key word and yet it's employed three times. The writer switches confusingly from *I* to *you.* The language of the passage is not exciting. No memorable pictures are projected. Yet the statement strikes with force because the boy speaks truly: his shoes and the tires of the car do become muddy. He gets yelled at by his parents and the car does not. The comparison surprises. Its candor draws a smile from the reader.

> *I never think I have hit it hard unless it rebounds.*
> SAMUEL JOHNSON

Trying to write honestly and accurately, we soon find that we have already learned habits of writing falsely. As small children we spoke and wrote honestly most of the time, but when we grew older, honesty and truth came harder. The pressures on our ego were greater. We reached for impressive language. Often it was pretentious and phony. It imitated the style of adults, who are often bad writers themselves. They ask questions. So in writing school papers, we asked questions: "Did you ever think what might have happened to South Africa if the Boer War had not been fought?" A false question. Most of our readers had never thought of that possibility. However well meant—a false question. In class, a young man is anxious to impress the teacher, so he begins his paper by saying:

> **The automobile is a mechanism fascinating to everyone in all its diverse manifestations and in every conceivable kind of situation or circumstance.**

His first remark is simply untrue. Cars do not fascinate everyone.

In this paper the writer has placed his vocabulary on exhibit (*mechanism, diverse, manifestations, conceivable, situation, circumstance*) rather than put it to work. An honest writer makes every word pull its weight. In this writer's opening sentence, the words *kind of* are not working at all. They could be dropped with no loss. What does he mean by "all the diverse manifestations" of a car? Cars don't occur in manifestations but in models. If the cars he's referring to are custom-made and not strictly speaking "models," then he should say he's writing about hybrid cars. At the opening of his paper, his reader has no inkling that he's talking about home-made cars. And nothing could be more untrue than the thought conveyed by the last phrase—that everyone finds cars fascinating "in every conceivable kind of situation or circumstance." When the valves need regrinding at 17,000 miles at a cost of $125.00, even the car lover finds the loved one repulsive.

Compare this writer's pretentious and untrue statement about cars with this account:

> **Thundering down a Northern Michigan highway at night I am separated from the rest of the world. The windows of the car are all rolled down and the wind makes a deep rumbling as the car rises and falls with the dips in the pavement. The white center lines come out of the darkness ahead into the beams of the headlights only to disappear again under the front edge of the hood. The lights also pick up trees, fenceposts, and an occasional deer or racoon standing by the roadside, but like the white lines they come into view only for a few seconds and then are lost in the blackness behind me. The only signs I have that any world exists outside the range of the headlights are the continous cheerping and buzzing of the crickets and the smells from farms and sulphur pits I pass. But the rushing wind soon clears out these odors, leaving me by myself again to listen to the quickly passing crickets I will never see. The faint green lights and the red bar on the dashboard tell me I'm plunging ahead at 90 m.p.h.; I put more pressure on the pedal under my foot; the bar moves up to 100 . . . 110. The lines flash by faster and the roar of the wind drowns out the noise of the crickets and the night. I am flying through. I can feel the vibrations of the road through the steering wheel. I turn the wheel slightly for the gradual curve ahead and then back again for the long straightaway. I press the pedal to the floor and at the same time reach down to touch the buttons on my left that will roll up the windows for more speed; the bar reads 115 . . . 120, buried. With the windows up, the only sound is the high-pitched moan from the engine as it labors to keep the rest of the machine hurtling blindly ahead like a runaway express train. Only I have the power to control it. I flick on the brights to advance my scope of vision and the white lines**

come out of the black further up ahead, yet because of the speed, they're out of sight even faster than before. I am detached from the rest of the world as it blurs past. I am alone.

HENRY HALL JAMES

This boy may have been driving at an immorally high speed—even for a relatively uninhabited region—but he was writing morally, because he was staying true to the feel of his experience. Writing this way requires a quick jump in the car and a zooming away before you remember all the driving habits you have picked up watching bad older drivers. Try writing for truth.

Never say that you feel a thing unless you feel it distinctly; and if you do not feel it distinctly, say at once that you do not as yet quite know your own mind.

SAMUEL BUTLER

WRITING FREELY WITHOUT FOCUS

WRITING ONE: Write for ten minutes as fast as you can, never stopping to ponder a thought or consider spelling, punctuation, or grammar. Put down whatever comes to mind. If you find you can't get started, look in front of you or out the window and begin describing whatever you see. Let yourself wander to subject, feeling, or idea, but keep writing. When ten minutes is up, you should have filled a large notebook-sized page. Remember you are hitting practice shots. If what you write is bad or dull, no one will object.

Save all the writing you produce while reading this book. Keep it in a manila filing folder so you can go back to it to revise it or look for paragraphs or pages that may be combined or expanded into stronger work. As time passes, you'll see your words differently and sometimes learn from them without doing further work.

Here's what one student wrote in ten minutes:

I still haven't gotten used to the dull routine of school. I still feel like I should sleep in the morning until I wake up—naturally. Usually the only things that get me up, even naturally, are an empty stomach and a full bladder. I haven't seen half the new TV shows yet. Those that I have

> **seen don't look too horribly bad. It's funny how the weekends always have the worst TV and the weekdays the best. My aunt's been in the hospital lately, so all my cousins are over. It's funny how all these "little kids" are now all grown up and almost ready for high school. I can still remember when I, as the "big cousin," always directed the tricycle rides up the street, always got to carry the money out to the popsicle man, and always got to go to the Santa Claus parade and stand on Grandma's shoulders while the rest groveled underneath.**

That free writing probably kept your attention because it was honest, but it's not memorable. You will probably remember the following free writing longer. In the third sentence the writer says, "this time" and with that phrase begins to tell a story. Most good writing, fiction or nonfiction, depends a great deal on stories—a long story, or maybe a number of little stories used as examples. Professional writers know The Secret of Once. It opens you and gets you going, telling of this real object and that uttered word, and soon you have created a world that compels your reader to enter it. For example:

> **My Grandma and Grandpa had always lived on a farm in Alabama. I used to love to go there when I was young. I loved the cows and chickens and the smell of grass. But this time things were different; I didn't smell the grass, or see the cows, or hear the chickens. Everything was still. The funeral was held the day after we arrived. I couldn't understand why one bunch of ladies sat around the body until I heard them talking. They talked about who cried the longest and who cried the least. I hear the same bunch gets around to all the funerals.**

That statement impresses but doesn't let the reader touch a cow or hear one chicken's feet scraping the doorsill of a particular chicken coop. And it doesn't tell who died.

A good part of the time you're writing, you must sense your reader out there. The poet William Stafford said, "When you write, simply tell me something." Vague advice, but valid. In a sense, you become your own reader while you write. You talk to readers and hear that talk yourself. When you acquire that knack, other persons will come along with you. Easy as this habit is to learn, many persons never learn it. They're like those who try to turn a piece of pottery on the wheel and never create a cup that holds coffee.

The following free writing forgets the reader out there, talks big, but doesn't tell the reader enough. It doesn't employ The Secret of Once.

> **I don't want to grow up yet! I'm too young to be burdened with all the responsibilities of adulthood. Someday I'll get married and have a home and children of my own, but for now, I'm going to enjoy every moment of my youth in freedom.**
>
> **I want to be a unique individual. I spent much of my junior high years trying to act mature, seldom allowing my real self to emerge for fear of non acceptance. I only succeeded in mimicking others. Life is so brief. When I think of all the time I've already wasted conforming, it makes me sad.**

Mr. Stafford would say, "Tell me something you did." This writing lacks an authentic voice. No individual person seems to be speaking, but rather a recording of excerpts from textbooks and magazine articles about contemporary youth. In contrast, here's a real girl speaking:

> **Everyone around here is having an awful time getting along with me. I'm being positively intolerable. Mom is trying really hard not to say anything in the wrong tone of voice, so that I feel kind of—what's that old-fashioned word, *ashamed* of myself. One day I'm in a great mood, and and you could yell at me all you wanted without making me mad or hurt. The next day (or the next hour for that matter) you could say "Good morning," then yawn, and I'd burst into tears. I suppose that is not awfully abnormal (at least that's what Mom says—in her psychological tone, "It's just a phase. You'll grow out of it.") By the way, that makes me mad, too. I don't like to have my life summed up in a series of phases. It seems like she's saying, "You can't help acting like an idiot. It comes natural at this age. But don't worry, you'll outgrow it. It'll pass."**

The writer of the next statement used The Secret of Once and puts the reader in the situation.

> **He swore at me. It was the first time he ever had. I deserved it but that didn't lessen the shock any. I had gone out on him, then lied to him about it. It was always easy for**

me to bring on tears when I was hurt by his actions, but this time I'd hurt him. I couldn't feel sorry for myself. My eyes burned. My fingers picked at my knee. I kept twisting my ring around my finger while he repeatedly and very calmly asked me to please get out. The quiet summer night and full moon seemed to mock my every word. Ironic. I wanted to explain but I couldn't. I wanted him to hold me but he seemed repulsed at my touch. I couldn't leave. Earlier, I could have tossed my head, laughed it off, maybe saved face. But I confessed. Playing on his mercy. He wasn't being merciful. Disgusted, as his elbow brushed my knee, he leaned over and shoved open the door. When I look at the black scar in the street, I can always hear the screaming tires and feel the force of his arm.

Most of these ten-minute free writings keep the reader awake. At times disconnected and perhaps meaningless for a reader, they are full of surprise, as so much writing is not. Some of their surprises came because the writers were not trying hard, but riding with the waves, letting strange and exciting things drift up from the bottom. Most are not finished pieces of writing to be published for an audience, but they come alive.

WRITING TWO: Write three or more of these absolutely free writings. Choose times when no one will disturb you, before breakfast or late at night perhaps. Go beyond ten minutes if the river keeps flowing. But don't expect anything. You're just warming up. Maybe none of your ten-minute writings will produce an interesting sentence. Don't worry. Write. And don't think about punctuation or grammar or style. Put down one word as a sentence if you wish. Maybe your writing will be completely uninteresting to others. As long as you are trying to write honestly and you are writing fast and steadily to fill up a page or two without stopping, you are on your way.

WRITING FREELY WITH FOCUS

Free writing involves no pressure on you. It never requires perfection. If you goof, you haven't lost the game or produced a work disgraceful in the public eye. You can forget the bad shots. They don't penalize you. If you produce a good passage, you can show it to other persons because you have it down on paper. You're luckier than the golfer, who can't take a shot off the practice tee home to show his family.

After a game of golf, an amateur spends hours complaining that she missed three short putts. Before a game of golf, a professional spends hours in putting practice. If she hits bad putts, she tries a different stroke, and when she finds one that produces good putts, she grooves it.

WRITING THREE: Now try free writing with more purpose. Stay on one subject as the writer did when she said that everyone thought she was being positively intolerable. But if you find that subject takes your mind off to another related subject, let yourself go to that. The one necessity in such practice is that you keep writing freely and quickly.

> *Thought is an infection. In the case of certain thoughts it becomes an epidemic.*
>
> WALLACE STEVENS

Here's a free focused writing:

> **The building was old and dingy. We opened the doors and an even older odor hit us; it smelled of must. I followed the group closely. I was afraid of this quiet solitary place. I walked through the halls peeking around every corner cautiously. I might bump into one of them. Through every open door I saw their faces and bodies. In beds. Sitting looking out windows. Holding dolls, silently humming. I couldn't understand. Would I end up here some day? I'd rather die. Being old was a torture, not the pleasure I'd thought it to be.**
>
> **After a slight tour of the building, we stopped to eat our sack-lunches. The food didn't taste very good. It was dried-up and molded—I couldn't erase the feeling. Even the bathrooms provided were old like the people using them. Oh God, I prayed, why do they have to live on?**
>
> **The clocks seemed to never move. Suddenly, walking through a sun-deck, I found her grabbing at me. Her bony little fingers clutched my arm. I was afraid. I imagined her bones cutting into my flesh. I wanted to jerk away. I looked in her face for a long time; she just stared. Her eyes were the first young things I'd seen. They reflected my friends and me. I saw it coming. I understood. That one big tear made everything clear. How much I loved her. She tried to rise. Her clumsy bars wouldn't let her. It was like she knew she'd die there. She touched my hair. "Angel-hair," she said. All I could hear as I walked away were sobs.**
>
> JANE LENARDSON

This passage speaks with authority. The writer passed on to her readers enough of what made her respond so that they could respond also. She found surprising realities and communicated them: old ladies holding dolls, young eyes in an aged head.

Free writing is random rehearsal. Don't let it become dress rehearsal or first night. If you insist that you speak in an honest, not phony, voice, and you write freely and fast, you'll write foolishly at times, and at other times with astonishing wisdom.

Here's another focused free writing:

> **I keep slugging that yellow rubber ball harder and harder. It's tattooed by the skin off my knuckles and comes back for another mark. My hands sting. The kids behind the net can't return those hard balls. Sweating. I gulp down a cold Coke and go over to the trampoline. This web is huge and the air belching from the pressure of bouncing bodies cools me off. It's my turn to show off. As I jump, my sweatshirt parachutes and my jeans come unsnapped. Enough of that. I charge Mike just as he throws a long pass at the rim of the basket. He misses. I run after it and bounce it in. Mike grabs it and I'm right behind him trying to steal it. I sink it from the middle of the floor. Stop it! Girls aren't supposed to do that.**

> *If you have had your attention directed to the novelties in thought in your own lifetime, you will have observed that almost all really new ideas have a certain aspect of foolishness when they are first produced, and almost any idea which jogs you out of your current abstractions may be better than nothing.*
>
> ALFRED NORTH WHITEHEAD

As you dash off these writings, don't plan ahead. Write. Spill out whatever comes to mind and eye. Put down honestly what you feel and see. A day after you have finished them, read them over aloud and underline those sentences which you think say something alive for a reader. If you find no such sentences, don't despair. Keep writing. If you find a great many consecutively lively lines, mark a vertical pencil stroke next to them in the margin. Soon you'll be writing more and more good lines.

> *. . . what is always provocative in a work of art: roughness of surface. While . . . [these*

writings] pass under our eyes they are full of dents and grooves and lumps and spikes which draw from us little cries of approval and disapproval.

E. M. FORSTER

Here's a young hunter's free focused writing. It speaks with terrifying truthfulness.

I had always wanted a BB gun, but I never had one until now. We were going out to a friend's farm near Paw Paw and my dad bought me one to take along. At first I took it home to practice. I thought it was a big thing to hit an empty Joy bottle from twenty feet.

After I got to the farm, the owner asked me to shoot some blackbirds for him. For a long time no blackbirds came around. At last one landed in a walnut tree in the yard. I walked under it quietly so I wouldn't scare it. The stupid thing just sat there begging to be shot. I fired my first shot. I saw the little gold BB fly past his head. Dumb bird. It still didn't move. I shot again and the bird's face reacted with pain. It fell over, hanging upside down by one foot from its branch. I shot again. It still hung there. I could see blood on its feathers even from where I stood. With the fourth shot it fell, its black feathers red.

Here's one more free focused statement by a beginning writer. In this book "beginning writer" refers to one who hasn't been frequently published. You may be talented but not yet know your worth because you haven't received responses to your work from a number of persons. Most professional writers are often writing freely. When producing by steady daily effort, they frequently break a log jam in the river of their associations and find their thoughts and words flowing rapidly downstream. Making anything well is a combination of conscious and unconscious production.

He doesn't have legs. Not ones that feel or move. It's been that way almost four years now. Wheels. I was scared to talk at first, felt like a kid asking what it is that everyone's talking about. But we did. We used to goof around and tell dirty jokes. I always felt a little fake. Dan and I took him to the bathroom every day. Had to be done in a special way. Were there once. Dan asked a question. I don't remember. I answered, "What do you think I am, a cripple?" That's

what I said. I didn't look at anyone, just the wall. For about half an hour, I felt very whole, but my stomach was tin foil. They were quiet, both of them. Quiet as being alone. I wished someone would cut off my arms.

. . . I sometimes begin a drawing with no preconceived problem to solve, with only the desire to use pencil on paper and make lines, tones and shapes with no conscious aim; but as my mind takes in what is so produced a point arrives where some idea becomes conscious and crystallizes, and then a control and ordering begins to take place.

HENRY MOORE, SCULPTOR

WRITING FOUR: Write freely for twenty or thirty minutes about something or somebody you stumbled upon once. Let yourself record the lumps and grooves, the dents and spikes.

The vital difference between a writer and someone who merely is published is that the writer seems always to be saying to himself, as Stendhal actually did, "If I am not clear, the world around me collapses."

ALFRED KAZIN

chapter 3 what is good writing?

HERE's a poem written by a high school girl.

hitchhikers
dive up
thumbs leaping
pleading narrowed eyes
against the rain
please dad
please stop
my hands curl
my voice muffles a drum in my throat
you speed up
against the wind
in the guilt-swish pass
every hopeful outstretched arm
little smile—

". . . our car's too small
for hitchhikers, and it's
against the law."
your eyes uncomfortable skirt around mine
sliding away from my gaze
like two slippery stones
another sorry thumber
vanishes into gray behind scape
with the shiny tire tracks
down the rain road

ROBIN RENSEVER

This is good writing. It puts the reader with the hitchhikers (their eyes narrow in the rain) and the girl in the car (her hands curl in frustration). The event happens for the reader as it happened for the writer ("the guilt-swish pass"). A few of the crucial words from father, not all the talk that probably took place in the car. Daughter hates father, but recognizes he feels "uncomfortable." So much said in so few words.

There is no wing like meaning.
WALLACE STEVENS

Any kind of writing improves as it approaches the skills with which Ms. Rensever wrote "Rain Road." For example, economy. The man who writes directions for opening and storing a jar of peanut butter improves as a writer as he learns to say more with fewer words. The writer for the Sears Roebuck catalog improves as she learns to dramatize more fully the product in use—to put readers there, seeing and feeling what they will buy. Here's a good piece of writing from the *Sears Spring Through Summer Catalog*.

> Dropped in mid-summer from a helicopter when loaded with 25 pounds of sand . . . also dropped when frozen at 20° below zero . . . IT BOUNCED. But Sears new exclusive Trash Can simply wouldn't break! (and because it's all heavy-weight plastic, there was *no noisy metallic clang*).
>
> Sears Best . . . because of these important reasons:
>
> Because Handy Bottom Grips plus side handles and lid handle for easy portability. No hand-cutting bail handle here.
>
> Because friction-fit Top stays on without twisting, fits snugly without getting stuck.

> Because No Seams. Holds water, won't leak. The utility area stays cleaner . . . won't be as likely to attract pests.
>
> Because Stands Boiling Water, "boiling" hot sun . . . "boiling" hot concrete. Made to withstand the weather.
>
> Treated with SANI-GARD to retard odor and bacteria . . . Won't "pick up" odors . . . resists the growth of fungi, mildew and bacteria that cause them.

In some senses, Robin Rensever's "Rain Road" cannot be compared with an advertisement for a trash can; its intention is different, its achievement greater. But the Sears writer comes closer to creating good literature than many ad writers. She doesn't shoot off a roman candle of unsupported adjectives—Magnificent! Unheard-of! Stupendous! Instead she tells clearly how the can was tested for durability. Like Robin Rensever she makes the reader believe, because the details she presents suggest that she knows what she's talking about.

Writing a sports report, "Orioles' 16 Hits Rout Yanks, 9-4," for *The New York Times,* Joseph Durso shows that like a poet he knows how to make his words speak to each other as well as to the reader:

> The barrage consisted of these consecutive elements: a triple to left by Russ Snyder (leading the Yankees to draw their infield in), a single past the infield by Frank Robinson, a single past the infield by Brooks Robinson and a home run past everybody by Powell.

Repetition and rhythm. Robin Rensever wrote "sliding . . . slippery . . . sorry . . . scape . . . shiny . . . down the rain road."

Steve Smith begins his column "Sport" in *Car and Driver,* September, 1966, with this paragraph:

> After completing our six-car comparison road test (elsewhere in this issue), we started back to the city on the Long Island Expressway, known variously as the L.I. Distressway, and the world's longest parking lot. It was a quiet Tuesday afternoon, so we weren't expecting much traffic. Soon, however, the three westbound lanes reached the saturation point, slowed to a crawl and then to a stop. Temperatures and tempers rose. Some of the traffic bled off onto the two-lane parallel service road, allowing about half-a-mile of progress before clotting. Somebody had the bright idea of trying three abreast, and traffic telescoped another few

> hundred yards. In desperation, drivers veered off the roadway onto the center mall and the outside verge, becoming trapped by cars that had pulled off to let radiators cool. Finally, those that were able inched north and south the width of the island, then turned east. Within three hours, every major artery into the city was hopelessly snarled. Nothing moved. The System had broken down once again.

Mr. Smith cites two humorous names for the Long Island Expressway, employs sound beautifully in ending his sentence "slowed to a crawl and then to a stop" and makes the words *bled* and *clot* speak to each other in a metaphor. Like Robin he seldom uses dull and empty verbs such as *have, make, is,* and *come.* Instead he says *telescoped, veered, trapped, pulled off, inched, snarled,* and *broken down.*

In *The Field Book of Ponds and Streams* (G. P. Putnam's Sons, 1930), Anne Haven Morgan writes:

> Mayfly nymphs are of many shapes and sizes; some have flattened heads and bodies and their sprawling legs are held akimbo as in *Heptagenia.* Active runners, like *Calliboetis,* are set high on spindling legs, while the little creeper, *Leptophlebia,* almost drags its low slung body.

Like Robin, Dr. Morgan employs adjectives that are not vague and inert, but precise and active: *flattened, sprawling, spindling, low slung.*

Guidebooks are usually crammed with fact but written without flavor. *The New York Guidebook* edited by John A. Kouwenhoven (Dell Publishing Company, 1964), includes a chapter by Jean Shepherd, a disc jockey, who writes:

> After midnight you can fuel up for your stroll at Riker's Corner House on the northeast corner of Sixth and 57th. By day it is filled with quick-lunch office types, but after midnight (it's an all-night, seven-day-a-week operation) there's as motley a crew as you can find this side of an average painting by Hieronymus Bosch. Good guys and bad guys, reverends and chicks, all assembled for a plate of scrambled eggs with onions, or a slab of chocolate cream pie. There are no tables, only a horsehoe-shaped counter, which is served from somewhere in the kitchen by an endless belt on a high podium in the center. At Christmastime the podium is covered with elves, brownies, and a tiny electric train that I once

> saw derail and crash into seven banana splits. The applause was deafening. In the spring, this same treadmill is decorated with plastic daffodils and rubber tulips, and so each succeeding season is celebrated amid the hamburgers. It's the only way some of the customers can tell what time of year it is. Many of them have not seen the sun since they were kids.
>
> Before you start east on 57th, look up Sixth Avenue. Two blocks north you will see the dark mass of Central Park, unfortunately an excellent place to stay out of after dark. There are romantics who will disagree with this. But there are equally large numbers of experienced patrolmen and unfortunates who have been mugged, who will tell you the truth.

Like all good writers Mr. Shepherd chooses from his experience what surprises him and will surprise his reader, and he delivers it in sentences that hammer the surprise: ". . . a tiny electric train that I once saw derail and crash into seven banana splits." He knows the strategy of using unexpected words together: "each succeeding season is celebrated amid the hamburgers." And he is not willing to gloss over truth in order to make Central Park at night seem romantic to tourists.

Writing is good not because of who writes it or where it appears. Shakespeare and William Faulkner have written badly at times, and good publishers have marketed bad work. Writing is good because of what it says, how it opens up a world of ideas or fact for readers. And how accurately and memorably it speaks, a voice issuing from a human being who is fascinating, surprising, illuminating. But still a person and a writer who does not always strike sparks.

> *failure . . . is the poet's only real business. The one hope is for a better and better failure . . .*
>
> JOHN CIARDI

Most good writing is clear, vigorous, honest, alive, sensuous, appropriate, unsentimental, rhythmic, without pretension, fresh, metaphorical, evocative in sound, economical, authoritative, surprising, memorable and light. If you set out to collect examples of good writing you'll be surprised to find how many writers you admire are humorous or light. *Hamlet,* a story of decadence and tragedy, is at the same time one of the lightest plays ever written. Mark Van Doren, a professor at Columbia University who encouraged many young persons in America to keep writing until they became successful authors, used to say in his literature classes that a great work of art possesses a quality of lightness. It's never like a ponderous public building that looks as if it's going to sink into the ground. Lightness can be achieved in many ways—by varying style; by continually lifting the reader with genuine, rather than trick, surprises; by not taking oneself too seriously for the circumstances. For example, directions for cooking need not be boring and deadly: Irma S. Rombauer and Marion Rombauer Becker take space in *The Joy of Cooking* to put some joy into their opening discussion of salads:

> I remember the final scene of a medieval Maeterlinck play. The stage is strewed with those dead or dying. The sweet young heroine whimpers, "I am not happy here." Then the head of the house, or what remains of it, an ancient noble, asks quaveringly, "Will there be a salad for supper?"

This in a cookbook. Here is a college teacher's dittoed instructions for her students:

> Trippers will meet at 7:15 (Kalamazoo time) in front of the Union. The bus will leave promptly at 7:30 a.m. There will be no watering stops between Kalamazoo and Chicago, so I strongly recommend that you all eat something vaguely resembling breakfast before we start—something substantial and comforting like a Hershey bar.
>
> At 11:15 (Chicago time) we will go en masse to the Berghoff for lunch. The Berghoff is a marvelous old German place where the food is good and the prices are low. I think that the $5.50 lunch will make you all feel genial and broad-minded about Chicago, the museum, and modern art.
>
> After lunch everyone is on his own in the museum. Museum fatigue is a very real phenomenon and I caution you to use some restraint in your viewing, taking the 20th century first and whatever else you can manage after that.

The teacher who wrote these directions didn't strain to be funny; she simply let her own voice take over instead of the voice of doom we often take on when we feel ourselves in a position of authority.

We can all find an honest voice (yet different voices for different circumstances) in which we can speak with life and vigor. Alan Levy, Bernard Krisher, James Cox, and Richard Flaste, the writers of the Signet paperback book *Draftee's Confidential Guide,* succeeded in conveying wittily their honest feelings about life in the army. On the first page they said:

> This book is not an exposé; it won't tell you the Army is rotten. The Army isn't rotten. It varies from post to post, but in each place it's the product of our country's needs and of the peole who are in the Army—including you. This book will give you quite a few hints, however, that may keep your own Army life from being rotten.

Later in the book they present excerpts from diaries they kept. The passages are dramatic. Persons speak and create tension between each other. Some of these excerpts show army life to be cruel and sadistic, but the last one ends with a note of tolerance that proves the writers were honest when they said earlier they believed the army isn't rotten.

> At formation this morning Sergeant B—— made us hold our rifles above our heads for 10 minutes. Then we had to lift them up with one hand and hold them for another five minutes. It seemed like hours. He looked at us and said: "I know what you're thinking of me. You're calling me all sorts of names. I'm not running a popularity contest, so I don't give a damn what you think. And whatever you're thinking —'gentlemen'—the same to you." . . .
>
> We always have our share of surprises waiting when we return to the barracks after a weary day at the range. Sometimes the inspecting officer turns our beds upside down. Tonight we found all our spit-shined boots muddied.
>
> We began bayonet training yesterday. Whenever we practice with the weapon we have to shout, "Kill . . . Kill . . . Kill." The instructor said anyone who didn't want to say "Kill" could say "Lollypop." No one did.
>
> The cadre and officers are puzzled that we haven't griped as much as we're supposed to—according to Army regulations, I guess. They're not too happy about our strange, passive attitude and consequently we haven't had a night off in a week. One officer said he didn't believe we were capable of showing any emotion. He said it was unhealthy not to let off steam. He directed us to growl for five minutes. We complied, but he wasn't satisfied. It wasn't sincere enough, he said, but he finally gave up.
>
> The worst thing about basic is not the KP, or the lack of sleep, or the harassment, but the fear of the unknown. Ev-

> eryone was afraid of the gas indoctrination chamber, the infiltration course, and the first day at the rifle range. But hardly anyone would hesitate to go through them now. Much of the griping in basic (and the diarrhea) is the result of anxiety. If we had known beforehand that everything had been planned down to the minutest detail in Washington, that hundreds of thousands of men had gone through the same thing before and were none of the worse for it, and that every safety precaution is taken, I think many of our fears would have been considerably calmed.

Part of the power in this writing comes from the lively words the authors have quoted.

If you feel you can never write as well as John Steinbeck, Charles Dickens, or the writers quoted in this chapter, you may be right. But you can write as well as you spoke at your brilliant best when you were five years old, and you can write as well as some of the catalog or guide book writers presented in this chapter—if you find a voice that rings true to you and you learn to record the surprise of the world faithfully. The free writing by beginning writers quoted in the preceding chapters displays many of the characteristics of good writing discussed here; for example:

Surprise: I sink it from the middle of the floor. Stop it! Girls aren't supposed to do that.

The author speaking in an authentic voice: I hear the same bunch gets around to all the funerals.

Economical use of words: The next day (or the next hour for that matter) you could say "Good morning," then yawn, and I'd burst into tears.

Words that put the reader there: My eyes burned. My fingers picked at my knee. I kept twisting my ring around my finger while he repeatedly and very calmly asked me to please get out.

Strong metaphor: I felt very whole, but my stomach was tin foil.

Words that speak to each other: . . . an *empty* stomach and a *full* bladder.

A record of the authentic voice of another person: "It's just a phase. You'll grow out of it."

Strong adjective: Her eyes were the first *young* things I'd seen.

Strong, full verb: The stupid thing just sat there *begging* to be shot.

Strong repetition: It fell over, *hanging* upside down by one foot from its branch. I shot again. It still *hung* there.

Powerful rhythms: I knew I hated him. Only a chair, a desk, and a man saying, "I'll be back in about a half hour," which really became three.

The persons who produced these free writings are on their way. They may need to master additional skills, but they have already produced many sentences that ring true and stay in the reader's ear.

> *The best writing, both prose and poetry, as Shakespeare pre-eminently shows, makes use, with condensation and selection, of playful, impassioned, imaginative talk.*
>
> SIDNEY COX

You may wonder how I can be so sure what good writing is. Not everyone likes the same authors or reporters. Readers will always disagree. When you sit in the circle of writers and responders discussed in the Introduction and Chapter 10 of this book, you'll devise your own standards. They'll differ somewhat from those of others in your circle and in other circles, but probably not on certain fundamentals. Those who have worked in the circle have studied the reactions of the members as they listened to writings being read aloud. From the expressions on faces, grunts of approval, sighs, actions signifying boredom, and spoken comments, they slowly came to believe that most good writings gain their power in these ways:

1. They do not waste words.
2. They speak in an authentic voice.
3. They put the reader there, make him believe.
4. They cause things to happen for him as they happened for the writer (or narrator).
5. They create oppositions which pay off in surprise.
6. They build.
7. They ask something of the reader.
8. They reward him with meaning.
9. They present ideas, actions, or details that are solid, like an apple with its core and flesh, and however small or momentary, are rounded and complete in themselves.

I hate anything that occupies more space than it is worth. I hate to see a load of band-boxes go along the street, and I hate to see a parcel of big words without anything in them.

WILLIAM HAZLITT

chapter 4 tightening

GOOD WRITERS meet their readers only at their best. If you should read the sentences in their wastebaskets, you would find them full of bad starts and complete misses. When you write, you can discard your bad tries and forget them.

Benjamin Franklin, who helped Thomas Jefferson write the Declaration of Independence—a skillfully revised document—once told this anecdote to Mr. Jefferson:

> When I was a journeyman printer, one of my companions, an apprentice Hatter, having served out his time, was about to open a shop for himself. His first concern was to have a handsome signboard, with a proper inscription. He composed it in these words: "John Thompson, Hatter, makes and sells hats for ready money." with a figure of a hat subjoined. But he thought he would submit it to his friends for their amendments. The first he shewed it to thought the word "hatter" tautologous, because followed by the words "makes hats" which shew he was a hatter. It was struck out. The next observed that the word "makes" might as well be omitted, because his customers would not care who made the hats. If good and to their mind, they would buy, by whomsoever made. He struck it out. A third said he thought the words "for ready money" were useless as it was not the custom of the place to sell on credit. Every one who purchased expected to pay. They were parted with, and the inscription now stood "John Thompson sells hats." "*Sells hats*" says his next friend? Why nobody will expect you to give them away. What then is the use of that word? It was stricken

> out and "hats" followed it, the rather, as there was one painted on the board. So his inscription was reduced ultimately to "John Thompson" with the figure of a hat subjoined.

You can cut out the necessary words in your writing in this way. The principle is simple: don't repeat words or ideas unless they strengthen what you want to say. "Hatter . . . makes hats" repeats *hat* to no avail. Don't tell your writer that "Mr. Smith is a man who—." The words *Mr. Smith* reveal that Smith is a man. Don't say "Lincoln School is a *school* that I really like." Look at what happens when a writer cuts out weak repetitions:

Original. He looked at Mike. Mike was his brother.

Tightened. He looked at his brother Mike.

Original. The beginning of the play shows Richard as a confident and strong man while the end shows him as a desolate and weak man.

Tightened. The beginning of the play shows Richard confident and strong; the end shows him desolate and weak.

Before you get carried away with cutting out weak repetition, remember that strong repetition is the heart of all good writing, in fact the heart of all good music making, hurdle racing, hammering, walking, or courting. Repetitions set up pattern. Only with pattern can you achieve emphasis and variety. Da-da-da, da-da-da, da-da-dum. That *dum* is smart because it comes after all those *da's*. It picks up its power as you wait through all those *da's* for something to happen. Repeat and vary. That is the secret of achieving significant form in all art and communication.

This book will demonstrate how the repeat-and-vary pattern strengthens writing in many ways, but for the present, consider only how to omit those repetitions in your writing which are not working powerfully, which get in the readers' way rather than drive them down your road. If you can learn to say in a few words all you want to say, with precision and fullness, you will delight yourself and your readers. We all love people who say a great deal in a few words. Most of us feel that life will be too short; so we praise a person who can hammer the nail with only three blows. We don't want to hear:

> In order that the ruling organization of a country that is committed to a democratic organization organized to give the people a voice in its procedures, and thinks of their well-being, shall not become disorganized and come to an end in these times . . .

And we don't want to hear:

> That government of the people and government by the people and government for the people shall not perish from the earth.

That's so much government that we can't hear the people. We want to hear

> . . . that government of the people, by the people, for the people, shall not perish from the earth.

That statement repeats *people,* not *government.* The man who wrote those words respected people and knew his *repeat-and-vary* principle. Further examples of how to repeat words powerfully will be presented in Chapter 9.

REVISING ONE: In your WRITING ONE and WRITING TWO papers, lightly circle all repeated words. Then consider each one. Do you want to retain it? If you want to omit it, draw brackets in pencil around it so that after you show the revision to others and give it time to cool off, you can restore an omitted word easily if you choose. Thomas Jefferson used brackets to recommend omissions to others, and most editors today follow him.

Life is the elimination of what is dead.
WALLACE STEVENS

The words *which, who,* and *that* often clutter up sentences. Good writers remove excessive Whooery, Whichery, or Thatery.

1. Mr. Rendew, Alice's father, [was a man who] actually liked to have his lawnmower go wrong so he could tinker with its motor.
2. George [is the type of man who] always shines his shoes before going downtown.
3. [The people that] I would like to tell you about [are] Father and Mother.

Other words, for example *all* and *what,* often fail to add meaning to a sentence and need cutting.

1. [All] I wish [is that] he would admit that passion has a respectable place in our lives.
2. [What I mean to say is that] no child should eat his grandmother.

The careless use of the word *thing* is more serious and damaging.

Original. The thing that enrages me is mosquitoes inside my open shirt collar.

Revision. Mosquitoes inside my open shirt collar enrage me.

3. [The] first [thing] I'd like to say [is] . . .

Original. Of all the things in the world I can't stand, boiled hot dogs are the worst.

Revision. I can't stand boiled hot dogs.

Why do schools turn out students so masterly in word wastery? Simple. Knowledge consists to some extent in naming and ordering things. So schools teach categorizing—how to place things in classes, species, etc. (Note that the word *things* is used twice in the two preceding sentences, but meaningfully, not emptily. These two uses of *things* are necessary and justifiable.)

Thus educated persons become addicted to such categorizing words as:

type	situation	phase	factor
kind	area	aspect	one

Often the words are not pulling their weight in a sentence.

Original. The first level of the poem gives the situation of a dull sergeant speaking to a group of new recruits.

Revision. The first level of the poem presents a dull sergeant speaking to a group of recruits.

1. The Queen realized that her life was not [a] carefree and spotless [one].
2. He was a typical [type of] fraternity man.

When a writer must categorize and generalize, these words are valuable, but often they are abominations.

Namery, another sickness, is the habit of naming things which do not need naming. Consider this passage:

> **Juliet and Rosalind are women who fall in love. This is one of the few similarities between these two characters. They are different in age, with Juliet being an impetuous adolescent and Rosalind being a mature adult. This difference is illustrated by the manner in which each character falls in love. Juliet rushes into romance and gets married as quick-**

ly as possible while Rosalind makes sure of her love for Orlando—a much more rational and logical choice than Juliet's.

This paragraph is devastated by Namery. The author says that Juliet and Rosalind fall in love and then unnecessarily says these acts are similar. He says the two are different in age and then later says one is an adolescent and the other an adult. He wastes completely the sentence:

> This difference is illustrated by the manner in which each character falls in love.

because the next sentence shows the difference specifically. The paragraph could be cut in half without losing essential meaning:

> One of the few similarities between Juliet and Rosalind is that they both fall in love; but Juliet rushes into romance while Rosalind makes sure of her love for Orlando. Juliet is an impetuous adolescent, Rosalind a mature adult.

Essentially Namery is a failure to recognize that one's audience may possess brains. The writer says:

> George came in with a new idea. It was a thought that had never struck his boss.

Readers don't need to be told that an idea is a thought. All they need is:

> George came in with an idea that had never struck his boss.

In schools, Namery usually involves a special vocabulary.

> The causes of the basic difficulties in the area of mathematics are manifold. Fractions present the student with an entirely new set of assumptions.

The introductory sentence stupefies the reader with its dull buzzing. The writer should have said:

> Fractions are hard to learn because they present students with new assumptions.

Too often writers introduce everything to their audience: "Now we are going to look at large cities and then we are going to compare them with small towns," they say, when all they mean to do is compare Chicago, Illinois, with Bad Axe, Michigan.

REVISING TWO: Take one of your free writings you like best and tighten it by removing all Whooery, Whichery, Thatery, and Namery.

When you examine your own writing for weak repetition, you may not be able to see it. You need a way of looking for it. Ask yourself where you have said something twice without meaning to. The following passage from a student paper shows weak repetition of both words and ideas. Try cutting it in about half.

> **Hands, did you ever notice how many different kinds of men's hands there are? I first began to notice hands when I found that all men's hands were not as large as my Dad's hands. They were large, strong, and forceful, yet always gentle like the man. His hand encompasses mine even now when he takes it gently yet firmly, as though providing it with a cover of protection against the outside world. But he has always been like that, strong and protective, yet gentle. When those hands hold a baby, the baby stops crying and is quiet as though calmed by their strength and gentleness. When those hands take a pencil and draw an idea, the lines are firm and confident. Other men seem to respond when they shake his hand to the friendliness and strength behind the handshake.**

The assertions in that passage are simple and unsurprising. They do not need a lot of repetition to be clear to the reader.

REVISING THREE: Look over two of your past writings for meanings unnecessarily repeated. For example:

> Valerie scrutinized my face [carefully].

The word *scrutinize* means to examine carefully.

Original. Richard has a consistently bad habit of not listening to what people are saying to him unless he is sure it will please him.

Revision. Richard consistently fails to listen to people unless he is sure they will please him.

The word *habit* means a consistent or frequent action. Because *consistently* is used, *habit* can be eliminated.

The ground felt [peculiar. It was] soft as clouds.

If the ground was soft as clouds, it must have felt peculiar, and the opening comment isn't needed. In the revision the writer hits us with her surprise. She doesn't waste a word telling us a surprise is coming. Note how the following statement is brought alive by simple tightening:

Original. I see a man whose face is hidden by shadow except where the sun reveals it.
Revision. I see the sun-lit half of a man's face.

You may properly think of wasting words as a form of dishonesty. People don't mean to do it, but when they do, they risk losing both their readers' attention and their trust.

A young author is tempted to leave anything he has written through fear of not having enough to say if he goes cutting out too freely. But it is easier to be long than short.

SAMUEL BUTLER

Start out with the conviction that absolute truth is hard to reach in matters relating to our fellow creatures, healthy or diseased, that slips in observation are inevitable even with the best trained faculties, that errors in judgment must occur in the practice of an art which consists largely in balancing probabilities—start, I say, with this attitude of mind, and mistakes will be acknowledged and regretted; but instead of a slow process of self-deception, with ever-increasing inability to recognize the truth, you will draw from your errors the very lessons which may enable you to avoid their repetition.

SIR WILLIAM OSLER

chapter 5 deceiving oneself

SOMETIMES writers set out to deceive their readers, as Roget's *Thesaurus* puts the words, to hornswoggle or bamboozle them, to throw dust into their eyes; to engage in window dressing, hanky-panky, chicanery, pettifogging, flam, bam, flimflam, or cajolery; to speak mealy-mouthed buncombe, to beat about the bush, to quibble, counterfeit, fake; to write two-faced, bare-faced, or smooth-faced; to tell taradiddles and whoppers, to gild the pill.

But more often they set out to tell the truth and speak seriously, as Eudora Welty advises them, and still they gild the pill and throw dust into their own eyes as well as the reader's. No writer knows how often he deceives himself and his reader until he becomes a professional and listens to the complaints of editors and readers. Then he often sees that he has unconsciously

(1) not written about what really motivated him to put pen to paper, or

(2) not spoken truly when he thought he was being faithful to the world he experienced, or

(3) told only a small part of the truth, or

(4) forgotten to tell the reader the facts that make convincing what he insists the reader must be overwhelmed by, or

(5) grandly asked questions that everyone knows the answer to, or

(6) apologized for not being an expert on what he writes pages and pages about, or

(7) used awkward and phony language that does not belong to him, or

(8) used six words where his reader needed only two.

The best writers commit these sins. You cannot rid your writing of them, but you can reduce them if you learn the identifying marks of the snakes and where they are likely to slither into your paragraphs.

Any writer, beginner or professional, feels pressed to imitate successful writers. Often the beginner echoes an idea she has heard before without remembering how the thought was imbedded in a fact of her life. She generalizes on her knowledge instead of putting her reader through the experience that led to the generalization. She presents a conclusion but doesn't tell the story that led her to it. Here, for example, is a poem published in a high school newspaper:

PLAY TODAY

Yes, my child, use this time for play,
Tomorrow will be too late.

Play with your soldiers, cannons and guns,
Use them while they are a toy.

Be happy that the world is not yours.
Tomorrow it will be, but today it is mine.

Let him live today as a time of freedom and play!
Tomorrow he will work and he will have no time to play.

This is a time for pleasure and a time so short,
So be a child of joy and of troubles forgotten.

Tomorrow is too late my child.
Tomorrow, you are a man.

The writer may have seen her small brother playing with soldiers and then her father came home from work too tired to do more than eat, read the paper, and go to bed. The thought she wishes to convey, that a child should enjoy his life of play while he can, is old and moldy. No reader wants to encounter it unless it is brought alive with power and originality. If the writer had revealed her brother and father in the uniqueness of their experience, she might have produced a good poem. In the following writing, note how a mother showed her child at play and opened the lid on a mystery. She did not deceive herself about what story she wanted to tell.

MY SORCERESS

My daughter is a spare-toothed, seven-year old sorceress. Her brown hair is too short for a ponytail, too long for anything else. Yet if her hair were cut, some of her magic power would disappear. Her sparkle and infectious laugh assure control of her victim. When her thirteen-year old brother says, "I hate your guts," she dances around him and chants, "I love you, I love you." Then she breaks a vial of laughter in the room and he is in her power. Although his words do not change, he has taken up her chant.

CAROLINE BROWN

Often an author generalizes on his experience but doesn't relate it: double mistake. One experience usually makes an unconvincing base for a generalization. Without the personal story, the writer may not be able to keep his reader awake. A writer must learn that his authority resides in his knowledge, not in an attempt to sound like someone else. What led a writer to begin writing often can tell him where his subject hides. The young man who began a paper with this paragraph (part of which was quoted in Chapter 1) probably didn't realize that he was faking his way through every sentence:

I consider experience to be an important part in the process of learning. For example, in the case of an athlete, experience plays an important role. After each game, he needs to acquire more knowledge and proficiency, thereby making him a better athlete. An athlete could also gain more knowledge by studying up on the sport, but it is doubtful if he could participate for the first time in a sport with study alone and without experience and still do an adequate job. I think that this is the very important point which Thoreau is trying to show. He is not opposed to education, but thinks that we can be educated many times better with experience. I have the impression that he feels

> **that it is better for most people to gain experiences and not waste so much time on unrelated things that will be of little value to them in gaining their goals more quickly in life.**

What spurred this boy to spend so many words telling the obvious fact that an athlete gains from experience? Who doesn't? Probably he was thinking of a football game in which he made three mistakes: missed a tackle because he hit too high, threw an interception because he couldn't see over the red-dogger's hands, and failed to make a clear signal for a fair catch. If he had put the reader dramatically through these experiences, he might have written a memorable paper. But he didn't. He wrote as if he were a philosopher instead of a football player, and his philosophy was old and dully stated.

> *. . . creativity is continual surprise, and only because it is surprise can it be truth. When we grow self-conscious we hide, we cloak, we disguise, we lie. So the true writer artist always hopes, through working swiftly with his emotions to spring forth the delights and terrors, to trap them before they escape.*
>
> RAY BRADBURY

Another way writers deceive themselves is to speak only to themselves and yet expect the public to be fascinated. This act might be called private writing. For example, a girl publishes a poem in a high school paper:

> SORROW
> MY TRUE STORY
>
> Now, I want to tell you people
> My true story and it's sad
> I will shout it from the hill tops
> How I really had it bad
>
> How I cried each night just for him.
> How I missed him when he left.
> I believed the lies he told me.
>
> Then his heart grew tired and restless
> And he soon stopped loving me.
> He would flirt behind my back
> And he thought I didn't see.

Now, I know he was unfaithful
But my hurt just wouldn't show
For I loved him, too much even
To ever let him go.

I wonder as I look back if
I did right, or was I wrong?
To let him think he deceived me
When I knew it all along.

He finally asked for his freedom
So, I had to let him go
Now my friends say to forget him

But they don't even know
That when I hear his name or see him
All the memories creep inside
Then my heart is filled with
Sadness and the tears are hard to hide.

I'm sure you recognize my story
For it happened to you too.
That's why I'm shouting from this hill top
How did it end with You???

The person who speaks in this poem cried, she missed her boy friend; he told her lies, he stopped loving her, he flirted behind her back. A pattern of experience that almost every girl has known, yet the writer tells not one convincing detail—what was the boy like? how did he treat her? Blatant or devious lies? Finally, she says, she let him go. Was she in a position to let him go? He had already gone in the sense of being unfaithful. She asks what might be a penetrating question:

I wonder as I look back if
I did right, or was I wrong?
To let him think he deceived me
When I knew it all along.

Does she really wonder? She accuses him of deceiving her and then admits deceiving him. If she had faced this question squarely and probed the reasons both deceived each other, she might have found truth valuable to herself and her readers. She says she felt such sorrow that she is now shouting from this hill top. "How did it end with You???" What does this question mean? It may be false, covering up some other question or attitude. Is she really interested in knowing how other students' loves worked out? Or does she mean only to suggest her superior knowledge—that love turned sour for her and will for others? In the next to the last stanza she says:

> But they don't even know
> That when I hear his name or see him
> All the memories creep inside.
> Then my heart is filled with
> Sadness and the tears are hard to hide.

Unless her friends are inhuman, they would expect that when she heard his name or saw him she would remember moments with him—whether she had despised him or loved him. But what memories? She never tells anything about this boy that convinces the reader she loved him or even knew him as a person.

> *"If the artist does manage to be ruthless with himself," said the voice, "must we not think of him as the luckiest of men? How many men can afford the luxury of being ruthless with themselves in their dreams of doing a perfect thing?"*
>
> JOHN CIARDI

You may deceive readers and yourself by attempting a trick ending or beginning, holding back the identity of someone or something when such holding back doesn't heighten meaning. The materials of a story or experiment should determine whether you're justified in reversing the natural order of events or holding back information that normally would be communicated at once. The readers are always out there. The best writers forget them at times, but finally remember that writing is to be read. Life is full of ambiguity. You're justified in building mystery into your work. But to pump false suspense into writing is to cheat your readers. Don't destroy the excitement in an experience by insisting to readers that they're about to be amazed. For example:

> **I began wading across the river on the sandbar. Deeper and deeper I went into the water. Up to my waist, then chest, then shoulders. The sandbar was narrow here—only about a foot wide. One misstep and off I would go. I was just about midway when IT HAPPENED.**

The IT forgets the readers. They weren't there. What actually happened may have been exciting, but the writer must give readers a chance to determine how exciting the happening was. Note how the story goes without the false suspense signal.

> . . . I was just about midway when I tripped. I fell, went under the water, and the sandbar disappeared beneath me. I was carried downstream.

Holding back is justified when the significance of a series of events or progression of ideas is enhanced by the mystery. For example, the following passage opens with a sentence that puzzles the reader:

> Grandma, Dad's stepmother, welcomed us warmly, but gave us whole wheat biscuits with our meals.

What is the point of whole wheat biscuits? A mystery. The next sentence reveals the answer:

> Many times we watched from another room as she served her own grandchildren the preferred biscuits made from white flour.

This is the way the experience came to the writer, as a mystery revealed later when she saw the white biscuits. She makes the reader wait for understanding, but the wait is rewarding. A writer should expect intelligent reading from his audience, but the line between writing privately and publicly is difficult to draw. Suspense is a common ingredient of life, but in writing it should not be artificially introduced. It should exist in the materials the writer has discovered.

And so with questions. They should belong to the writer and his body of materials or he should not ask them. "Did you ever fall down a basement stairway while eavesdropping and land in your sister's boy friend's lap?" The answer is easy. "No, I never did." Not only does this question give away what might be a smash ending to a humorous story, but it is not really meant. Ask questions when you mean them, when you have really wondered about what they ask. Avoid them when you know your readers know the answers. "Are children wiser than grownups?" The reader knows the writer is going to say next: "Yes, sometimes." But the writer deceives herself about her job. She shouldn't be running a question and answer show. She probably wanted to tell her reader about a time when she saw a child act wisely. She should forget the hanky-panky and get on with the story. A writer who frequently asks lame questions ultimately becomes as irritating as a six-year-old child who prefaces every assertion with the words, "Mom, you know what?"

Closely related to false questions are apologies and irrelevant introductions. Editors will tell you that most manuscripts they see wind up three times before they deliver the ball. Begin the paper. Wind up once and throw the pitch. The difficulty with beginnings comes from that sticky old relationship with readers. Will they believe me? Will they like me? How can I impress them with my wisdom or honesty? One sure way to depress readers is to apologize before starting a long article.

> I may not know much about politics, but I'm sure of one thing.

A reader may be tempted to say, "If you don't know much about politics, why are you writing this long article about it?" Modesty is one thing and false modesty another. To pretend you know almost nothing of a large subject you're writing about is inexcusable in a writer, but to admit that you don't know this or that bit of information, or that you're not sure of your understanding on one point, is proper and even persuasive to the reader. For example, Stephen Spender, poet and critic, writing about another man's poem, says:

> The idea—if I understand it—is that the poet, through allowing his isolated self to die, enters into that life . . .

Mr. Spender admits that the poem is hard to understand; he doesn't deceive himself or his reader.

Naturally, beginnings are difficult for a writer because they establish or fail to establish a strong relationship with the reader. Often writers don't know all the persons who will read their work. And even when they do, they can't be sure how each reader will comprehend their sentences. When you're uneasy about being understood, you often act pompously, speaking words that you haven't really made your own. And so you don't find your own voice. Everything becomes strained and artificial rather than easy and sure and winning. The urge to impress readers at the outset is so powerful that in their first drafts of a piece of writing writers feel obliged to make sweeping statements about mankind when they actually have a much smaller story to tell. For example, here is a professional writer beginning an article in a magazine about high-performance boating:

> Time has a way of perpetuating events, situations and people. As one event dies another is born. As one situation dissolves, another is conceived. As one person disappears, another appears. The cycles of life's activity renew themselves constantly.
>
> In the unlimited circle a few years ago sports reporters bemoaned privately the loss of colorful figures. Lee Schoenith had mellowed from blustering "bad guy" of the pits to Chairman of the Unlimited Commission. Bill Muncey, Peppery Willard Rhodes and their *Thriftway* retired, and with them went the possibility of fiery hassles and pungent statements. Col. Russ Schleeh of plumber's helper fame left the sport (and Air Force) for staid duties behind a desk of industry. And so it went. "Story material," said one tired writer, "is lacking—and that's an understatement."
>
> Into this void strode big, bouncing, boisterous Bernie Little and his beautiful buoyant, bewitching four-seater, *Tempo*.

The opening paragraph of this article is highly pretentious. Everyone knows that people die and are born, and rise to fame and retire. The writer speaks these obvious truths in a voice that should belong to a prophet. All she is trying to do is introduce the story of Bernie Little, an attractive racing boat driver who appealed to her for his humor and manliness.

Nothing will help you more as a writer than finding a voice right for you, your material, and your audience. This writer didn't find it here. After beginning in prophetic voice, she shifts in the third paragraph to corny repetition of "b" sounds. But she wrote well in other parts of her article. In the opening she experienced a common difficulty of all writers—finding words that speak honestly and validly.

When revising, you must test every word for its pitch: does it hit the note you're aiming for? Does it say what you meant it to say? The simplest word can be falsely used. *And* looks innocent, but often gets writers into trouble.

> She came by our house swinging her ever-present black parasol *and* Dad was trying to fix the fertilizer distributor so he could get the potatoes planted faster.

And is the wrong word there. Ordinarily it joins like or equal things. The woman swinging the parasol and Dad fixing the fertilizer distributor are not equal or related until the writer brings them together. The *and* could be dropped and the sentence made into two sentences. Or *and* could be replaced with a word like *while*.

Frequently writers employ the loose, imprecise language of casual conversation which will not stand scrutiny as it must if it is to be writing that tells the truth and speaks seriously. A writer says:

> I saw the victim lying beside the car, his left leg separated from his body and blood all over the highway. I was rather shaken . . .

Rather is here a false word and should be omitted. In this use it belongs in the family of expressions like *not exactly* and *not too nice,* permissible in informal conversation but often sloppy and inexcusable in writing.

> Again and again he had lied to his daughter about what her fiancé had said about her. As a father I guess he wasn't exactly nice.

No, not exactly.

Phony language like this creeps into the best writers' work. They must be ever on guard against it. They like the sound of their sentences and don't listen closely enough to hear that they have said:

> Johnny was hanging suspended from the highest branch.

or

> The talk has a tranquilizing effect on him.

when they could have made the same point in fewer words:

> Johnny was hanging from the highest branch.

and

> The talk tranquilizes him.

The ways of deceiving yourself about what you're saying are too numerous to illustrate completely here. One more conversational habit that may lead you into trouble:

I *did* have to disarm one student last year.

Something interesting *did* happen when the sisters came to that camp.

Sometimes, but rarely, this use of *did* to emphasize a verb signals the reader that what is being told now is unexpected. Something said earlier implied otherwise. But usually the writer will save words and lose no meaning by saying:

I had to disarm one student last year.

Something interesting happened when the sisters came to that camp.

"Something interesting did happen" sounds dull. Make it happen. If it was so interesting, tell it so the readers will be fascinated. Hit them with the surprises you've collected. Don't weaken your sentences with excessive *did's.*

I hope you did like this chapter on Deceiving Oneself and that it did teach you many valuable and important things that you did find interesting.

But to have a full kit of auditory patterns curved to real emotions we do need to listen. We need to listen, with inside matching on our own part, to those whose phrases fit their inner state. We are lucky if we listen less to lecturers and experts, more to farmers, mechanics, truck drivers . . . laundresses, and children out of school.

SIDNEY COX

chapter 6 people talking

"YOU WANT to go or don't you?"

"Where?"

"Where? What difference does it make? We're going with the guys."

"Well—"

Nothing much gets accomplished in that dialogue but it probably made you want to know what was going to be said next. Conversation is so much our lives: waiting for sentences to clear, asking when they don't, and then waiting for the answer to our asking. Two people talking together create constant tension. Will these words do? Will those words help?

Conversation is responsive, like hitting a ball back and forth over the net quickly. Even when a speaker doesn't answer the other's questions, as in the dialogue above, the refusal is still a response. That's one of the reasons conversation makes writing more intense: it builds suspense. Another reason is that it gives the sound of life.

On paper you can put down all kinds of conversations. For example, listen to your mother—or any mother—talking to her eight-year-old son when he rushes in from school at 3:00 P.M.:

"Hi, Mom. Guess what."

"Hi, Bobby. You hungry?"

"Ya. Hey, guess what. Next Monday all the guys are bringing their S.S.P.'s and racing um in the hall. You gotta get me a new S.S.P. Sidewinder cuz mine's broke. Will ya?"

"No! Christmas was only four weeks ago and I'm not buying any toys now."

"Aw Mom, you gotta. I'll be the only guy without a racer."

"Now Bobby, how many times must I tell you, your being the only one without an S.S.P. is not a good reason for getting one. It sets a pattern of the need to conform to what is important for someone else. It robs your character of individualism. I know you probably don't understand all of what I'm trying to say right now but someday you'll see I'm right."

"Mom?"

"What, honey?"

"Your nose wiggles funny when you talk."

RUTH FENTON

That conversation will speak to many parents—help them see how pompous they get at times. It shows the delightful candor of children, who haven't learned well enough yet how to be diplomatic and dull. Maybe that's the age—about eight—for here's another such boy, this time aged seven. The writer is the mother:

"Hi, David, how are you?"

"OK, I guess. Didn't have a good day at school, though."

"Oh? what happened?"

"Nobody likes me. John wouldn't let me play on his football team at recess."

"Um, wonder why. You always have before. Did you say or do something to make him mad?"

"Nope. He just said, 'Brown, you can't play today.' "

"Didn't you ask why?"

"If I had, he would have said, ' 'Cause you're too stupid.' Nobody likes me."

"David, you know that isn't true."

"Yes it is. Mrs. Strand wouldn't ask me a question either."

"Well David, I know everyone in the class can't be asked a question every day. There just isn't enough time."

"Mom, there are thirty-two kids in my class. Everyone else was asked a question."

"Oh good grief, David, *everyone*?"

"Well almost. She doesn't like me, either. You don't even like me, do you, Mom? You just yelled at me."

"David, why don't you go in your room and play awhile?"

(He gives a big grin.)

"OK, Mom."

Those are conversations. Two persons exchanging words, listening to each other, responding. Like most good writers the authors wrote out of close knowledge. If they had been writing of someone they hadn't known, for example, diplomats in Washington, they might have distorted the dialogues because they couldn't use their ears as they wrote.

You can quickly tell when a written conversation is phony, delivered in Engfish. The supermarket cashier is saying, "Oh, it's been delightful to have you as our customer today, Miss Watkins." Or the bank manager is saying, "O.K., Watkins, you write the check properly, we give you the bread."

When you write conversation, try for truth to the feeling and ideas expressed by persons in real situations. Try also for the true sound of each speaker's language—or languages. We're all language-using animals. You speak the native language of your country. You also speak several dialects that belong to a part of your country or the social groups you associate with at school or work or play—the gang from 14th Street or the guys at the Aerospace Company. And you speak an idiolect, or personal language, which is yours alone. It has a distinctive sound. It's spiced by a word or two you or someone else in your family made up, or an original grammatical construction you fell into at age four and never climbed out of. That's also true for everyone else in the world. Here's another real conversation:

John: **You're so crazy I love you.**
Carol: **That's three times you've said that.**
John: **You are crazy, you know that?**
Carol: **That's not what I mean—think about it.**

John: Oh, I know what you mean.
Carol: Those words don't come easy for you, I can tell.
John: No, they don't.
Carol: It almost scares you while you're saying it.
John: You're crazy, Carrie, for the fourth time.

There's a great deal of *love* in those lines but the word is mentioned only once.

> *I notice particularly the cadence of their voices, the sort of phrases they'll use, and that's what I'm all the time trying to hear in my head, how people word things—because everybody speaks an entirely different language . . .*
>
> FRANK O'CONNOR

The above dialogue was presented in dramatic form, like a play, with nothing but the spoken words and the names of the speakers given, and therefore it didn't need quotation marks. But in most writing, conversation must be marked off clearly. And so must the speakers. If you run together the spoken words and the narrative, you may confuse your reader. Example:

We got into the elevator and I stood as far away as possible. His eyes felt my body. He came toward me, slowly, arms extended, fingers stretching, stiffened, ready to grab me. What's the matter? You afraid I'll rape you? He laughed. Uh, no—uh, I'm shy. We left the elevator and entered a dimly lit hall. I wondered where he was taking me. What are you studying here, Doug? Tool and Die. Oh, how long you been going here? Eight months. Aren't you going to hold my hand? Um, uh—remember? I told you I was shy.

With no indication of who is speaking, the passage becomes hard to follow. To prevent this confusion, conventional ways of punctuating and paragraphing conversation have been established. In the following story, which contains conversation along with narrative, you can see how the above passage is unconfused by the indention of a line every time a person begins speaking. And quotation marks indicate which words belong to that person, to differentiate them from the author's narrative words.

FOR A WALK?

The bus pulled up in front of the State Technical Institute and Rehabilitation Center. I said to myself I don't want to go in there and talk to those boys but I knew I did or I wouldn't have come. What would I say? I didn't know how to talk to strangers, especially boys.

The sixteen members of my group walked into a lobby filled with young men anxious to see the faces and bodies of some young women.

At first, for moral support I stayed with some of the girls I came with. After about an hour I ventured off by myself to find the restroom. I was approached by a tall, thin boy wearing bell-bottoms that were too short and a baggy green shirt. His hair nearly covered his face.

"Wanna go for a walk?" he asked.

"Uh, ok. Your name is Doug, isn't it? I met you earlier."

"Yea. I don't remember your name."

"Kathy."

We got into the elevator and I stood as far away as possible. His eyes felt my body. He came toward me, slowly, arms extended, fingers stretched, stiffened, ready to grab me.

"What's the matter? You afraid I'll rape you?" He laughed.

"Uh, no—uh, I'm shy."

We left the elevator and entered a dimly lit hall. I wondered where he was taking me.

"What are you studying here, Doug?"

"Tool and Die."

"Oh. How long you been going here?"

"Eight months. Aren't you going to hold my hand?"

"Um, uh—remember? I told you I was shy."

"Oh yea, I forgot. You're shy."

We walked into a well-lighted lobby where there were two other people and a grotesque statue that I raved about until he could tell I was insincere. I resigned myself to walking another dark hallway. We reached a dead end in conversation and space. I stood on my tiptoes to look into the window of an auto shop. When I lowered myself from the window and turned around, his lips brushed the back of my head.

I began slowly walking away. "I have this industrial

arts class for elementary school teachers and we're gonna get to work with wood and metal and electricity and—"

"You don't like me, do you?"

"I don't even know you. You're a nice boy, and very friendly, but like I already told you, I'm shy and don't know what to say."

As we continued walking, I could feel a nervous headache beginning to grow above my eyes. I felt selfish and inexperienced. I was wounding his ego and all I could think of was what a bad time I was having.

"You going to hold my hand now?"

"No I—"

"I know. You're still shy. Well, I don't believe you."

We were approaching the familiar crowded lobby. I suggested we sit down. Immediately we were joined by Doug's friend Gary, who was confined to a wheelchair. After the "What are you studying's" and the "Where are you from's" our conversation died. Gary suggested that somebody say something. After he said it a second time, I knew I was a failure. I thought it was just Doug I couldn't talk to. Gary was much more pleasant, but I couldn't talk to him either. I decided I was a shallow person and had lived a sheltered life. The ache in my head became a pounding, and even though I'd had a three-hour nap that afternoon, I was exhausted. I kept watching the clock because I wanted to get out of there and never come back. I still had thirty minutes.

We went downstairs to shoot pool, but there wasn't an empty table. We just stood there.

"What's wrong?" Doug said.

"Nothing, I just have a headache."

"You don't like it here, do you?"

"No. No. It's not that. I just have a headache and I'm tired."

"I have to go call my mother. Wanna come to my room?"

"Well, uh—it's almost time to leave. I'd better go find Judy."

He walked away, wheeling Gary with him. I could hear them talk and laugh. They were laughing at me.

Two other points about writing conversation: professionals identify a speaker with phrases like *said John* only when necessary, and they don't keep nudging the reader with Insistery ("Go to hell, said John *angrily*"). If John says "Go to hell," he's probably angry. If he isn't, you have to do more than simply say, "said John gently." You must establish by the context of the whole conversation and the character of the relationship between the speakers that "Go to hell" in this instance is a gentle, comradely comment rather than an angry dismissal.

The spoken words in the following lines were taken from the above story "For a Walk?" They appear right after the first three paragraphs. Here below they are handled amateurishly, with unnecessary explanations and identifications beyond the spoken words. In the story they were handled expertly—the readers given no more than they needed.

> "Wanna go for a walk?" Doug asked questioningly.
>
> "Uh, OK. Your name is Doug, isn't it?" said Kathy obligingly. "I met you earlier."
>
> "Yea," he said matter of factly. Then he added, "I don't remember your name."
>
> "Kathy," she said shortly.

In the original passage, the author didn't employ these words in her version: *Doug, questioningly, said Kathy obligingly, he said matter of factly, Then he added, she said shortly.* If there are only two persons in a conversation, seldom do they need to be identified. If three or more, readers are more likely to become confused at times; but the fundamental remains —don't insult readers by giving them more than they need.

WRITING FIVE: Write two dialogues that carry truth that counts for you and voices that speak truly and individually.

It's helpful for beginners to write their first conversations in dramatic form, with the names of speakers preceding each spoken line. Then they won't be encouraged to clutter their writing with explanations and comments like "he said disgustedly."

Here's another sample of a dialogue that in every way asks a lot of the reader; two college roommates are talking.

MOVE

> **"You're going to move tonight?"**
>
> **"Yes, I might as well get it out of the way before classes get started."**
>
> **"Are you sure it wasn't anything that I said or did?"**
>
> **"I've explained that to you so many times! It's not you. It's your people."**
>
> **"OK, OK. Is there something I can do for you?"**

"Yes, you can close up my record player."

"All right. Did you say you were going to room with Darleen?"

"Yes."

"Is she militant?"

"That's not really a good term, but she is. Your tact is terrific."

"Do you agree with her?"

"In some ways. Jan, she's one of my people."

"I'm not blind. Here's your record player."

"Thanks. Have you seen my James Brown album?"

"I think Darleen borrowed it."

"That's right. You know it has to be this way, don't you?"

"I can't say that, but I'm trying to understand."

"Well, look at Barbara Jean. How many Blacks have you seen talking to her lately?"

"I haven't really noticed."

"You've got to notice, Jan! There is no middle of the road, or at least there won't be."

"Have they been giving you any static about living with a White?"

"This is my own decision."

"Now you're not noticing!"

"Well, I guess I'm ready."

"Maybe I'll see you around, huh? You don't have to tell anyone that you lived with a Honky."

"To be shoor, Miss Jan, ah wunt do dat!"

"Bye."

"Good-bye."

People talking. They say so much more than their words say.

Shams and delusions are esteemed for soundest truth, while reality is fabulous. If men would steadily observe realities only, and not allow themselves to be deluded, life, to compare it with such things as we know, would be like a fairy tale and the Arabian Nights' Entertainments.

HENRY THOREAU

chapter 7 fabulous realities

MOST OF US go through each day looking for what we saw yesterday and we find it, to our half-realized disappointment. But people who daily expect to encounter fabulous realities run smack into them again and again. They keep their minds open for their eyes.

Asked to expect surprise, a number of students explored their nearby worlds for fabulous realities. Here are some they found:

1. I was speeding along the highway when I saw a small yellow sign.

   SLOW
   MEN
   WORKING

   It was followed by a larger one in black and white, reading

   YOUR HIGHWAY DOLLARS
   AT WORK

2. At a football game yesterday at Waldo Stadium a blind man sat next to me listening to his radio.
3. I stood in the checkout lane behind a boy who looked about sixteen. He waited for the clerk to begin ringing up his package of Pall Malls, then reached out and added five packs of bubble gum.

4. Ever since Rennie found out that Jane, his co-worker, doesn't like him, he tries to upset her when they are together. I asked him why he did this. He said, "I hate intolerant people."
5. At the Allegan County Fair I approached the cotton candy stand and told the girl I wanted pink. After she gave it to me she turned to get my change and I noticed a piece of cotton in her ear.
6. Today I found a dead bird in the gutter with its mangled wing held in place by "Magic Transparent Tape."
7. A drunk teenager trying to cross West Main at Michigan assisted by a little old lady.
8. I excitedly opened my only two valentines from males. They were just alike.
9. A girl with a deep V in her blouse holding her books over it.
10. A man returned to his parked car to find its hood and fenders gashed and crumpled. On the dashboard he found a piece of folded paper. Written in a neat feminine hand, the note said: "I have just run into your car. There are people watching me. They think I am writing down my name and address. They are wrong."
11. A small boy, obviously lost, walked up to a security guard at Hudson's department store, and asked, "Did you see a lady walk by here without me?"
12. A pregnant woman carrying a globe of the world in front of her up a steep sidewalk in the city.
13. In the middle of a heated argument with me, my wife goes to the refrigerator, gets a bottle of ginger ale, fills two glasses, gives me one, and continues the argument.

Each statement surprises. It's not fairly surprising, but absolutely surprising, because it's unique. A robin sitting in the April snow in Illinois or Massachusetts wouldn't qualify as a fabulous reality. In those states a late short snow often occurs after robins have arrived.

Tension is necessary to make a fabulous reality. Two things that don't belong together touch in some way. And their touching creates waves of further suggestion that aren't stated. In the middle of the young man's argument, his wife interrupts him, but not to put him down, rather to make him more comfortable. The argument is heated; she gives him a cold drink.

When I went to those great cities I saw wonders I had never seen in Ireland. But when I came back to Ireland I found all the wonders there waiting for me. You see they had been there all the time; but my eyes had never been opened to them. I did not know what my own house was like, because I had never been outside it.

BERNARD SHAW [*Keegan speaking*]

COLLECTING THREE: This weekend keep a piece of paper or notebook in your pocket or pocketbook and jot down five fabulous realities you see. When you have a chance, write them in sentences. Keep revising them until you have built up to the surprise rather than given it away weakly. Note that most of the above fabulous realities (1) place the happening in a particular setting, (2) put the reader there through telling details, (3) make the action happen for the reader as it happened for the writer, (4) do not waste words, (5) do not explain, but present facts and force the reader to find the surprise, (6) put the kicker at the end.

Note how the facts in this fabulous reality do all the telling by themselves.

> **A pimply-faced, dirty, barefooted, greasy, string-haired girl smoking a cigarette and eating a peanut butter and jelly sandwich riding a crowded elevator at the University of Michigan while reading *How to Win Friends and Influence People.***

COLLECTING FOUR: Collect five or more additional fabulous realities. Don't be easily satisfied. Tension. Punch at the end. Uniqueness. Implications or suggestions that spread beyond the statement.

The looking and discovering involved in producing fabulous realities isn't a trick or an exercise. It's the way good writers see. Because their eyes aren't tired, their readers turn their pages with surprise. In *People of the Abyss,* a book about the city of London, Jack London wrote:

> From the slimy spittle-drenched sidewalk, they were picking up bits of orange peel, apple skin, and grape stems, and they were eating them. The pits of green gage plums they cracked between their teeth for the kernels inside. They picked up stray crumbs of bread the size of peas, apple cores so black and dirty one would not take them to be apple cores, and these things these two men took into their mouths, and chewed them, and swallowed them; and this, between six and seven o'clock in the evening of August 20, year of our Lord 1902, in the heart of the greatest, wealthiest, and most powerful empire the world has ever seeen.

Note that Jack London is here not just telling an unusual incident but is writing toward an idea—that the great English capital city did not save [illegible]ns from degrading poverty. Surprising realities suffuse good [illegible] and articles as they do good stories. One of the reasons students in schools seldom write powerful themes or essays is that they mistakenly think good nonfiction writing is abstract and dull. Actually, the best writers of nonfiction (articles, essays, autobiography, history, etc.) continually surprise their readers with fabulous realities.

When you read accounts others have written of surprising realities, like Jack London's, you may feel they were lucky but you were never blessed. But reality is often fabulous for the person who remains awake.

> *He [Thoreau] knew how to sit immovable, a part of the rock he rested on, until the bird, the reptile, the fish, which had retired from him, should come back and resume its habits, nay, moved by curiosity, should come to him and watch him.*
>
> RALPH WALDO EMERSON

The unfamiliar frequently appears amazing, as does the familiar when it is scrutinized more closely than usual.

WRITING SIX: Write a fabulous reality that is a page or more in length. You may already have found one that you can expand. Or you may have done a free writing that you can work up into a fabulous reality.

Here's such a free writing done by a high school student:

THE REPORTER

The news last night was about the dam breaking. A reporter was talking to a boy who was about ten or eleven years old. The boy said, "My mom told me to get out of the house because a flood was coming. As soon as the water hit the house, it collapsed." He stopped; he was trying so hard to keep from crying that he couldn't go on. The reporter said, "Then what happened?" The boy said, "Then, then my mother, my two sisters and brother, were drowned." It made me sick when that reporter made him tell what happened. Couldn't he see that it was about to kill the kid by talking about his family? I don't like reporters; they always have to probe into people's lives.

This piece of writing would gain if it employed point 4 of the requirements for a fabulous reality: making readers work to find the significance of the event on their own. Suppose the last three sentences were dropped so that the tale ended with the kicker. But without the last three sentences a reader might miss the point. Maybe if the phrase "The reporter said" were replaced with "The reporter kept pressing," the reader would be cued sufficiently to see how the writer felt about what was happening.

While the writer is sharpening this tale so that it becomes a fabulous reality, he might use conversation paragraphing to make more apparent the change of speakers. And he might think about cutting one of the *about's* in the first two sentences. That kind of repetition is common in speech and writing: we say a word like *about* and use it again because it has printed itself on our language machine. Sometimes the second printing is powerful; here it is not. As so often happens, the move to delete a wasted or weakly repeated word leads to an improvement in other phrases. In this account the writer says "a boy who was about ten or eleven years old." He doesn't know how old the boy was. One year's difference won't count with the reader, so the writer might as well say "a ten-year-old boy." Here's a tightened version of the story:

THE REPORTER (*Revised*)

The news last night was about the dam breaking. A reporter was talking to a ten-year-old boy who said, "My mom told me to get out of the house because a flood was coming. As soon as the water hit the house it collapsed." He was trying so hard to keep from crying that he couldn't go on.

The reporter kept pressing. "Then what happened?"

"Then, then my mother, my two sisters and brother were drowned."

Now the passage requires the reader to see that the reporter's question should not have been delivered at that time. It infringed upon the boy's privacy agonizingly. Surprising that anyone could be that cruel? But true. A fabulous reality.

Here's another longer free writing that isn't pointedly a fabulous reality, but behind its lines lies the irony that in this setting, where a patient is supposed to feel one way, she feels another.

PATIENCE

I've always gotten along pretty well with doctors, until last Friday, anyway. I swung open the door and was immedi-

ately confronted by six pairs of eyes—a young guy on crutches, an old woman with her daughter, a lady in her twenties, and another lady with her baby. Everyone seemed to look me over as if I were a cow for sale. The receptionist greeted me with a large toothy smile, and I said hi. I proceeded to give her my name, address, telephone number, have you ever had thises and have you ever had thats, stopping every now and then to repeat myself.

I then took a seat and picked up a copy of *Sports Illustrated* and began to wait, and wait, and wait. I waited for an hour and ten minutes. I must have read the magazine twenty times.

Finally a plump little nurse came out and said in a witchy tone of voice, "Casarri, please." She escorted me to a room and said, "Strip down to your underwear and put this on." She handed me a hospital gown and left.

I did what she told me but then made a mistake—I sat in the aluminum chair. Oh! was that cold. Again I waited, but this time for only ten minutes. Those gowns are so starchy if I moved I cut myself. The doctor did show up but not for long. He did a few quick taps here and a pull there, then off to the X-ray room. Again I waited and again I sat in a cold aluminum chair. After X-rays I went back to the room and waited. That's all I seemed to do. Wait.

Some young guy brought the X-rays back, but alas no doctor. So he made some wise-ass remark as he slapped a picture on the viewer, like, "Bet you've never seen your back before." I had to chuckle to make him feel good and to get him out of there. I don't think I could have taken any more of those intern jokes. When the doctor finally came back, I had gone through the X-rays and could have told him what was wrong with me. He looked at them this way and that and then wrote down a prescription while mumbling some witchcraft incantation like "Oooo, EEEE, ah ah ah wellllll, maybeee." Then he wrote something in some foreign tongue and handed it to me. I looked at the piece of paper, then I looked at him. I couldn't read it but I didn't want him to know that. He then left me standing there —half-naked, with a piece of ancient hieroglyphics in my hand, wondering what was going on.

That's an unusual story. It's beautifully quick and humorous at times and overwritten at other times. Where a patient is supposed to feel secure because she's in the land of scientific techniques, she feels the opposite. The waiting becomes ludicrous, the aluminum chairs cold, and the impression grows that she's in the hands of a witch doctor. A first step in cutting would be to drop the phrase "proceeded to" in the fifth sentence and simply say "I gave her . . ." You might consider other ways to tighten this writing. It's worth working on, for it makes a large point about how patients feel with doctors.

Here's another passage which takes on the power of a fabulous reality:

KISS

I first kissed a girl in the fifth grade, during basketball season. I decided it had to be this cold November night. With the north wind blowing, it had to be done in a car or on the south side of the gym. I got to the basketball game late. We held hands until half time, and that was when I decided it would have to be now. We went out to my parent's car with my best friend and his girl friend. Rita and I just stared straight ahead. I was shaking so badly with fear that I couldn't get any words out. She broke the silence finally by saying, "We better go in or our parents will be looking for us." So I made a deal with her. We could go in as soon as we went on the other side of the gym. The first thing I remember her saying was, "Well, we are on the other side of the gym." I tried to kiss her but missed. So I led her over to a foot high rock. I climbed up so I could reach her, and finally kissed her for a second but then it felt like a long time.

Another giveaway opening, but with the first five words cut and a new title supplied, this would be a fine fabulous reality. It puts the reader in the action with short, building statements. The last statement of the passage, "but then it felt like a long time," is more an explanation and less an action than the endings of most successful fabulous realities, but here the words create a sufficient surprise to make the story work.

Life is routine more than it is fabulous. Without the steadiness of the expected, newness is impossible or chaotic. But most of us would gain from confronting and recognizing a great deal more newness than we do.

If you stand right fronting and face to face to a fact, you will see the sun glimmer on both its surfaces, as if it were a cimeter [scimitar], and feel its sweet edge dividing you through the heart and marrow . . .

HENRY THOREAU

Sit down before fact as a little child . . .

THOMAS HENRY HUXLEY

chapter 8 writing case histories

FOG IS BEAUTIFUL from above or outside—rolling, wispy. But once your car enters it, your journey becomes nightmare. Where you are, how fast you are going, what direction, or what other vehicle will loom up, you don't know. You can't drive at a reasonable speed and you may very well slide into a ditch or river before you know it. There is simply too much unknown.

This is what happens often to students in school. You should take your journeys on the back of your hand or in your own yard. And simply tell us what you know. A case history of how you carried your papers on your route one morning, of how you prepare for school in a family of seven in a house with one bathroom, of how you got ready to play your first game of varsity basketball. A day, a week, an hour—some interval of your life through which you take us as you carry out one connected action or watch someone else or something else go through a process. No fog should be involved.

You don't have to be a professional writer to tell a case history with authority and power. You have only to know your journey intimately and carry some attitude toward it which enables you to select details that keep the history alive and significant—something more than a bad list of names and dates. Michihiko Hachiya, a medical doctor in Japan, was wounded on August 6, 1945, by the first nuclear explosion directed against human beings. The next morning he awoke to groans of patients and a new Hiroshima. He told the story of his experiences, a simple case history of what happened to him then.

> Dr. Katsube looked me over and after feeling my pulse, said: "You received many wounds, but they all missed vital spots."
>
> He then described them and told me how they had been treated. I was surprised to learn that my shoulder had been severely cut but relieved at his optimism for my recovery.
>
> "How many patients are in the hospital?" I asked Dr. Koyama.
>
> "About a hundred and fifty," he replied. "Quite a few have died, but there are still so many that there is no place to put one's foot down. They are packed in everywhere, even the toilets."
>
> • • •
>
> Downstairs, I ran into Mr. Hirohata sitting on a bench and down beside him. Mr. Hirohata had been employed in the Telephone Bureau and was at work in the building when the explosion occurred. Despite the fact that he was less than four hundred meters from the hypocenter, Mr. Hirohata escaped injury.
>
> "How did you avoid injury when nearly everyone around you was killed or hurt?" I asked.
>
> "The thick concrete wall of the building protected me," answered Mr. Hirohata, "but people standing near the windows were killed instantly or died later from burns or cuts. The night shift was just leaving and the day shift coming on when the explosion occurred. Forty or more were killed near the entrance. About fifteen employees in the construction department, stripped to the waist, were outside taking gymnastics. They died instantly.
>
> "Doctor, a human being who has been roasted becomes quite small, doesn't he? Those people all looked like little boys after the explosion. Is there any reason why my hair should be falling out and I feel so weak? I'm worried, doctor, because I have been told that I would die and this

has already happened to some people I know who didn't seem to be hurt at all by the *pika*."

"Mr. Hirohata, I don't believe you need worry about yourself," I answered, trying to be reassuring. "Like so many others, you've been through a dreadful experience, and on top of that have tried to work night and day here at the Bureau. What else could one expect? You must go home, stay absolutely quiet in bed, and get all the good nourishing food you can."

This excerpt from a 233-page book shows that Dr. Hachiya wrote down his experience in incidents and conversations as they came to him. He called the book *Hiroshima Diary: The Journal of a Japanese Physician, August 6–September 30, 1945*. He told what he did, what others did, whom he saw, what they said to each other. In writing a case history, put the reader there, right in the process, the place, the action. If you see a man riding a bicycle with a broken red reflector on its rear bumper, don't write: "I saw a man riding a damaged bicycle," but "I saw a man riding a bicycle with a broken red reflector on its rear bumper."

If you record the details of a process or experience and then write them into a case history, in one sense you are an authority. You may not know more about that process or experience than some others, but your written record commands respect by its truth to particular fact. Here is a case history written by a student:

THE BIRTH OF A LAMB

As my father and I fed our ewes at night, I could easily pick out which ones had serious thoughts for the long night ahead. Their ears would be streamlined like the wings of a jet. Their sides would be concave from their backbones like the sides of the pup tent. After we finished chores, I would climb into the straw mow where I would be the king looking down on a command performance. Tonight I would watch a miracle people never have the opportunity to see—watching the coming of a new life.

I couldn't tell how long the birth would take. If it were hard, it might take three or four hours—only an hour if it were easy. First came the water bag. I was surprised to see it because in my excitement I was looking for the lamb. My anticipation bounces me over many surprises because I remember only the end.

The bag was pliable like a transparent sack made of

rubber bands. It held nearly a pint of antifreeze colored liquid. As the birth progressed, the water bag bounced lower and lower like a spider coming down his web. When the bag touched the dirty straw in the pen, it acted like an anchor as it pulled the rest of its container from the ewe. This accomplished, it opened, spilling its deep, purple antifreeze onto the straw like a fallen handkerchief full of BB's that has been held by the corners. The new element sponging through the dirt-freckled straw united the freckles into a solid dirty brown.

A gummy material followed the water bag, threatening the worn straw again. It was thick and sticky; it looked and felt like petroleum jelly with gum added. The work was coming heavier to the ewe as a pair of black hoofs covered by a slimy plastic bag emerged. The ewe pushes from her front shoulders down. I can follow the strain down to her rear shoulders, then up again as she relaxes. She holds her breath and pushes so hard that her lips curl outward, sometimes emitting a little "ma-at"—not a "blat" like most people think.

The nose and eyes are out, but the hardest part remains. The straining eases now. The anxious ewe thinks her labor is over. She gets up expecting to find the lamb behind her, but finds nothing. She licks the spot where his head has touched and lies down to try again. Once the lamb is out past his shoulders, the rest is easy. Now I sigh and realize that I've pushed and strained with the ewe for the last hour.

The lamb doesn't need me, but I rush down from my throne, stumbling because my eyes see only him. He lies coughing to clear the phlegm from his throat. I reach into his plastic puddle and force my fingers into his throat, clearing it.

The mother communicates with me. A recognizable smile unites me with her feelings. I could have had the birth and she could have been the king.

She doesn't have a doctor to hand her the baby, so she forces herself up to lick off his sticky coating. Our union of feeling ends; she's a sheep and I'm a curious little boy. I can't understand how the slimy plastic sack tastes. Too many people can't understand.

MAX SLISHER

Writing a case history will point you in the opposite direction from which this high school student went when he wrote the following comment for his school newspaper:

DAYS GONE BY DON'T RETURN

Everyone has heard the expression from their parents, "Well when I was young . . ." What parents need to realize is that life is different now; the problems of teenagers are still present, but the problems are new and different.

Today's teenagers are pressured more than any other generation has been before. A constant threat to this age is one of worrying about college and being "in" a crowd at school.

These problems existed when parents of today were younger, but not to the extreme that they do now. A job today requires a college education; before, this was not necessary.

Teenagers are more socially conscious now than in past generations. Fads must be met, the new places must be visited, the group must be followed in order to be considered "in."

Times change; with them come joys and problems. Life for the teenager seems easy to most parents but it is difficult. New problems arise before old ones are solved. It is a never-ending battle of pressures and difficulties.

Maybe a good point, but never made convincing. Had this writer presented a short case-history of a student learning to observe a fad, or visiting one of the "new places that must be visited," or going through the actions necessary to become "in" with a group, he probably would have produced a valuable piece of writing.

> *The momentum of the mind is all toward abstraction.*
>
> WALLACE STEVENS

WRITING SEVEN: Write a case history of some job, process, action —what happened through a period of time. An hour working with a computer, a day in the body shop, one swimming lesson you gave a five-year-old, one vacation day when you did "nothing" for eight hours. If possible, take notes as you go through the experience, or right after the act, and record details you can remember.

Choose an action that is fun or misery for you, exciting or boring. Speak factually most of the time, as did Dr. Hachiya and the author of "The Birth of a Lamb." Make your readers respect you as an authority on this action by the way you reveal its intimate workings, but remember not to lose them in meaningless technical terms.

Pack in the detail but make it add up to reveal the essence of the job, or your feeling toward it. A case history should be useful and fascinating. You can make it alive by remembering to keep asking "So what?" as you assemble materials and write. When readers finish your history, they should go away with one or two major impressions in mind, and possibly feelings, as well as a memory of close details.

Note how the following case history of a few minutes at a music festival reveals the feelings of a performer and a judge. Like all good writing, it doesn't oversimplify. It centers on the embarrassment of one person and goes deeply into its complex causes. And so humorously.

REED

Maybe I could faint again. I did at the Solo-Ensemble Festival. Almost, anyway. That's where instrumentalists memorize a solo and play it for a rating from some judge who knows all about whatever instrument it is and spends all his Saturdays listening to the same solos over and over. But I was playing along on mine and hoping I'd remember the next note because I'd only memorized the piece the night before and I kept getting short of breath and gulping. Pretty soon I felt faint but I thought I better keep going instead of being one of those whimpering fainting females. I began wondering what would happen if I did faint right there.

It would wreck the reed for sure. The reed is what makes the noise. No reed, no sound, and the hellmost torture for a clarinetist is wrecking a reed because the good ones cost forty-five cents apiece and only come in boxes of ten and only two or three of these will work with luck, and two or three won't work at all and the rest will just kind of thud a lot.

So when I thought of falling over on my good reed, I decided I better stop, so I asked the judge if I could stop for a while, except I said "Sir, I feel faint." The judge was a heavy man who looked like he should have been bald, but he wasn't. Anyway, my accompanist hadn't heard me and it was the end of a rest and I was supposed to come in again,

so she kept playing my cue over and over. I walked over to the judge's desk and said I felt faint and wanted to sit down. He wore black glasses and looked at me over them like what was I doing stopping in the middle of a piece like that? I was supposed to just play and not interrupt his judging routine with sudden stops. He took my elbow and my clarinet, which he put on his desk after checking the make of instrument and mouthpiece I had because he was a devoted clarinetist and probably hated fainting whimpering females. I hoped then that I was using a fifteen dollar Kaspar mouthpiece some character sits around making by hand in Ann Arbor, except he's retired now. This is like my mother telling me to always wear pretty underwear in case I get hit by a car and have to go to the hospital. Maybe she said that because once she fell down the stairs and broke her leg and was embarrassed to tears at having to ride all the way to the hospital in an ambulance with ugly underwear.

The judge kept my elbow and showed me to a chair. He told me to "take a whole bunch of deep breaths." While I was doing that, a group of people came into the room because they thought I was through playing. It was supposed to be a science classroom regularly except that Saturday when clarinetists performed in it and people were only allowed to come in between performances. When I got up and started in the middle of the solo it puzzled them a little, but when I was through they clapped anyway and the judge told them they hadn't heard very much, but the rest was just as good. That's one of those devious, double-sided comments people say and leave a person wondering exactly what they meant for some time afterward. I volunteered to play the whole thing again but the judge kind of shoved me out to the hall and collapsed in a chair.

LOUISE FREYBURGER

If you prefer, you may write a history of someone else's actions. Choose what you can observe firsthand, clearly and completely—an incident or event you can sit and watch like a cat. Take notes. Ask questions if necessary. Get the facts right.

You might sit in a library and write down what you see for an hour. Sit opposite the circulation desk, close by, where you can hear and record what the clerk does and says in a half hour.

Think of what your finished writing will look like. Choose a process or event small enough in time and limited enough in scope that you can cover it with satisfactory thoroughness. Don't write a case history of your high school career or a year's performance by the basketball captain. Each would require volumes. Aim at a paper of two to six pages, double-spaced if typewritten, a little more if in longhand.

REVISING FOUR: When you have finished your first draft of the case history, put it aside for a day. Then read it aloud to see whether any leading idea or feeling emerges. If you find one stirring a little, consider cutting out those parts that do not touch this idea or feeling, and adding more details that strengthen it.

If you care about what you write, and know or observe it closely, you'll reveal to your readers things they don't know. Stay awake when you observe. If you or other human beings are in action, the chances are high that you will be recording some fabulous realities.

One professional caution: Change any real names in your case history to fictional names. What if your work becomes published, or passed around locally? What you consider an unbiased report of how Mrs. Smithweather, the science teacher, swore at John Saunders in lab may not strike Mrs. Smithweather in that way. If you had money, she might properly sue you for libel. Some real names you must keep in your writing or its point may be lost, but inspect all names and weigh the need to change them. Samuel Butler wrote a long book which became the classical English story of a sensitive son and a tyrannical, self-righteous father. Butler's real father was a sadist to him, but he refused to publish this book until after his father had died. And then it came out as a novel, with Butler's father carrying a fictional name. Butler himself died before *The Way of All Flesh* was published and he never knew that he had written one of the finest novels in the English language. The least you can do is protect Mrs. Smithweather and yourself by changing names.

> *It is much easier to sit at a desk and read plans for a billion gallons of water a day, and look at maps and photographs; but you will write a better article if you heave yourself out of a comfortable chair and go down in tunnel 3 and get soaked.*
>
> STUART CHASE

Repeat: *to double, re-double, renew, parallel, echo, match, mirror, reproduce, regenerate, reincarnate, multiply, revive, reaffirm, reassert, accentuate, emphasize, build, hammer, slap, thump, beat, bang, punch, jab, convince, charm, lull, caress.*

chapter 9 repeating

WEAK AND STRONG REPETITION

IF SOMEONE you love keeps saying "I love you," the repetition is beautiful. But if someone you dislike keeps saying "I love you," the repetition is unbearable. And there are places and moments where you don't want to be told you are loved. Even the heartbeat, with its repetitious but slightly irregular liveliness, can become monotonous—for example, if recorded day after day in a laboratory.

Repetition can comfort or bore, clarify or confuse, astound or outrage. Consider these repetitions:

> **I think Ethel was rebelling when she refused to follow my suggestion. She was rebelling against her ability to recover, her ability to heal, her ability to retain her youth. She had lost her youth, yet she was still fighting. Fighting for a lost cause.**

They clog the passage rather than emphasize what needs to be emphasized.

Professional writers read their work aloud to themselves and to others. They hear repetitions their eyes don't see. You need to find ways of getting inside your writing and hearing it objectively. One way is to read it aloud and listen for repetitions, which are easily detected. Those that you're surprised to find are usually weak: you didn't intend them. They may become valuable to you as flags indicating other failures or surrenders. If you didn't notice them before, you probably missed other weaknesses.

Often weak repetition blooms when writers try to impress their readers, as in this passage:

> **When one sits before an open hearth and can see the flames shooting from the burning wood, hear the crackling of the fire as it engulfs its source of fuel, and feel the warmth given off, one enters another "world," a "world" which is quiet and peaceful . . . You may ask why we spend so much time by the fire, and that should be a difficult question to answer. But I believe it is the "mystery" of the fire that intrigues us. This "mystery" of the fire has a way of captivating your thoughts and putting you in a trance-like atmosphere.**

Here words appear close to each other in ineffectual repetition. The writer puts quotation marks around the words *world* and *mystery*—which she uses in the commonest way—and insults her reader. Instead of saying the crackling fire "engulfs its *wood,*" the writer says "engulfs its *source of fuel.*" She's so afraid of repetition that she went to ridiculous lengths to find a synonym. Wood is fuel, but here the general subject of fuel is not being discussed. If the writer can't stand to hear the word *wood* repeated, she should remove its first use, not its second. Then the passage would read:

> When one sits before an open hearth and watches the shooting flames, hears the crackling as the fire engulfs the wood, and feels the warmth given off . . .

Avoidance of repetition sometimes leads writers to silly substitutions for a key word in a passage. If the principal subject of your writing is *cats,* use the word *cats* frequently. Don't say *cats,* then *felines, furry friends,* and *four-legged bundles of fur.* Sports writers often sin with this "elegant variation." For example, a good sportswriter in a student newspaper began his article with *The Rich track team.* Then he calls them by their name *The Olympians.* Next he says, "Then *the squad* began to show." Up to that point his variation in naming is inoffensive, but next he says:

> Still improving, the Central cindermen then overran T. F. South and Lockport West, finishing the season in grand style. The Olympians captured nine firsts . .

By that point the paper's regular readers are probably fatigued by the writer's attempt to avoid repetition, and an outsider is probably lost, wondering whether *the Central cindermen* still refers to *the Rich track team* or to one of their opponents.

Writers who have found a voice that belongs to them repeat words with power, not weakness. If they want to hit a word hard, they repeat it. Dr. Seuss does:

> Then Horton the elephant smiled. "Now that's that . . ."
> And he sat
> and he sat
> and he sat
> and he sat . . .
> And he sat all that day
> And he kept the egg warm . . .
> And he sat all that night
> Through a *terrible* storm.

Thomas Paine, the pamphleteer who helped persuade colonists to join George Washington's army, wrote:

> I call not upon a few, but upon all: not on this state or that state, but on every state: up and help us; lay your shoulders to the wheel; better have too much force than too little when so great an object is at stake.

These repetitions helped create the United States.

In Shakespeare's *Macbeth,* Macduff speaks to Malcolm, reminding him of the sad state to which Scotland has fallen under the rule of the murdering King Macbeth:

> Each new morn
> New widows howl, new orphans cry, new sorrows
> Strike heaven on the face, that it resounds
> As if it felt with Scotland and yelled out
> Like syllable of dolor.

Here the *new* murders husbands, fathers, happiness, and creates widows, orphans, sorrows. It is not at all like the *new* which appears on so many packages of detergent, toothpaste, and shampoo in the supermarket. Manufacturers think the word will sell their product and they change the product ever so slightly once a year, or change it not at all, and stamp *new* on the package. Too many *new's* on packages have killed the force of them all.

Professional writers usually avoid starting a sentence with the same word that ends the preceding sentence:

> I found out his name was John. John was an engineer.
>
> The last topic on the program was rehabilitation. Rehabilitation is an urgent matter in Michigan because prisons are overcrowded.

In the second or third draft, professional writers look for repetitions of this sort—they know they will be there—and expunge them. But frequently they achieve their best repetition unconsciously. An idea or a fact, often epitomized in a key word, dominates their minds. They repeat it when they write.

A good way to utilize repetition without being dull is to shift the form of the repeated word, or play with it in some say. Here a writer makes the word *uncivilized* speak to the word *civilized:*

> **I don't like picnics. That's against the great American tradition, I guess. I don't like to combine the civilized way of eating with uncivilized surroundings.**

When you write out a first draft hurriedly, you may find one key word appearing again and again. Before you eliminate the repetitions of it, think twice. Some of the repetitions may give strength to your writing and let the reader know what objects or ideas dominate your thought. Here's a memory of childhood that needs cutting. It contains too much good writing to be allowed to remain in this state marred by weak repetitions. But some of its repetitions are essential; for example, of the word *outside,* which is central to the writer's point. (Some of the major repetitions are indicated here in italics.)

> **Summer seems more fun during childhood. I remember those *screen-door days*. The back *door* to my house was covered with two sections of *screen* that bulged from being pushed by an endless chain of small hands. I doubt that the *door* was ever shut without a *bang;* in fact it seemed to be there for the sole purpose of shutting with a *bang*. To butt out that *door* without hearing the familiar b-r-r-zing *BANG*! would have been as unnatural to me as giving my sister some of my candy—well almost. I was always in a great hurry to get *outside*. Summer is an *outside* time. I had an *outside* mind. I could only think in *outside*. Sometimes in my haste to join my mind *outside*, I would fly at the *door* only to discover, too late, that a security-conscious grand-**

mother or some such menace of childhood had locked it. I would come to a tire-tearing halt, like a cartoon car stopping on a dime. I had to peel my face off the *screen* like a waffle, and looking very much like one only with much smaller squares. I would *cuss* at whoever locked the *door*. If I did not know who the culprit was I would *cuss* at everyone just to be on the safe side. However my anger was silent, or mutterings at best. My mother's children left much to be desired where brains are concerned, but she did not rear any of us to be *stupid*, at least not so *stupid* as to be caught *swearing*. My father was a great strong *swearer*. He could invoke deities and conjure up demons that made my bottom sore before the *belt* was even off his waist. I was always puzzled by the fact that I could say "*god-darn*" this and "*god-darn*" that depending on whatever I wanted *God* to mend, and yet "*goddamn*" always removed the belt from my father's waist. The sin was in the "damn" not in the "God." I always wondered what God thought about it and how big a belt he had.

MICHAEL MANUEL

In this reflection on childhood, the notion of *outside* is crucial to the story because it's the urge to get outside quickly that led the boy to swear and to confront his father and think upon the effects and causes of profanity. But too much emphasis on *outside* and the screen door makes the ending discussion of profanity seem like an afterthought rather than the major subject the writing builds toward. Here's a revision of the story with a number of the repetitions cut out:

The back *door* to my house was covered with two sections of *screen* that bulged from being pushed by an endless chain of small hands. That *door* seemed to be there for the sole purpose of being slammed. To butt out it without hearing the familiar b-r-r-zing BANG! would have been as unnatural to me as giving my sister some of my candy.

I could only think in *outside*. Sometimes in my haste to join my mind *outside*, I would fly at the *door* only to discover too late that a security-conscious grandmother had locked it. I would come to a halt like a cartoon car stopping on a dime and would peel my face off the *screen* like a waffle. Then I would cuss—at everyone, just to be on the safe side—but silently, mutteringly. Mother did not rear us to be so stupid as to be caught *swearing*.

> **Father was a great strong *swearer*. He could invoke deities and conjure up demons that made my bottom sore before the *belt* was off his waist. I was always puzzled because I could say *"god-darn"* this and *"god-darn"* that, depending on whatever I wanted *God* to mend, and yet *"god-damn"* always removed the *belt* from Father's waist. The sin was in the *"damn"* not in the *"God."* I always wondered what *God* thought about it and how big a *belt* he wore.**

Repetitions remain but they are necessary, therefore not tedious but powerful. To gain their full effect, some words should not be repeated at all. The writer should save them strategically for one best moment. In the above story if the word *bang* is to sound loud, it should be heard only once.

Rhyme is a form of repetition, of sound, not word. It can be used in prose if the writer remembers that its effect there is customarily humorous. Lilian Moore wrote a book she called *A Pickle for a Nickle* in which she had Mr. Bumble say truly, "Boys like noise."

REVISING FIVE: Examine your story about childhood. Omit the weak repetitions and consider adding strong repetitions. Use penciled brackets so that you may restore words or phrases should you later change your mind.

WRITING EIGHT: Dash off two 10- to 15-minute free writings in which you play frequently with repetition. Repeat words in as many different patterns as you can. Repeat a word three times in a row, then repeat it as the key word in three phrases: "He was a bumbling carpenter, a bumbling father, a bumbling fisherman." Then separate the repeated words even more from each other. Try repeating all kinds of words—verbs, adverbs, prepositions, adjectives, nouns, etc. Use a word once with one meaning and then with another meaning. If you feel stalled, study advertisements in magazines and commercials on television to find still other ways to repeat. Study poems; almost all good ones repeat words skillfully. In all your practice in repeating, do not make up nonsense phrases or sentences that are lists of words unrepresentative of thoughts or feelings in you. Try always to say something you mean but play while you do that. Play around—seriously.

PARALLEL CONSTRUCTION

One of the fundamental beats in all good writing is parallel construction, which is based on repetition. No competent writer's ear is deaf to it. Take this statement:

> George liked Jean and often walked beside her on the way to school. Jean was also sometimes accompanied to school by Ronald, who also liked her, but who often could be seen walking behind her.

Here's a shorter version:

> George liked Jean and often walked beside her on the way to school. Jean was also accompanied by Ronald, who walked behind her.

But it's still awkward. Seeing that the sentences compare George's and Ronald's walking with Jean, the professional writer would cast each part of the comparison in parallel form:

> George liked Jean and walked beside her to school. Ronald liked Jean and walked behind her to school.

Tightened and paralleled in this fashion, the sentences now emphasize that Ronald was bashful. They could be paralleled in another way:

> The boys liked Jean. George walked beside her to school and Ronald behind her.

At the same time that most parallel patterning throws into simple and dramatic comparison two or more ideas or persons or things, it shortens a statement so severely that it requires work from the reader. This is an ideal combination of qualities: challenge and delight.

If you wonder how your words will strike your readers, you need only ask how they strike you as you pattern them. If you find yourself unchallenged or bored, you should know you're not writing well. Your words should speak to you as well as to your audience—and to each other. Parallel patterning helps give them voice. Note how this writer's words speak to each other:

> **I like to bounce when I get into bed, and pick up my pillow and throw it down, then pick up my head and drop it into the pillow, like someone picking up a little kitten and dropping it in some out of the way place so that it won't get *under* foot. Good thing I've got the upper bunk . . . I couldn't be any more *out* from *under* foot.**

Train your ear so you hear a word when you write it, and then ask whether it needs an answer from another word soon. Here's a beginning writer listening as she wrote:

> Why not be natural, free, untimed, unlimited?

Here's a professional advertising writer listening while writing:

> You ought to watch Longchamps meat experts buying beef for your dinner. They stride through the refrigerators, sniffing and poking each rib on the rack. They know what's what. So butchers give them their best. Well marbled steaks, tender as butter. Naturally aged meat, with a rich, beefy taste. Longchamps experts are tough. That's why Longchamps steaks are tender . . .

All writers who want to hammer an idea employ repetition and parallel construction. A high school girl gets out her hammer in the following article from the Lakeview High School *Crystal* of Battle Creek, Michigan (May 6, 1966):

> NASTY NAZI SYMBOL OR HARMLESS FAD?
>
> **Most teenage fads are inoffensive and short-lived. A current fad in Battle Creek is far from inoffensive and should be stopped at once.**
>
> **Teenagers are adorning themselves with symbols of German militarism such as German army helmets. Some are wearing an Iron Cross on a chain around their neck. Elsewhere, the Nazi swastika is in style.**
>
> **These symbols recall the death of 291,000 Americans and the slaughter of six million Jews.**
>
> **They recall an upheaval during and after the war, started by a man who used the swastika as the symbol of an evil philosophy.**
>
> **Human memories are short, but not so short that they blot out this devastating period of history.**
>
> **These military symbols are probably just an expression of rebellion. Some kinds of rebellion are healthy. This kind is sick.**
>
> JANICE NEMRAVA

Here are some parallel patterns in the writing of professionals. Read them aloud to yourself and put them into your reservoir of sounds. Later when you are writing, you may hear echoes.

1. Every day, the sun; and, after sunset, Night and her stars. Ever the winds blow; ever the grass grows. Every day, men and women, conversing—beholding and beholden.

RALPH WALDO EMERSON

2. We have rates by the hour, day, week, month, or by the job.

DICK'S KALAMAZOO JANITOR SERVICE,
YELLOW-PAGES ADVERTISEMENT.

3. Other people cannot see what I see whenever I look into your father's face, for behind your father's face as it is today are all those other faces which were his. Let him laugh and I see a cellar your father does not remember and a house he does not remember and I hear in his present laughter his laughter as a child.

JAMES BALDWIN

4. Cut flowers at proper stage of development. Dahlias when fully open; gladioli when first floret is open; peonies when petals are unfolding; roses before buds open. In general, cut while in bud.

The Pocket Household Encyclopedia

5. Remember that young uncooked spinach makes a good salad; that cooked buttered spinach and grapefruit salad are an ideal reducer's luncheon; and that cooked spinach greens are superb with Hollandaise Sauce . . .

IRMA S. ROMBAUER AND MARION ROMBAUER BECKER

WRITING NINE: Write two 10-minute free writings comparing two objects, acts, or persons. Let yourself drift frequently into parallel patterns. Don't try to make every sentence parallel, but seize upon whatever opportunities present themselves.

Before you start writing, read this passage by a student playing with the ideas in this chapter:

> **I get the feeling that I repeat myself. I get the feeling that I repeat other people. I get the feeling that other people repeat me. I get the feeling that other people repeat things about me. I get the feeling that I get a lot of feelings.**

. . . the mere act of reading aloud put his work before him in a new light and, by constraining his attention to every line, made him judge it more rigorously. I always intend to read, and generally do read, what I write aloud to some one; any one almost will do, but he should not be so clever that I am afraid of him. I feel weak places at once when I read aloud where I thought, as long as I read to myself only, that the passage was all right.

SAMUEL BUTLER

chapter 10 the helping circle

BY NOW you have probably learned to write in circles. First, you write for yourself, and then read aloud your writing and listen. It sounds different, as if it had made a circle and become someone else's writing. You can judge it better.

Second, you read it to a friend or member of the family. Now it sounds different than it did when you read it to yourself. You begin to sense how the writing may come across to persons who didn't share the experiences and feeling you wrote about. The listeners don't have to say anything, but simply be there—and the writing becomes an object apart from you. You're getting objective about it.

You can ask the listeners to tell how they felt when the writing was read aloud. But that presses them. What if they weren't moved by it? or couldn't follow it? They hate to say anything that may hurt. That's why—especially in the beginning—you're lucky to work in a large circle of responders. They feel less strain in speaking frankly of the writing than do persons in a group of three to five. They know there will be others who will agree with them, and some who won't. The differing opinions make the comments easier for you to take. You can carry them home with you, and later decide which you will use or ignore.

So the circle—at times it will frighten every writer--is your third best resource. The first is your own experience (including your thoughts, feelings, and knowledge picked up from others). Second is your skills as a writer. And third is the help the circle can give you to hone those skills.

In the beginning of a course, writers are unsure. They should be given only encouragement. So the group agrees to comment on what they like in initial free writings. If they don't like a piece of writing they hear, they say nothing. That's not a lie. It's a helpful decision not to talk. If they like anything about the writing—a word, phrase, ending, idea—they say so. Perhaps the writing puts them in an event fully enough to call up a similar feeling they thought no one else had experienced. After three or four meetings, when enough free writing has been done that everyone or almost everyone has heard praise from the circle, the prohibition against negative comments may be dropped.

Think of and look at your work as though it were done by your enemy. If you look at it to admire it you are lost . . . If we look at it to see where it is wrong, we shall see this and make it righter. If we look at it to see where it is right, we shall see this and shall not make it righter. We cannot see it both wrong and right at the same time.

SAMUEL BUTLER

Now imagine yourself in the circle. The following piece of writing by one of the members has been read aloud to the group after the reader has read through it once already.

IT'S SUNDAY

It's Sunday, and I'm in church. The Mass has just started, and it's particularly warm and crowded. The lady on my left is wearing great amounts of a stifling dime-store perfume, and the little old Italian woman on my right smells strongly of garlic mingled with whiskey. One of the women in front of me (I think she's wearing last year's hat with new plastic flowers) just pointed out to the other that

> **Madge Russell sewed the rip in her black coat with brown thread. Oh, and the good mother in the last pew hasn't stopped slapping her six children once to participate in the service.**
>
> **Lucy Dowden, the first one in line for communion, has been seeing her husband's best friend for the past two weeks—or so they say. And look at that lady in the third pew, the elderly one in shocking pink. She forgot to zip up her dress all the way. The kids in back of her are showing no mercy. They're carrying on so loudly that everyone's noticed her now. Sally and Deb are up there talking—probably about poor Mr. Cronson's ulcers. They think he has them because his daughter had to get married.**
>
> **The two women in front of me are gossiping so intently that they have huge perspiration rings under their arms. I wonder who they're talking about now. Maybe if I kneel up straighter I can hear. Why, they're talking about me! The nerve of them! Why don't they just take part in the Mass instead of looking around and minding everyone else's business? Some of the biggest hypocrites go to church on Sundays, don't they?**

In the circle no one calls on you. You speak up if you have strong feelings. Truthfully. The moment you or anyone else in the circle makes a phony comment to please the writer or teacher, or to show off knowledge, the power of the circle is diminished. It may not be killed, but it's weakened; and such wounds will continue to disable it unless energy is restored.

As you are listening to the story being read aloud, try to read your reactions. And when the end comes, check in on your feelings, as if you were connecting the jack plug for the earphone to your transistor radio. Then you can simply report your feelings. You don't have to say something you think the teacher wants to hear, something profound. You don't have to use literary terms. The writer doesn't care about them. She or he wants to know whether the paper has scored with you, made you believe, moved you enough that you may remember the writing tomorrow or next week or month. If you don't know why you liked or disliked it, the writer still wants to know that it moved you. You don't have to give the reasons. The writer would like to know them, but will take the general reaction if that's all that's offered. If you say you liked the piece, and don't know why, perhaps another in the circle will help you see why. And thus you will both help the writer.

Here's an honest response—mine—to "It's Sunday":

"I liked it. I was led along by all the unfriendly remarks about the people in church—and I believed them, maybe because of details like 'huge perspiration rings under the arms'—and it all began to get pretty ugly for me. Then I was surprised at the turn at the ending: 'They're talking about me!' I didn't know it was going to go that way and I'm glad it did. I believed so much in the people in church, and I despised them along with the author. So when she (or he) showed that she was herself being talked about while she was calling the others hypocrites, I not only knew she was a hypocrite but that I have been one like that myself."

At that point, I would stop talking. That's enough. Give someone else a chance.

In the circle, Lisa says—thinking about how much tightening has helped her own writing—"I think you could do without the word *particularly* before *warm* and the word *strongly* before *of garlic.* When your nose meets garlic and whiskey together, the smell must have been strong."

Carol says, "I like it. It makes me laugh. It's so real." And the writer feels wonderful. She wants to go home and write another story.

Ted says, "The little things—forgot to zip up that shocking pink dress all the way, and the daughter had to get married—I liked them. It's very short, but it gets a lot said." And the writer feels like writing more stories.

Francis says, "I'd like to see the last three sentences dropped altogether. I already got the idea that if the other people in church are hypocrites because they are looking around and minding everyone else's business, then the writer was also hypocritical. Because that's what she was doing, too."

Mike says, "Well, yeah, you and I may be smart enough to get that, but maybe some reader wouldn't be. I'd like to see it end the way it does, just to make sure."

Carol says, "Don't be so sure other people are going to be that dumb. I'd like to see the story end with 'Why, they're talking about me!' That makes a great ending—wham!"

Gerald says, "I think it's a fine piece of writing. I agree that the details are terrific—like 'kneeling up straighter' so she can listen. But I'll have to say, and I hate to say it, that the whole thing doesn't grab me as much as it did some of the rest of you. I'm tired of writings making fun of people in church."

If left there, the discussion may now have turned for the writer. We are all sensitive. At that point the writer might have gone home thinking that the initial praise for her writing was not representative. She may have remembered the comments about the words *particularly* and *strong,* the two assertions that her ending was weak, and the last comment about picking on churchgoers. And she may have been discouraged from working further on this writing or giving her full effort on subsequent papers.

But the fact may be that everyone in the circle except the last speaker, Gerald, liked the story a great deal. Those who made small suggestions were only trying to help make what they thought a fine story perfect. So it is helpful for the members of the circle to try to sense how full a response the writer is getting. Just the comment "I thought it was great" or "I really liked it" from half or more of the group will ensure that the writer's confidence is not destroyed. And the danger on the other side must be considered also: if most persons were not moved by the writing, the writer should be told. No need to insult her, a great need to help her keep going as a beginning writer—but still truth from the circle.

As the course progresses, the members of the circle will become more and more adept at helping. At any given moment they will perceive who needs encouragement, who needs facing up to weaknesses. A supposedly helpful coment this week may be damaging, although two weeks from now it may be helpful. You can wait until a writer can use this suggestion or that.

> *He [Ezra Pound] was a marvelous critic because he didn't try to turn you into an imitation of himself. He tried to see what you were trying to do.*
>
> T. S. ELIOT

Not all writings that come before the circle will be as short and clear as "It's Sunday." The following story, for example, strikes me as exciting. But it doesn't satisfy me, and I don't know what to suggest to the author about it.

OLE EDNA

Good ole Edna Mulloney. When I try to picture her all I see is knees. She used to sit at the table on the platform in study hall, her knees, top of her hose, and garters showing under a skirt that was too short. And her toeless shoes with the little bows. Next I see her sagging bust in a tight sweater. She always wore suits with a sweater and there was always a wrinkle across the front of her skirt. It was either too tight or just wrinkled from sitting. She had fuzzy, wild

gray hair and an automatic or mechanical pencil—anyway the kind you put lead in. Not a wood one. That pencil. It was so much a part of her as an arm or leg. While she talked and gestured, it clicked. It flew across the room the day she slapped Red Tompkins across the face. She seemed flustered because she'd lost control. I don't think anybody made a sound for the rest of the period. There was quite a buzz around school about it but nothing ever happened. That was 7th or 8th grade. And she used to send me up to the Ag Room when she caught me chewing gum in class. The Ag Room—tiny, and it had a skylight. It was a condemned part of the building on the top floor. Mr. Cannon, the principal, would be there teaching the Ag Class—about 10 to 15 junior and senior boys. I just knocked on the door, said Mrs. Mulloney sent me, and sat down, hoping he wouldn't say much. And he didn't. He just went on teaching class. I can't remember that he ever asked me why I was there and I was there pretty often. Eventually she stopped sending me up to the Ag class. I know I didn't stop chewing gum. I think I just became better at concealing it. The walls were really ugly, tan on the bottom, cream on the top, the colors chosen by the same person who chooses the colors for prisons. Big ugly windows with dirty tan or green shades except once in a while when I'd look out and the sun was shining and the trees and the grass were so green.

Mrs. Mulloney lived in East Linden and raised cocker spaniels. I don't think she had any children. She taught Latin and had studied in Rome. I remember my mother telling me she was a very fine, well educated teacher. She had studied abroad. That doesn't necessarily make her a good teacher. I liked her Latin class but I can't remember much about her English class except that we had to write our autobiography and try to begin it some other way than I was born in so and so on such and such a date. That autobiography was really dull. Engfish. All it had was dates and places and not what I felt, which would have made it the story of *my* life. Anyone can make a list of dates and addresses. I knew it was uninteresting but I couldn't figure out why. In school nobody cared what I thought. All they were interested in was what they thought I should learn.

In the Helping Circle your job is not to show off. I've learned better from Professor Don Graves of the University of New Hampshire when I've invited him to join the Helping Circle in some of my classes. If a writing doesn't strike him hard, he tries to figure out what's missing. If he had heard "Ole Edna" read aloud, he would probably have thought, "There's some great stuff there about Edna Mulloney, but something's wrong about the writing. It starts describing Edna, slides into her failure as a disciplinarian to stop the writer from chewing gum, goes on to show how Edna accepted Engfish and dullness in a student's autobiography, and ends with a condemnation of school. Is the subject of that paper Ole Edna or school?. Either it ought to stay with Edna or be a paper about school with Edna used as the main example."

But as a responder in the circle, Don Graves wouldn't say that. Rather he would ask a question that led the writer to improving the paper rather than feel embarrassed about its weakness. He wants people to feel good about the strength of their work and then go on to make it stronger. So he would probably say, "What is it that you wanted to say in that paper?" and the writer would say "I wanted to remember Ole Edna for my readers." Or "I wanted to show how school often isn't interested in the students' own thoughts. It wasn't just Ole Edna that prevented me from speaking my own thoughts. It was all those boring tests and exercises as well. 'Read the book. Give back the teacher what it says.' "

While the writer had been saying that, Don would have written it down, so he could read it back to her. "Why don't you put that in your paper also?" Don might have said. Now the writer had enough to use as a frame for the paper. Start with a condemnation of school, give Ole Edna as a prime example of bad teaching, and finish up with an echoing comment about school.

In the Helping Circle responses like Don Graves's make a writer feel good. If something is missing in a paper, his question often brings it out of the writer at that moment. Don might say, "You tell about how the other persons present at this event felt, but how did *you* feel?" And then the rest of the story spills out. You can learn to ask such questions yourself. The writer of a paper says she suffered terribly when her dog died, and she described her feelings beautifully but forgot to show readers the dog. As a responder, you don't need to say, "I can't sympathize with your sorrow—although you describe it wonderfully. I don't miss the dog along with you because I never get to know it." All you need say is, "That must have been a wonderful dog to make you feel so bad about its death. Tell us more about it." And while the writer is speaking about the dog, take notes, and read them back to her. Probably those statements would fit perfectly into the paper. Then you can say, "Why don't you go home and write down still more memories of your dog? That will make a terrific paper."

In the circle an intelligent question is so much more valuable to the writer than a put-down criticism. If some part of the paper confused you or seemed weak, you can ask the writer, "What were you trying to accomplish in the beginning?" or "in the end?" Or "Why did you put the description of your grandmother before the description of your dog?" The answer to such a question may well go like this: "Well, I don't know. I guess I just got sidetracked on Grandma, even though the paper was supposed to be about my dog. On second thought, I think I'll drop the whole description of Grandma, and just get into what the dog and she did together at the picnic."

Questions like these put the responsibility for thinking through a paper and rewriting it where it belongs—on the writer, not the responders. And they leave a positive effect. Not, "Oh God, my paper was such a failure in class!" but "I can't wait to start rewriting my paper. I know I can make it so much better."

A writer is unfair to himself when he is unable to be hard on himself.

MARIANNE MOORE

As a member of the circle, you are party to a contract. Others will help you. You must speak up and help them. If only a few members respond and the others remain silent, there is no circle. If one person dominates, soon others will not listen, no matter how wise the comments. This group can become literally a circle of energy. You have probably seldom experienced a relationship like this in which a group of people are praising your work and helping you make it better—or saying it's weak and helping you make it better. Over the weeks and months that helping spirit builds. It can give you the confidence to do what you've never done before, if you'll take part in the circle. When everyone is responding to others' writing, then the writing and the responding improve.

If you don't keep up in your writing, but continue to comment on others' work, they'll eventually resent your remarks. They'll think: "You're not pulling your weight here. What right have you to tell me what's wrong with my writing?" If you write powerfully and consistently and receive praise from the circle but refuse to help others, they'll resent you for two reasons: You're not being fair, and as a powerful writer you are especially qualified to help the rest of them.

The most surprising outcome of working in the circle is that your remarks about the other person's writing will help your own writing. When you comment on how a writing might end better or why its metaphors are strong, you're printing that thought about writing on your brain more sharply than when you simply have the thought. Speaking it under the pressure of the group makes it yours, perhaps forever. One day writing a metaphor or an ending, you'll think of what you once said in the circle, and your help to another person will become help to you.

SOME REMINDERS TO CIRCLERS:

1. Avoid beginning comments about a writing with small points. First, let the writer know your large reaction, especially if it's positive. Then later in the discussion bring up the small suggestion; for example, to cut a word or change a phrase.
2. If you are the leader in the circle, don't let an argument drag on about a point that has been discussed fully. You can say, "Well, John has now been given several alternatives. He can take them home and decide which one he wants to use in rewriting his work, or he can turn down all of them." The circle is not a debating society but a gathering of helpers.
3. If you find yourself talking too much or too little, remember that the most helpful responders present their best thought—the one most apt to surprise and be useful. They resist the impulse to make obvious comments.
4. If you feel reluctant to talk, think of your responsibility to others. Responsibility—ability to respond. There is no other you in the world. No other person with the same set of past experiences. Only you can say what you feel and think, what *your* response to a writing was. That is what every serious writer is looking for: the effect of the writing upon individuals. You can't say anything wrong if you truthfully report your response to the work. And you may help a lot.
5. When your paper is being read aloud by someone else, watch the responders in the circle and try to determine what their involuntary responses—their laughs and sighs, grunts and groans, and changes of posture—are saying about individual parts of your writing.
6. As a responder you can sometimes draw out another responder who is reluctant to speak fully his feelings. "You said the story was too cute. Can you say more about why you felt that way?"
7. As a writer listening to comments on your own work, you may turn off the help if you start defending your writing too quickly or vigorously. "Well, I didn't mean by that ending to suggest I knew it all." Or "Maybe you're just too dumb to understand that

passage. You know one of the eight fundamentals of writing is to make the reader work." That sort of response may generate attacks rather than help. Wise and strong writers look everywhere for help. They want to make their writing as powerful as it can be. At times, they encourage a responder to tell them more and more. To a hostile or highly critical remark they may say, "Yeah, O.K.," or "Thanks." They should be thankful for any comments. They can't expect that every comment will be helpful. They know that at times they have been hurt and irritated when their work is being discussed and then later at home, with time to simmer down, they have found that some of the suggestions they resented are valuable, and they use them.

8. Here's a trap to watch out for. If you hear a writing read in the circle about a grandmother, you may begin thinking about your own grandmother and then say, "I liked your story because my grandmother's like that, too." That's a human reaction and touches one of the reasons we write: to show each other we have had similar experiences. But by itself it's no proof that the writing was strong. When a paper read in the circle turns you to your own experience, check it out carefully. Did it put you in the writer's experience powerfully? Did the grandmother—or whatever—come alive, or was she merely a trigger for your memory?
9. When there's too much writing to be read and helped in the circle, break the circle into smaller circles. If a paper is read in one of the smaller groups that demands hearing by the whole group, make sure it gets a later hearing, or publishing on the bulletin board or in a handout for everyone.
10. When you are the writer taking comments from the circle, remember that you are the final authority about your own work. No one can insist that you follow the advice you get. You are to weigh everything you hear and use what you think will help your writing. But weigh—don't throw it back before you put it on the scale.

COLLECTING FIVE: Lest this chapter should remain too general, here's a specific matter that every responder and writer should ponder [Good echo of sound—*responder, ponder?* No. And now that I look at that sentence closely, I see that the command "every responder and writer should ponder" is insulting to my readers. Sounds like Mother dressing the kids for church. And I don't need the comment about the chapter perhaps remaining too general. Just give the facts, Macrorie, without the lecture. So I'll start again]:

You can help people in the circle find worn-out expressions in their writing. You don't need to pounce on them gleefully and scornfully. You can simply say calmly, "And I found several clichés—Line 5, 'in the final analysis'; last paragraph, 'with tender loving care.' " And the writer can remove them later if she sees fit.

Copy in your journal a dozen or more clichés you find in print and in the writing of your classmates. Here are some examples, along with fresh expressions which possess their own unique truth. Some of the latter were written by junior-high students:

CLICHÉS

1. out of the clear blue sky
2. cold shivers up my back
3. eyes glued
4. down in the dumps
5. racked our brains
6. broke my heart
7. lump in my throat
8. safe and sound
9. well aware
10. one and only
11. last but not least
12. not a care in the world
13. heavy as a rock
14. light as a feather

FRESH EXPRESSIONS

1. That man is hairless as a window.
2. If this kid was a dog, he looks like he's been chasing parked cars and punched his nose in.
3. Her mouth looks like she has been eating red candy and got it all over.
4. His eyes look like you picked them up from a kids' marble game, big and brown.
5. It was quiet in the woods and smelled of hot pine trees.
6. His wooden leg was lying on the bedroom floor by the side of his bed, on the rug, like a faithful dog.
7. I watched her trace the path of the blood [on a medical chart] and felt my heart pumping.
8. All the colors outside are muted as if someone forgot to dust off the trees and grass.
9. I turned my head to the side, resting it on his shoulder and could feel his warm Listerine breath on the back of my neck.

There was a Boy . . .
many a time
At evening, when the earliest stars began
To move along the edges of the hills,
Rising or setting, would he stand alone
Beneath the trees or by the glimmering lake,
And there, with fingers interwoven, both hands
Pressed closely palm to palm, and to his mouth
Uplifted, he, as through an instrument,
Blew mimic hootings to the silent owls . . .

WILLIAM WORDSWORTH

chapter 11 remembering childhood

ACHIEVING DISTANCE

REMEMBERING childhood is not childish, but wise and sweet and necessary. We go back because we loved those years of play. We go back because remembering moves us closer to the children around us today. We go back because in writing through these years we gain a second life.

The best writers take this journey. Mark Twain wrote *Huckleberry Finn,* a novel about a boy with a gifted tongue, who once said:

> It would get so dark that it looked all blue-black outside, and lovely; and the rain would thrash along by so thick that the

> trees off a little ways looked dim and spider-webby; and here would come a blast of wind that would bend the trees down and turn up the pale underside of the leaves; and then a perfect ripper of a gust would follow along and set the branches to tossing their arms as if they was just wild; and next, when it was just about the bluest and blackest—*fst!* it was as bright as glory and you'd have a little glimpse of tree-tops a-plunging about, away off yonder in the storm, hundreds of yards further than you could see before; dark as sin again in a second, and now you'd hear the thunder let go with an awful crash and then go rumbling, grumbling, tumbling down the sky towards the under side of the world, like rolling empty barrels downstairs, where it's long stairs and they bounce a good deal, you know.

J. D. Salinger wrote about another boy with gifted tongue, who cherished his little sister Phoebe:

> She was laying there asleep, with her face sort of on the side of the pillow. She had her mouth way open. It's funny. You take adults, they look lousy when they're asleep and they have their mouths way open, but kids don't. Kids look all right. They can even have spit all over the pillow and they still look all right.

And the best poets go back to childhood. May Swenson went back like this:

THE CENTAUR

The summer that I was ten—
Can it be there was only one
summer that I was ten? It must

have been a long one then—
each day I'd go out to choose
a fresh horse from my stable

which was a willow grove
down by the old canal.
I'd go on my two bare feet.

But when, with my brother's jack-knife,
I had cut me a long limber horse
with a good thick knob for a head,

and peeled him slick and clean
except a few leaves for the tail,
and cinched my brother's belt

around his head for a rein,
I'd straddle and canter him fast
up the grass bank to the path,

trot along in the lovely dust
that talcumed over his hoofs,
hiding my toes, and turning

his feet to swift half-moons.
The willow knob with the strap
jouncing between my thighs

was the pommel and yet the poll
of my nickering pony's head
My head and my neck were mine,

yet they were shaped like a horse.
My hair flopped to the side
like the mane of a horse in the wind.

My forelock swung in my eyes,
my neck arched and I snorted.
I shied and skittered and reared,

stopped and raised my knees,
pawed at the ground and quivered.
My teeth bared as we wheeled

and swished through the dust again.
I was the horse and the rider,
and the leather I slapped to his rump

spanked my own behind.
Doubled, my two hoofs beat
a gallop along the bank,

the wind twanged in my mane,
my mouth squared to the bit.
And yet I sat on my steed

quiet, negligent riding,
my toes standing the stirrups,
my thighs hugging his ribs.

At a walk we drew up to the porch.
I tethered him to a paling.
Dismounting, I smoothed my skirt

and entered the dusky hall.
My feet on the clean linoleum
left ghostly toes in the hall.

Where have you been? said my mother.
Been riding, I said from the sink,
and filled me a glass of water.

What's that in your pocket? she said.
Just my knife. It weighted my pocket
and stretched my dress awry.

Go tie back your hair, said my mother,
and *Why is your mouth all green?*
Rob Roy, he pulled some clover
as we crossed the field, I told her.

These persons wrote of childhood at the height of their mature powers. If you are under twenty, you need even more than they to write of childhood. Writers require about seven years of distance between them and the events they recall. Then they're unfamiliar enough with them to feel the need to relate them fully for their readers and for themselves. If they write of yesterday's or last year's events, they usually remember them so well they leave them shrouded in their nearby intimate memory, which the reader does not share. James Boatwright, editor of *Shenandoah* magazine, says that few writers in their teens can write strongly of anything but their childhood. You may hope he's not right but you should start where you are most likely to achieve success. Don't search for tasks in which you'll probably fail. Proceed, as this book suggests, from success to success.

But don't expect to write well about the love affair that you are in the midst of, or have just mailed a letter to break off. One principal figure in that situation you can't see. At least one. Probably two. You are "involved." You don't surround it. You suffer or you triumph; you do not comprehend.

Later, all those feelings will become your knowledge. They will be of your knowledge and your wisdom when they no longer possess you. Your subject must be something you possess and can move all the way around. The former feelings that come together in your subject may include the most glorious or devastating that you ever had. And you will re-experience them. But you must emotionally enclose and dominate them.

SIDNEY COX

Consider the skill with which this high school student wrote of her childhood. Her name is withheld because she is writing candidly of her family.

BIRD

I sneaked back into my room, waited. I heard the light thud on the stairs. The floor creaked. The dress hangers swung squeakily on the door as it opened, then closed. I counted to ten, held my breath, listened. A soft shuffling sound came from the darkened room next to mine. Then with the squeak of springs came the shrill cry. A click. A spurt of choked sobbing began when the light went on. Rapid thuds sounded across the floor, door slammed, footsteps pounded down the stairs.

When the sound was gone, I crept from my bedroom to the stairway. Holding myself with my feet, I stuck my head through the bars and leaned down over the ledge. The room at the bottom of the stairs was dark, but I saw a light shining from the kitchen. Still, I could only hear a disturbed mumble and irregular sobs. My head was feeling heavy and since my position didn't let me hear the talk below, I inched back to bed without anyone else hearing.

I didn't think Suzie would act like that. She was a smart big sister, not the sissy type to get upset by a dead bird on her pillow. After all, the soft, smelly part had rotted off long before I found the bird. Now all it was was a delicate spine and skull with a few feathers sticking out at the neck. I liked it because of its pink and purple colors. No one else liked it. But my mother let me keep it when I told her I would keep it in my bedroom with my piece of driftwood. She didn't like my driftwood, either. Suzie had

> **even handled my bird before. Now she had probably smashed its spine when she lay on it and maybe pulled some of the feathers off. She had been downstairs now long enough to stop her crying bit and to tell on me.**
>
> **I heard someone; maybe she was coming. I started to go tell her that I didn't think she was going to take it so hard. But, no, it was a heavy, steady beat on the stairs. The sound came near my closed door. Silence. The beat, steady again, moved into Suzie's room. I fell asleep as the sound closed in on my room, but I woke up the next minute to see my father staring down. He had turned my bright light on, so I squinted up, looking sleepy and innocently asked what was going on. I knew that was a bad question when I saw my bird in his hand. He replied by asking where my driftwood was. I told him and he got it. And I told him I didn't see why everyone was making such a big fuss about the bird. He gave me the usual line about "never do that again." Then he told me how Suzie was really upset and that she was going to spend the night on our play room davenport. He left without really scolding me. He probably didn't see how my bird could scare anyone, either.**
>
> **I didn't really believe that Suzie would stay on the davenport all night. And I thought she would want to come get mad at me herself. So I fluffed my pillow, lay down, and waited. All I heard was the garbage can lid slam down.**

The humor of this story comes from the writer telling matter-of-factly of her childhood outrage at her sister's refusal to enjoy going to bed with a skeleton of a bird, yet at the same time letting the reader know that now she knows her sister had reason to be upset. The writer tells the reader enough, but not too much. She puts the reader there, listening for the sister's reaction down below. She makes the bird really dead, remembering "the smelly part had rotted off," and liking it "because of its pink and purple colors." She chose surprising attitudes to write about; so she keeps the readers off balance while telling them consistent and believable truth. She knows that bird and her family. When her father comes up the stairway, the reader probably expects a bawling out. Instead, father disapproves without scolding, and thus comes over as a real man, not a stereotyped parent.

This story is almost professional in its skill, but it could be polished further. It communicates sounds precisely: "a spurt of choked sobbing," "The beat, steady again, moved into Suzie's room." Almost every sentence makes readers want to know what's going to happen next. And yet the repetition of *thud-thuds* and *squeakily-squeak,* all in the first paragraph, is weak.

Here is another young person's story about childhood:

ORANGE

A pitcher of orange drink fell over in the refrigerator and trickled out onto the floor, creeping along, where the tile meets the green of the living room carpet. I hate orange pop. It makes me think of our church picnics, which always had an over abundance of that too sweet nectar—the junk that kids consume by the gallon and end up vomiting up by the end of the day under some dwarfed tree in the corner of a baseball field. I was a champ at it—only I intermingled bottles of orange drink with cups of soft, white ice cream that slid down my throat (after the tenth or so) like chunks of plaster of Paris. Still I shoveled it in and then ran in the races. I won, of course, to the delight of my ego and the sorrow of my stomach.

Splash! We were in the creek. About a half dozen of Mrs. Sallay's Sunday School sweethearts couldn't make it through the day without plunging into the muddy creek while walking the narrow branches stretched from bank to bank. I never missed the fun, year after year. Was I sick by the end of the day! I remember clinging to the trunk of a very small friend, watching fat, bald shirtless men loudly oppose the young boys in softball. While the women squealed at flabby forms puffing around third base, I threw up my ten bottles of orange pop, now the gravy over my once-downed lumpy ice cream. The day was complete. I could go home.

GEORGIA TODHUNTER

A reader probably would not say that the writer of "Orange" was making up this story. It contains the authority of closely recorded fact: a "dwarfed tree in the corner of a baseball field," orange drink and white ice cream that "slid down my throat (after the tenth or so) like chunks of plaster of Paris." Parts of the story may have been made up but they are true to life, deeply. "Orange" is a fine piece of writing but probably would not be published in a magazine because it does not develop any incident through time, as does the following memory of childhood:

THE PIRATE SHIP

I can still remember the time two of my buddies, Jim and Tom, and I decided to leave home. We were all avid Captain Kidd fans, and we decided to build a pirate ship and make our fortunes by looting and plundering other vessels.

After three agonizing days of searching for a ship, we discovered an old discarded casket crate drydocked in the cemetery. It was ideal. Just large enough to hold all three of us and yet small enough to make the fancy maneuvers demanded of a pirate ship. Finding our ship solved one problem, but getting it back to our hideaway created another, because it was well guarded by Mr. Snod, the groundskeeper. We waited until he went into his office for lunch to avoid capture and then charged the ship and overpowered the sole crew member, Snod's angora cat.

We hoisted the ship upon our wagon, lashed it down securely, and set out of the cemetery full sail, knocking over two small tombstones due to the faulty navigation of Tom who was steering the wagon. This part of the operation went along without a catch until we started down a long hill a block away from my house. One minute we were towing the ship and the next minute it was towing us. About halfway down the hill, the ship got second wind and lurched ahead, breaking our grips on the rope.

Twenty crushed tulips and one trampled hedge later it came to rest in my mother's flower garden. Now more than ever, if we had a reason for leaving home, this was it.

We tried to fix the mangled tulips by breaking uncooked spaghetti sticks into pieces and inserting them into the stems, hoping to make them straight again. After twenty-five minutes of failure we gave up and dragged the ship into the back yard and tried to get it seaworthy before one of my parents discovered the disaster area in the front yard.

I went into the basement and rummaged around until I found some tar and old rags. Dipping the rags into the tar, we managed to seal up the slits in the ship. By now we looked more like the Br'er Rabbit tarbaby than pirates.

Our mast and sail were made up of my mother's clothesline pole and a white sheet she had hung out to dry. We needed a Jolly Roger to identify our ship so we bor-

rowed Jimmy's grandfather's V.F.W. flag. We nailed spikes into the bottom of the ship to prevent sharks from eating us up.

All good pirate ships had a ram to destroy other ships at close range, so we had to have one, too. After a lot of fast talking I persuaded Tom to lend us his father's moose head which would serve as the battering ram. We needed a cannon for long range warfare and we found it in my father's pump-type fire extinguisher, which we first emptied and then refilled with soap water. This would blind the crews of other ships long enough for us to make use of our twelve-point battering ram.

At last we were ready. Tugging and straining, we lifted our coffin onto the wagon and embarked toward the river to launch it, taking the short-cut through Mr. Freeland's backyard and Mrs. Murphy's flower garden. The ship was now top heavy from the sail, and the moose head fell off the wagon every fifty feet or so. Every time our ship fell, the nails in it would gouge the ground.

By the time we had crossed Mr. Freeland's lawn and Mrs. Murphy's flower garden, they looked like battlefields ripped apart by bombs. We used everything in sight to cover these areas. Tables, chairs, incinerators, toys, wet laundry, lawnmowers, bikes, play pens, empty milk bottles, and a sleeping dog. But to no avail. Within minutes, Mr. Freeland and Mrs. Murphy attacked like dive bombers, forcing us to abandon ship and flee for our lives.

Where could we run, what could we do? Head toward my house and the ruined front yard, or surrender and face the wrath of Mr. Freeland and Mrs. Murphy? We never got to make a decision because we were intercepted by our parents, who had discovered the disaster in their front yard and were following our poorly disguised trail. Trapped, we surrendered and tried to explain our actions. It was useless. Our tar-covered pants were yanked off and we were flogged all the way home. Our ship was destroyed and we were confined to our room indefinitely, let out only to eat.

Whenever I see Jim or Tom today, we stop and look at each other with that knowing smile and say, "It woulda' floated!"

MICHAEL MAY

The writer chose his details skillfully: they never become tedious; they take the reader on the dry voyage. The ship metaphor is continued in the telling of the story: the crate is *drydocked,* the wagon faultily *navigated,* the crate made *seaworthy,* the flag is a *Jolly Roger,* they *embarked* toward the river. The story is more than just a tale of a day's play: it shows how kids become engrossed in playacting and run smack into their parents' world without realizing they come from another.

WRITING TEN: Choose from your childhood a moment you can't forget and write it down. Put the reader there as these three stories do. You may tell of the experience in simple narrative—this happened, then that happened—as did the writers of "Bird" and "The Pirate Ship." Or consider a persistent joy or annoyance in your childhood and find examples which illustrate the feeling as do the events of "Orange."

BEGINNINGS AND ENDINGS

Most good published pieces of writings have been created in several drafts—each version tighter and sharper than the last. What you see in print is almost never the first effort. No professional writer expects to dash off a piece of writing that is beyond improvement. Each version she thinks of as preliminary to another better version until finally she has had enough of drafting and says, "Done."

About eighty percent of the time, professional writers and editors find that the beginning of their first draft is no beginning at all. It's a mess, a series of false beginnings in which the starter's pistol goes off once, then twice, and the runners burst from their blocks only to stop and come back again. A writer must expect those bad starts because when she first meets her readers she has been thinking through *all* that she wants to tell them, not just the beginning of it. So she tells them too much—what concerns the end of the story or the chain of ideas, as well as the beginning—or too little, on the false assumption that the readers have just gone with her on this journey of reflection. In fact it can't for the readers be a journey of memory. It must be a trip into an unknown woods in the partial dark where the stumps and branches leap at their feet and the hanging spider webs clutch their faces.

Look at the first draft of your story. Is there some place on the first page where the reader could begin satisfactorily? Look for a spot where the story itself starts up, not simply where you began to write.

I write my first version in longhand (pencil). Then I do a complete revision, also in longhand . . . Then I type a third draft on yellow

> *paper, a very special certain kind of yellow paper. No, I don't get out of bed to do this. I balance the machine on my knees. Sure, it works fine; I can manage a hundred words a minute. Well, when the yellow draft is finished, I put the manuscript away for a while, a week, a month, sometimes longer. When I take it out again, I read it as coldly as possible, then read it aloud to a friend or two, and decide what changes I want to make and whether or not I want to publish it. I've thrown away rather a few short stories, an entire novel, and half of another. But if all goes well, I type the final version on white paper and that's that.*
>
> TRUMAN CAPOTE

In its first draft, "The Pirate Ship" began like this:

> I can still remember the time two of my childhood buddies and I decided to run away from home.
>
> Even today I'm still not sure what happened to bring about this idea of ours.
>
> Anyway, since we were all avid Captain Kidd fans, we decided upon building a pirate ship . . .

The second sentence is all wrong because it confusingly returns the reader from childhood to today. The third shifts again to childhood with an apologetic "anyway," a word persons use in conversation when they have become mixed up in telling a story. The writer has the advantage over the speaker: he can unconfuse himself by rewriting his story until he gets it right for the reader. If he presents confusion in the final draft, he had better have intended to represent confusion or he is a lazy writer.

As "The Pirate Ship" appears in its complete and revised form, it begins competently and moves in a clear line. The writer introduces himself and his buddies, says they decided to build a ship, and then tells in ordinary narrative sequence how they searched, found, built, and launched their vessel—on land. What happened first, second, and so on. The revised opening is adequate. It might be more powerful written this way:

> My buddies, Jim and Tom, and I searched for three days for a ship. We looked in Mrs. Grigg's junk pile beside her garage. The old steel swing wouldn't do, too heavy [and then

> more examples] . . . We were Captain Kidd fans and had decided to build a pirate ship and make our fortunes by looting and plundering other vessels.
>
> On the third day, we discovered an old discarded casket crate . . .

This opening sounds more like a story and less like an explanation or lecture. An opening should start something going. If possible, arrest readers with your beginning. Make them feel as if you've pulled them over to the curb and are getting out of the patrol car. Create tension, suspense, or surprise, or begin an action that carries along the readers, making them continually ask: "What next?"

One of the simplest ways to create a good beginning is to look down the first page until you find an arresting line and cut out all that goes before it. Or move it into first position. Few writers, beginners or veterans, can throw a high hard one on the first pitch. They have to warm up first, and they shouldn't present their readers with the beginning practice tosses they made in the bullpen. Anton Chekhov is considered by many critics the best of all modern short story writers. Notice how in his published draft—we don't know how many earlier drafts he threw in the wastebasket—he began two stories:

> MY LIFE
>
> The director said to me: "I only keep you out of respect for your esteemed father; otherwise you would have been sent flying long ago." I replied: "You flatter me, Your Excellency, in assuming that I am capable of flying." And then I heard him say: "Take that gentleman away, he gets on my nerves."
>
> IN THE RAVINE (1900)
>
> The village of Ukleyevo lay in a ravine, so that only the belfry and the chimneys of the cotton mills could be seen from the highway and the railroad station. When passers-by would ask what village it was, they were told:
>
> "That's the one where the sexton ate up all the caviar at the funeral."

And here is Reynolds Price, author of the novel *A Long and Happy Life,* beginning a story:

> THE WARRIOR PRINCESS OZIMBA (1961)
>
> She was the oldest thing any of us knew anything about, and she had never been near a tennis court, but somewhere

around the Fourth of July every year, one of us (it was my father for a long time but for the past two years, just me) rode out to her place and took her a pair of blue tennis shoes.

These three beginnings to stories don't go off like cannons, but neither do they go *poof* like a puffball kicked in the woods. They say something. They don't beg, or back up, or curtsey. Whether you're writing stories, articles, editorials, or answers to an examination, start solidly.

In writing an opening beware of the windy generalization:

> Everybody likes hot rods and I am no exception.

Not true. Many persons detest hot rods and consider them the most likely transportation to Hell. Don't turn off the reader by pretentious or coy behavior. In the beginning you establish your voice. If you begin squeaking like a monkey or thundering like an elephant, you have ruined your chances with the reader, who will be astounded later to find you writing in natural human voice. Beware of phony introductions, voice changes, and unnecessary apologies.

An opening often gains by being new, surprising; but if your writing is crammed with surprises all the way through, you may do well to begin quietly and conventionally. You don't have to amaze or stun or mystify your readers at the beginning. But you have to avoid alienating them with emptiness, phoniness, or unsuccessful attempts at humor. You may simply begin factually:

> East High School is located two miles from the center of the business district in Clarksville.

but don't use that fact unless it makes a point relevant to your story. Later in this story, the distance from the school to the business district should come up.

Think hard how your reader will take your first words. Consider this opening:

> What's going on? This question might have gone through the minds of the grocery store owners when the students of Mr. McMahon's psychology class went to the different stores for an assignment that was done over vacation.

"What's going on?" is a question that might be asked by anyone in any situation. Here the reader is required to wait too long before the question gains any significance.

Revision: "What's going on?" said the grocery store owner when he saw twenty-five students from Mr. McMahon's psychology class walking up and down the aisles writing in their notebooks. They were carrying out an assignment during Thanksgiving vacation.

When you've found or created a good beginning to your story, consider its ending. At both ends of a piece of writing, writers are driven to explaining, almost as if they wanted to give advice to readers on how to read what they have written, and nothing is worse than advice. If the Explainery comes at the beginning, it's lost on readers who don't know the story yet. If it comes at the end, it tastes like soggy bread. The readers have read the story and are insulted by being told what they have read.

The first draft of "The Pirate Ship" ended like this:

> And since we had taken the "short-cut" across our neighbor's lawns, I'd say that it was approximately four phone calls and one crushed fence later that our parents finally caught up with us.
>
> Our ship was contrabanded and we "pirates" were sentenced to three long weeks of reforesting various islands, along with a looooong lesson from the "Board of Education"!

When the writer read his first draft to other students, they told him they wanted to know more about what happened on the journey through the neighbors' lawns. They didn't like the tired joke about a Board of Education being used to spank the boys. It was a pun that didn't spring from the experience itself, a canned joke. Discussing his story with critics, the writer said, "We really were upset to be stopped by our parents. Why, even today, when I see Jim or Tom, we look at each other and say, "It woulda' floated!" The critics and the writer knew instantly that he had stumbled on to a fine ending.

Study the ending of "Bird." It asks the reader to guess the significance of the garbage can lid slamming down. The story ends: a lid is put on it.

Look over your story for a spot near the end which is exciting or surprising. Or consider stopping a little before you believe the reader expects you to. Near the end find a good detail, an example of one of the main feelings or ideas in the story and chop everything else off that follows it. Or move the good passage to the end position. Don't drool an ending. Wipe your mouth, say the last word. Leave the reader.

[George Bernard Shaw often sent his early drafts of his plays to his friend Ellen Terry, the actress, for criticism. Once she said she feared to suggest changes on his manuscript. He wrote back:]

"Oh, bother the MSS., mark them as much as you like: what else are they for? Mark everything that strikes you. I may consider a thing fortynine times; but if you consider it, it will be considered 50 times; and a line 50 times considered is 2 per cent better than a line 49 times considered. And it is the final 2 per cent that makes the difference between excellence and mediocrity."

chapter 12 sharpening

REHEATING a piece of writing after it has cooled, tempering it, and sharpening it is enjoyable—if you know how. Otherwise it may turn out worse, brittle or misshapen. Look for the common sicknesses or dullnesses professional writers try to eliminate: Is-ness, It-ache, There-ache, excessive use of adjectives, adverbs, and passive verbs.

Consider this column of opinion printed in a high school newspaper. Its first paragraph makes its point dramatically; its verbs are vigorous and its adjectives full of meaning.

[THE FEMININE ERA]

Waltzing down the corridor in a velvet-collared, ruffled shirt, clutching a pink hairbrush, a teenager hurriedly skipped into the school lavatory between classes and began labor over a hair-do with side-swept bangs for four and a half minutes of agony and disgust; the door was marked "BOYS."

Is this the beginning of a new feminine era today among the boys of our country?

As they walk down the hall fussing and swishing with their hair with an occasional pat on the bangs, it becomes more apparent that this is a generation of feminine men coming up.

Once it was the style for boys to carry small combs in their hip pockets; now it's brushes, brushes with pink and baby blue handles.

By a recent poll it was revealed that until a few years ago, a boy got up in the morning, ran a quick one-stroke combing through his hair, jumped into the same old pair of Levis he'd taken off the night before and headed for school in less than ten minutes.

Today, an act like this would be considered a tragedy in a boy's life if he wasn't allowed at least a couple of hours to himself for the care and parting of his hair.

It seems that of the both groups, the boys are more conscious than girls about subtleties of dress.

Although occasionally they are apt to go a little more overboard, when they begin wearing ruffled embroidered shirts and more cologne than girls do perfume.

Boys have adopted hair styles popular with the girls . . . The boys have joined the co-eds in going to the "mod" or "natural" look with moderately short hair and side-swept bangs that shade their eyes.

Today, it is not unusual for a receptionist at a beauty salon to pick up the phone and find out that it is a male customer who wants to make an early appointment to have his hair thinned, washed, set, and then sprayed for a big school event coming up. In some parts of the state, there are even special beauty salons for only the male customer.

Why this drastic change? Is it because the boys see the feminine world as a privileged one, and they want to join it too?

Is it the feeling that the demands of the traditional masculine role are more than they can tolerate and they are abandoning it? Whatever the reason may be, "BOYS," stand up and hold your role as a "MAN."

Through the first 38 lines, this writing makes a strong case. Then it asks several good questions which it fails to probe or answer. It ends in a thicket: asking boys to fulfill their traditional role without understanding why it may be changing or whether it should change or whether males were at other times just as feminine in personal habits.

The author, a girl, is quick to condemn boys for following feminine hair and clothes styles. She neglects to admit that many girls of the time follow masculine hair and clothes styles.

The column needs rethinking. But for the moment, consider only how its expression might be sharpened in lines 7 through 45. It suffers from Is-ness, a dullness marked by weak uses of forms of the verb *to be.* If *am, is, are, was, were, shall, will,* or *been* connects trite or empty adjectives or vague nouns, it probably needs replacing with a verb that carries more meaning. Often a form of the verb *to be* can be eliminated from a sentence without losing any meaning. Write down all uses of this verb in lines 8 through 46 and study whether or not eliminating them would strengthen the writing. Here's the way a professional editor might make such an inspection:

Lines 5 and 7: adequate *was* and *is.* Don't change.

Line 11: Is-ness. Revise sentence:

Original. As they walk down the hall fussing and swishing with their hair with an occasional pat on the bangs, it becomes apparent that this *is* a generation of feminine men coming up.

Revision. As they walk down the hall swishing and fussing with their hair, occasionally patting it on the bangs, they embody a new generation of feminine men.

Line 13: Is-ness *(was).* Revise sentence:

Original. Once it *was* the style for boys to carry small combs in their hip pockets; now it's brushes, brushes with pink and baby blue handles.

Revision. Once boys carried small combs in their hip pockets; now they carry brushes with pink and baby blue handles.

Line 16: Is-ness *(was).* Revise sentence:

Original. By a recent poll *it* was revealed . . .

Revision. A recent poll revealed . . .

Lines 21 and 22: Is-ness *(would be, wasn't).* Revise sentence:

Original. Today an act like this *would be* considered a tragedy in a boy's life if he *wasn't* allowed at least a couple of hours to himself for the care and parting of his hair. (34 words)

A difficulty in this sentence is that the expression "an act like this" doesn't refer to any words preceding.

Revision. Today a boy denied a couple of hours to himself for the care and parting of his hair would consider himself tragically mistreated. (23 words)

REVISING SIX: Circle other uses of the verb *to be* in "The Feminine Era." In considering possible revisions, try to eliminate empty nouns and verbs, and replace them with persons or things which act through vigorous verbs. The revisions exhibited above do away with these weak expressions:

> it becomes more apparent that this
> it was the style
> by . . . it was
> an act like this would be considered a . . . in a boy's life

Note that these expressions contain no power or color. They consist of abstract and lifeless words, necessary and useful at times, but here pale and empty.

One way to transfuse red blood into a sentence anemic with Is-ness is to substitute a metaphorical verb for *is*. For example:

Original. The poor dog *is* an inferior because he *is* not a symbol maker, says Western Man.

Revision. The poor dog *wags* his tail as an inferior because he *is* not a symbol maker.

Here the second part of the statement retains an *is*. If it were eliminated by saying "because he doesn't make symbols" the sentence would lose part of its balance and parallel construction: "an inferior . . . a symbol maker." So you can see that you should not eliminate *is's* wherever they appear without considering how they are functioning.

Shakespeare was a master of the metaphorical verb. In *Macbeth* he made Malcolm say:

> This tyrant whose sole name *blisters* our tongues,
> *Was* once thought honest.

Suppose Shakespeare had written with Is-ness:

> This tyrant whose sole name *is* a blister on our tongues,
> *Was* once thought honest.

Again, one use of the verb *to be* is enough in the statement.

REVISING SEVEN: In one of your past longer pieces of writing circle every use of the forms of the verb *to be*. Consider which need to be eliminated and revise the sentences in which they appear. Remember that Is-ness stands for a *weak* use of a form of *to be*. No writer can write many sentences in a row without usefully employing *is*.

It-ache and There-ache are dullnesses marked by unnecessary uses of *it* and *there*. They are often associated with Is-ness. Diagnosis of It-ache and There-ache in "The Feminine Era":

It-aches in lines 10, 13, 16 were eliminated along with the Is-ness.

It-ache in line 24:

Original. *It* seems that of the both groups, the boys are more conscious than girls about subtleties of dress.

Revision. The boys are more conscious than girls about subtleties of dress.

There-ache in lines 37-38:

Original. In some parts of the state, there are even special beauty salons for only the male customer. (17 words)

Revision. In some parts of the state, special beauty salons serve only male customers. (13 words)

REVISING EIGHT: See if you can find other examples of It-ache and There-ache in "The Feminine Era." Often you will discover you have already eliminated them in dealing with Is-ness.

You are hunting for uses of *it* and *there* which do not carry solid meaning, but act merely as convenient handles for introducing other expressions. Sometimes they operate well as handles. They're hard to replace in these two sentences:

> It's cold out tonight.
>
> There are only four houses on the other side of the street on our block.

Too often, vague uses of *it* and *there* lead a writer to wasting other words as well:

Original. It is the task of the school to train all the students.

Such an It-ache as that may be cured by making a noun the subject of the sentence. At the same time, an editor would probably change the possessive construction "of the school" to "school's," a more informal but vigorous expression:

Revision. The school's task is to train all the students.

A sentence doesn't ache from a healthy use of *it* or *there*. For example:

> The ball rolled and rolled until it hit the fence.
>
> "He's sitting over there," said the witness, pointing.

In these sentences *it* represents the ball and *there* tells a place. These are different uses from those involved in *It is* and *There are*.

Now look for It-ache and There-ache in the longer paper you examined in REVISING SEVEN and make the needed changes.

Dullness also results from the excessive use of passive verbs.

Passive. It was brought to our attention by the manager that we had not sent out the invoice.

Active. The manager told us we had not sent out the invoice.

Passive. The play was a performance that was observed by George with amazing indifference.

Active. George observed the play with amazing indifference.

Passive verbs suggest that nobody is doing anything. Just sitting around being acted upon.

Passive. The object that was stepped on by me was a ladybug with lavender spots.

Active. I stepped on a ladybug with lavender spots.

Passive. The scheme was conceived by John at four in the morning.

Active. John conceived the scheme at four in the morning.

Dullness may also be imparted to sentences by excessive use of the verbs

make	go	get
have	move	come

They are not full of specific meaning. Circle each use of them in your writing and question it: can the verb be replaced with a more particular and meaningful one? For example, *making* might be supplanted by

constructing	gluing	joining	stringing
building	piling	digging	sticking

and many other verbs. Even these are fairly general; for example, a writer might say "I *cemented* two stones together" rather than "I stuck two stones together." Choosing more precise and vigorous verbs puts life into writing because life is particular, not general.

Like Is-ness, the shoddy use of *make, have, go, move, get,* and *come* leads to a frightening waste of words:

Original. This land *has* the appearance of being arid.

Revision. This land looks arid.

These verbs frequently seed sentences with unnecessary nouns.

Original. He finally *came to* his decision. He would run.

Revision. He finally decided he would run.

You should remember that these suggested revisions are made out of context. The last revision above saves three words from the original sentences, but if the author's purpose was to slow down the reader and delay the divulging of the decision, he might better use the original version, which carries a different rhythm.

Beginning writers often insist on establishing the ownership of an object with the verb *have* before they let the owner use the object. Good way to clog the story.

Original. He *had* a bicycle. He rode it to work every morning.

Revision. He rode his bicycle to work every morning.

The principle involved in sharpening is to fill words with precise meaning or get rid of them. Beginning writers splatter adjectives and adverbs like buckshot. Consider this passage:

> **I summoned up courage and *boldly* set forth through the pathway. Suddenly loomed in sight five male patients sitting outside only a few feet from me. Too late to turn back, I consoled myself with the idea that an attendant was probably *unobtrusively* hidden from view but there, nevertheless, for protection.**
>
> **Then the thought dawned on me that I was in the wrong and didn't deserve protection because I was trespassing—there were blockades which I had ignored, set up in front of the pathway. The patients, perhaps sensing my *nervous* anticipation, *possibly* evident in my *faltering* steps and *nervous* eye movements, said "hello" to me.**
>
> **My *natural* reaction to this situation bothers me. In Psych class we consider mental patients just "sick people." I don't want to be guilty of sharing the *common* feelings of the general public.**

Here in line 1, *boldly* is unnecessary with "summoned up courage" and "set forth," both expressions which imply boldness. In line 5, *unobtrusively* is unnecessary. Seldom does anyone hide obtrusively. In lines 10 and 11, *perhaps* is an honest word but the other italicized words overdo the notion of sensing nervousness. A sharp cutting is needed.

Original. The patients, perhaps sensing my nervous anticipation, possibly evident in my faltering steps and nervous eye movements, said "hello" to me.

Revision. Perhaps sensing my anticipation in my faltering steps and nervous eye movements, the patients said "hello" to me.

In line 13, *natural* is not an accurate word for what the writer wants to say. *Instant* or *stereotyped* would make more sense. In line 15, *common* is unnecessary. *Sharing* and *general* say enough by themselves.

Remembering the *repeat-and-vary* principle, good writers avoid ruts. They don't allow themselves to supply for every verb an adverb and for every noun an adjective until the pattern becomes monotonous and the words flabby. They avoid or change dead patterns like these:

> He slowly walked up the stairs, nonchalantly pushed on the door, and casually entered the room.
>
> At the picnic were sticky-fingered children, rosy-cheeked mommas, and large-stomached fathers.

When they finish the first or second draft, good writers test the adjectives and adverbs: are they pulling their weight? Do the other words around them render them unnecessary? See how freshly and powerfully Shakespeare uses an adverb in giving Regan, King Lear's daughter, these words about her father:

> 'Tis the infirmity of his age: yet he hath ever but *slenderly* known himself.

Powerful adverbs and adjectives are not beyond you. On the whole, the writer of "The Feminine Era" made her adverbs and adjectives count. *Velvet-collared* and *ruffled* and *side-swept* are doing their jobs. But in lines 26-27, the writer fell off the ship with the expression "a little more overboard." One can go overboard, but not more or less overboard.

A fundamental in using adverbs and adjectives is not to let one of them smother the effect of another strong word. Don't let your straight man steal the attention from the comic. If you write

> She was *unusually* hideous.

you have lessened the force of *hideous* by making the reader attend to the weak word *unusually*. If you write

> It was a tremendously tall skyscraper.

you have lessened the force of *tall*. In fact, both *tremendously* and *tall* are tired and should be replaced with words that fix the height of the skyscraper in actual or metaphorical scale.

> I stood a hundred feet away and yet my neck ached from looking up to the top of the building.

This chapter has talked about weak uses of certain words. All of them may be used adequately or strongly by a skilled writer. Note in this beautifully phrased passage from "Self-Reliance" that Emerson uses many strong verbs but also forms of *to be.* He plants four adjectives within the space of seven words. He finishes with a sentence that carries the normally vague and weak verb *go.*

> Travelling is a fool's paradise. Our first journeys discover to us the indifference of places. At home I dream that at Naples, at Rome, I can be intoxicated with beauty and lose my sadness. I pack my trunk, embrace my friends, embark on the sea and at last wake up in Naples, and there beside me is the stern fact, the sad self, unrelenting, identical, that I fled from. I seek the Vatican and the palaces. I affect to be intoxicated with sights and suggestions, but I am not intoxicated. My giant goes with me wherever I go.

The power of this passage comes from its ideas as well as from its expression. Emerson is true to his thoughts and feelings, and therefore his words carry surprise. The words that precede or follow ordinarily weak verbs like *to be* or *goes* are full of meaning—*intoxicated, giant, fool's paradise.*

Sharpening writing is not as black and white a matter as this chapter suggests. Many of the changes dictated here are debatable, and only a person considering the total context of a word or phrase can see whether or not it should be retained. Find ways of probing your sentences so that you see alternative ways of stating them. *Is, there,* and *it* frequently are wasted and breed other unnecessary words. But they are good words in their place. You will find writers as brilliant as Bernard Shaw using *it is* when the words are not absolutely necessary, as in the quotation at the head of this chapter:

> And it is the final 2 per cent that makes the difference between excellence and mediocrity.

This *it* doesn't ache much. It could be eliminated and the sentence written

> And the final 2 per cent makes the difference between excellence and mediocrity.

but the words *it is* in this passage act as emphasizers. They slow down the reader and make sure he gives attention to *2 per cent.*

The moral of this chapter is not to do away with all uses of the cited words, but to learn where to look for possible weak spots in your sentences. I originally wrote the first sentence of the paragraph above in this way:

> Sharpening writing is not as black or white a matter as this chapter makes it appear.

Spotting the *it* in the sentence, and thinking about removing it, he saw that he could drop three words, *makes, it,* and *appear,* and substitute only the word *suggests.*

REVISING NINE: Look over two of your past free writings and attempt to eliminate from them weak passive verbs, empty verbs like *make* and *have,* the overuse of adjectives, and the unnecessary use of intensifying words like *tremendously* and *great big.*

the point at which experience becomes form . . .
KENNETH CLARK

chapter 13 creating form

PATTERNS

A RECENT TEXTBOOK on writing says:

> Since learning to outline is one of the most important steps —perhaps the most important—in writing well, we want you to make at least four outlines.

The man who wrote that must never have talked to a real writer. Eight out of ten writers say they never use outlines and the other two say they use them only in late stages of writing, in the second or third draft when they have all the materials captured and need only to rearrange them strategically.

In the first place, outlines freeze most writers. Professionals are looking for ways of breaking up the ice and poking around in new waters. They want writing and ideas to flow.

I have often at the beginning of a book found myself very uncertain what I would do, and appalled at the difficulty of knowing what to put where, and how to develop my incidents. I never have that feeling now because I have always found that there is some one point or other in which I can see my way. I immediately set to work at that point and before I have done and settled it, I invariably find that there is another point which I can also see and settle, etc., etc. . . .
SAMUEL BUTLER

In the second place—Wait a minute. The second place. By their form, outlines always imply there will be a second place. Maybe there won't be. Or shouldn't be. I.a., I.b., II.a., II.b. "Express all your points in the outline in the same style, all complete sentences or all phrases." The Outliners are full of stuff like that. They get writers so interested in the form of the outline that they quit thinking of the writing they're outlining.

Yet readers need some form or they become confused, get lost, give up. Making anything—a table, a fishing fly, a piece of writing—involves a struggle between form and content. Only the dull assembly-line maker can avoid that struggle by drawing up a perfect plan, or outline, before beginning creating. Punched out, every one the same, no surprises anywhere. A good planner allows for departures from plan, sidetrips down alleys full of discovery. The best trip you ever took in your life—could you have written an outline for it beforehand?

Yet the reader and writer need form, some direction, some overriding mood, or they will sense only chaos. When the folks at home send George on a trip, they expect more than a bagful of chaos spilled on the kitchen table when he returns.

Many professionals say that the more experienced they become, the more certain they are of where they're going before they start. But they still keep their eyes and ears open as they go, hoping for fortunate accidents.

Beginning, you may find a direction, even a conclusion, flowering in your mind. Then all you do is find experiences to embody it and bring it alive. But if there isn't an example or experience clinging to the idea or direction when you first get it, the chances are you'll never bring it alive. Better start with something already alive and kicking. A butterfly caught and squirming in the net, wings flapping wildly. Not a lot of preserved specimens lined up in the glass case neatly and systematically labeled.

But the glass case is good. Something to enclose the things flapping around in your mind and experience. Place something else with the butterfly. Does it go with that butterfly? Or does it contrast in some significant way? Is it a leaf in shape—half of the butterfly? And then a bird. Look at it. How do its wings differ from the butterfly's and the leaf's? Let these pieces of experience knock around against each other in the case and in your mind.

> *It doesn't matter which leg of your table you make first, so long as the table has four legs and will stand up solidly when you have finished it.*
>
> EZRA POUND

If what you're thinking about doesn't fit into a case, you may simply jot down the elements in a list, informal, like the one you take to the supermarket.

Any piece of writing needs a point. What that means is hard to say but easier to sense. People know the meaning of the word when they listen to a person talk on endlessly through boredom into sleep, and someone says, "He talked on and on but to no point." What *point* is and why it is needed can be seen by reading most term papers written in high school and freshman college classes. They have subjects but no points. For example, Harry Smithers writes "about Switzerland." His paper is dead already. The facts he has read about Switzerland or the things he has seen in Switzerland do not make a paper simply because they concern one country. What about Switzerland? Do any of the facts he has collected do anything to each other? Contradict? Surprise Harry in some way when compared with facts he knows about other countries? If he thinks he'll write about Switzerland because the library has a number of books on it, or because no one else has written about it recently in school, or because he once heard that watches are made in Switzerland, his paper is doomed. When he starts in on a good piece of writing he'll have an itch or he'll never scratch hard, with purpose and enjoyment.

Switzerland might be Harry's subject, but never his point. To cover Switzerland would be to write an endless number of volumes, describing its government, postal system, watchmaking industry, role in European and world wars, people's dress, food, social customs—all with that dreadful emptiness of a travel brochure or a bad children's encyclopedia. Take this statement by a writer in a political magazine:

> The Swiss make watches, speak many languages, act as peace arbitrators, never commit themselves to the cause of right in any war, and act as holding companies for all sorts of high-level financial wheeling and dealing, aiding persons all over the world in avoiding taxes and financial responsiblity.

Maybe this statement isn't true. But it's full of assertions, of points that could be pursued with genuine curiosity. It wasn't made by the Chamber of Commerce trying to attract tourists, but by a man puzzled and inquiring who said what he truly believed. If you came upon this statement as the opening paragraph of an article, you would probably suspect that the writer was going to take you on a journey.

An editor of a university press once said that most Master's and Doctor's theses submitted to him for possible publication were unpublishable. No one would want to read them, he said. Some contained ideas and material that could be brought together with point if the authors could bring themselves to see why anyone might want to know what they had found in their research. When he came upon such theses, the editor said he returned them to the writers with the query: "So what?" If the writers could rewrite their theses so that they answered that question, they had made what could be justly called *books*.

To construct a good piece of writing you need to go somewhere in it. If you haven't taken a journey, no amount of outlining or structuring can make the writing live. Whatever the type of writing—article, essay, story, case-history, poem—it must contain surprises and questions. Else it will remain dead for you and the reader. They must be genuine surprises and questions. Many beginning writers are affected by the worst, most gimmicky writing. They spin a long description of a man they have known, disguising who he is and where they have known him, and then in the last sentence they say: "There he was, smoking his pipe in the big rocking chair in the living room—my father." Surprise is valuable, but it must make a point or give truth to experience. This trick ending about Father does neither. If the writer told of a man exhibiting behavior shockingly unlike his father's, then as indication of the shock the writer himself felt, he might properly hold back the identity of his father until the end. First-rate writers produce surprise after surprise for their readers, in their expression, in the events they record, in the thoughts they come to through comparisons.

What shape will you give a piece of writing? Or better yet, what movement? It needs a pattern. Formlessness is too hard on human perception. You'll lose your readers if they have no hint of what journey you're taking them on. They need surprise and wondering but they can't stand one question after another with no intimation of answer or direction. As a writer you need form, a limit which will force you to invention. Henry Ford didn't say one day, "I think I will invent something great" and then build one of the first American motor cars. He was thinking about a form—a wheeled, self-propelled vehicle; and a purpose—faster travel on roads than was provided by horse-drawn carriages.

What is the right form of your piece of writing? There is no manual in which you can look up the answer. Like all good questions, this one can't be answered simply. If you remember that a good piece of writing is composed partly through plan and partly through accident which the writer keeps herself ever ready to exploit, you may guess that a good form involves both discipline and freedom for the writer and the reader. It gives the reader a feeling that he can see the path at times, at other times that he has to work hard to open it up. Occasionally it will lead him astray on exciting side trips. Give the reader a small sense of direction for the journey, but don't keep nudging him in the elbow—This way! No! Over there! Now back again!

Professional writers are often mystified by the way they put together writing. They know it has a form but they seldom know its origin. They're afraid of outlining because they want things to happen to them as they write. Nevertheless their final draft usually possesses sure form, a movement that gives power to the events they have written about. Some emphasize freedom to discover. Some emphasize the need for plan. James Thurber said of Elliott Nugent, with whom he wrote the play *The Male Animal:*

> He could plot the thing from back to front—what was going to happen here, what sort of situation would end the first-act curtain, and so forth. I can't work that way. Nugent would say, "Well, Thurber, we've got our problem, we've got all these people in the living room. Now what are we going to do with them?" I'd say that I didn't know and couldn't tell him until I'd sat down at the typewriter and found out. I don't believe the writer should know too much where he's going. If he does, he runs into old man blueprint—old man propaganda.

Because Thurber wrote this passage doesn't mean that he never paid attention to the shape of his writing. He rewrote his stories dozens of times until he got them moving right.

Probably the reason professionals are so unsure in discussing form is that good form always comes out of the materials of a particular piece of writing. As you gain experience, you'll come unconsciously to a sense of form for your materials. Always you'll hold in mind a few simple, fundamental forms that will limit you wisely and give your readers a sense of certainty among all the surprises.

> *A plot is a thousand times more unsettling than an argument, which may be answered. It is not a pattern imposed; it is inward emotion acted out. It is arbitrary, indeed, but not artificial. It is possibly so odd that it might be called a vision, but it is organic to its material: it is a working vision, then.*
>
> EUDORA WELTY

Here are a few such fundamental forms or patterns of movement. They may be useful if you don't let them bind you. Allow one to dominate your complete piece of writing and at the same time introduce several of the others to shape small pieces of the same work if you wish.

(a) *Simple Comparison.* X is different from B. You may show how X's arms differ from B's, then the legs of both, the shoes, etc. Or you may describe X completely and then B completely. As you make your observations and as you write, keep thinking: So what?

(b) *Before and After.* It was *this* way once. Now it is *that* way. You may emphasize the difference. You may ask why the difference. You may tell how the difference came about.

(c) *The Journey.* I (he, or it) started here and went through this experience or that country and came out there. Chronologically. First this happened, then that.

You may present the whole matter as story, or occasionally interrupt to explain significance. Show. Give the story. Tell. Explain why or discuss the significance of an act. But don't interrupt a story to tell or comment unless you do so frequently and regularly.

The Journey pattern is useful in writing about ideas (as well as events) which are apt to become confusing to the reader unless controlled. If it's your idea, you may show where it came from, how you took it on, and what you did with it over the years or days. If it means a good deal to you, the tale of your journey with it should be exciting, for the truth is that the journey was full of surprises—traps, bogs, a mountain with a view.

(d) *David and Goliath.* David has only a slingshot and courage against a gigantic warrior armed with spear and shield and wearing a coat weighing as much as five thousand shekels of brass. Any little or deprived or disadvantaged person against great forces. Who will win?

(e) *Will It Work?* An idea, a plan, an invention new and untried, or old but now standing against the established order—a variation of the David and Goliath story. The odds are against it because it is not now the accepted thing. Will it win through?

In deciding upon a form, you need constantly to juggle

1. the needs of your materials (which may cry out for a certain treatment),
2. the weight of your purpose,
3. the limitations and potentialities of your medium (is it a letter, an article in a picture magazine, a paper to be read aloud or silently in class?),
4. the knowledge and needs of your audience.

But your urges should come first. Please yourself or please no one. Following your own bent, you may give your readers something they've never seen before, but like. Yet, at the same time, you must remember you're writing to other human beings, who can be bored, who are often insulted by gimmicks, who have normal human needs for rising excitement, for hoping that every trip they take will pay off.

THE HOOK

A good device to remember is the fishhook. It rises slowly and then hooks back, so it will dig in and stick. It is barbed. Its curve points back to its beginning, to remind itself and the reader where it came from.

In the light of these comments on form and movement, consider some of the writings in this book. For example, "Reed" in Chapter 8, is a Journey. A girl feels faint while playing her clarinet at a competiton. Step by step she leads the reader through her travails, over to the judge's desk, to a chair for rest, and back to the performance where she takes up where she had stopped. She is much like the hero of the *Odyssey,* apparently modest yet actually prodigious. Visitors wander into the room as she starts playing the unfinished half of her piece. They come in like foreigners, and the judge, like Jove, must explain what is happening. The Hook is that the innocent, fainting girl changes into a successful performer and the dignified authoritative judge into a human being who "collapsed in a chair." Surprise.

Tension. It creates life. When it's not present, no movement —death. You know the person, old or young, who spills a story in great oceans of tedious and irrelevant detail. "Stop! stop!" you say to yourself. "You began telling me about how you fell out of the tree at Aunt Louise's but now you're listing the names of all the trees in her woods!" Good writers know more than they present. But they give the reader only the intersection points where X and Y spark. Or where After is a surprise in relation to Before. Don't tell the reader that John or Algernon is a man unless the other one is a bear with long claws on all four feet.

So there are no sure-fire formulas for shaping a piece of writing. But you can help your writing if you keep the pressure of form upon yourself—if you keep asking:

Where is this going?

Does it arrive somewhere?

Does it add up?

Is something happening between things here?

Have I made clear, directly or indirectly, why I wanted to write this?

What did I want to say? Did I get it said?

WRITING ELEVEN: Choose one of your free writings you like and shape it more powerfully. You may have to expand or contract it radically. Does it already follow one of the patterns discussed in this chapter? Can you improve it with a Hook?

WRITING TWELVE: Look over your story in which you remembered childhood and your case-history. Can you improve them with a firmer pattern of development?

In subsequent longer papers you write as you work through this book, try early to find a form that belongs to your materials, your purposes, your audience.

Life is not free from its forms.

WALLACE STEVENS

. . . childhood word-play, adolescent slang and double-talk, often derivative, but natural and exciting. In general the schools have made it their business to kill this kind of playful interest, and they have had the backing of society in this effort . . . most professionals with highly developed skills are fond of playing with those skills.

W. NELSON FRANCIS

chapter 14 playing with words

TOO OFTEN we act as if we were put on this earth to die. In conversation we paralyze each other with interminable repetitions, clichés, tedious details. Then we write down our dullness so it will live beyond the moment.

We could act as if we were put on this earth to live, to carry ourselves buoyantly.

Take phrases you have heard before and twist them to see what happens. Maybe nothing. Maybe something. Silly, like the words of a disc jockey on radio station WBBM Chicago?

> Mostly fair in the morning followed by mostly cloudy in the afternoon followed by mostly evening.

Like most quick-minded word play, this statement started with no point and ended sharp. Not only does the twist "followed by mostly evening" delight because it surprises, but taken as a whole, it joshes weather reports, their dullness, their heavy repetitiveness.

Americans are taught in school to groan when they hear a pun. Yet all the brighest writers love puns.

ROMEO: I dreamt a dream tonight.
MERCUTIO: And so did I.
ROMEO: Well, what was yours?
MERCUTIO: That dreamers often lie.
ROMEO: In bed asleep, while they do dream things true.

The most intelligent persons play with words, seriously. Intelligent readers and listeners laugh with them.

BOOK TITLE: *Up the Down Staircase*
PLAY TITLE: *Who's Afraid of Virginia Woolf?*
TV COMMERCIAL: Who said you can't teach an old dog food new tricks?
TV COMMERCIAL: Certs has the best taste I ever ate.
NEWSPAPER ADVERTISEMENT: Where does Lazy Maple Bacon gets its remarkable taste and aroma? From some sap in Vermont.
BUSINESSMAN IN CONVERSATION: You've buttered your bread. Now lie in it.

The word player takes the old and turns it. Like this:

Join the Navy and see Norfolk.

Or this:

He's three-square.

Or this:

Life is just a bowl of pits.

These three twists on tired aphorisms and slogans were written by a beginner in writing. Probably she heard the first one from a sailor but the other two are hers. She took the mealy old paste of these expressions and twisted them like pretzels. They came out crisp and salty.

The secret of productive play is simple: let yourself go. All great persons—artists, scientists, engineers, architects, cooks, designers—fool around. If their play produces something usable, they use it. If not, they feel no pain or guilt. You can't feel guilty about play and become a creative person. In this game you must be loose with language. Sinful. Show no respect for the tried and blue. But don't expect all your play to produce chocolate gems. Many mudpies, much unsorted, unexciting sand and gravel.

More often than you will anticipate, you will stumble upon hidden wonders, both nonsensical and sensical. Note that the girl's twists on old sayings made sense, possessed point. Join the Navy and see the world. Often the promise of romantic travel in the Navy sours in the drabness of a stateside training center. He's four-square. Often a man expected to be solid and trustworthy turns out missing one side. Life is just a bowl of cherries. Not usually. So the twists led to truth, as well as to fun. When E. M. Forster decided to publish a book of essays showing some of the faults of democracy in Great Britain, he named his book *Two Cheers for Democracy.*

WRITING THIRTEEN: Try playing with words.

1. Twist a cliché. Here are some clichés.

    (a) Everything is peaches and cream.
    (b) It is both a pleasure and a privilege.
    (c) It's raining cats and dogs.
    (d) They worked long and hard.
    (e) The woods were a white fairyland, covered with a blanket of snow.
    (f) He danced with the greatest of ease.
    (g) Please give me your undivided attention and keep a stiff upper lip.
    (h) Make a concerted effort. Don't run around like a chicken with its head cut off.

Think of seven more clichés and list them. Choose five from yours and those printed here and play with them. A student who felt worse than "something the cat dragged in" wrote "I felt like something that dragged in the cat." Henry Thoreau went beyond a cliché in this statement:

> If you have built castles in the air, you work need not be lost; that is where they should be. Now put the foundations under them.

And so did William Hazlitt:

> Miracles never cease, to be sure; but they are not to be had wholesale, or *to order*.

A college student twisted three tired expressions in this way:

> Home is where the garbage is.
> Love Is a Many Splintered Thing.
> I want a girl just like the girl that turned down dear old Dad.

2. Take figurative, metaphorical words and phrases literally. Look at some of your free writings, or begin a free writing and stop when you can twist a metaphor by reading it literally. Anne Haven Morgan was hearing "A bird in the hand is worth two in the bush" when she said this about bullfrogs in *The Field Book of Ponds and Streams:*

> The way to catch them by hand is seize them very firmly by both hind legs, for a bullfrog "in the hand" is strong and apparently much larger than the same one in the pond.

In the following passage, note how a beginning writer took literally the metaphorical word *outgoing* and the phrase *on her shoulders:*

> **A girl friend once told me that I wasn't outgoing enough. I thought she was very wise, always cracking books—a good head on her shoulders. So while I was out going to house council, sorority meetings, and working on committees, she stayed home and worked on my boy friend—another good head on her shoulders. Of course this put me out quite a bit and I decided some drastic steps should be taken. I told her that she wasn't outgoing enough herself, so she took my advice and stepped out, going with my boy friend.**
>
> SHARON BUTLER

Write a paragraph or two in which you twist words in this way.

Word players are not so much playing chess as just playing around. They may decide to put the play to practical use, but they don't need to any more than they need to publish the first three bad drafts of a piece of writing. The more you play with words, the more often you will find playful statements crossing over into serious expression. E. E. Cummings, an American poet, constantly sawed up his words and tacked pieces on them. He looked at the word *mankind* and decided to write it *manunkind.* Then he used that new word in the first line of a bitter poem about the evils people have committed in the name of progress. It begins:

> pity this busy monster,manunkind

This was not simply a trick by Mr. Cummings. For years he had written against war and human cruelty.

WRITING FOURTEEN: Play with titles of articles or books, with titles for your own writings. First study newspaper and magazine article titles. Note the puns, the newly created words. Here are some examples:

(a) *How to Cheat on Personality Tests,* by William H. Whyte, Jr.
(b) *A Problem of Design: How to Kill People,* by George Nelson
(c) *Arms and the Boy,* by Wilfred Owen

"Arms and the Boy," a title of a poem, plays on the first line of Virgil's *Aeneid,* which begins: "Arms and the man I sing . . ." The poet is suggesting that the reader should remember that boys rather than men are often killed in war.

(d) *The Beast in Me and Other Animals,* by James Thurber
(e) *Bed of Neuroses,* by Wolcott Gibbs
(f) *Golf Is a Four Letter Word,* by Richard Armour

The word play in all these titles is pointed. It makes a reader think twice and see significance. When Sidney Cox, a writing teacher at Dartmouth College, published a book of reflections and musings about writing —not a program of specifics for learning to write—he called it *Indirections: for Those Who Want to Write.* He was playing on the word *Directions.*

> *. . . the light of magic suggestiveness may be brought to play for an evanescent instant over the commonplace surface of words: of the old, old words, worn thin, defaced by ages of careless usage.*
>
> JOSEPH CONRAD

Try to write the truth in your language and at the same time let your words speak to each other. One day a student playing with words wrote:

> **November, and the cornfields are brown and broken and they rattle in the freshening wind. Meanwhile across the**

> **cornflakes heavy voices grumble the usual. A word of meaning drowns in a sea of crunch.**

When he handed this paragraph to a teacher, he appended this comment:

> I was just playing with words and sounds and pictures. Somehow it reminds me of T. S. Eliot's coffee spoons [in "The Love Song of J. Alfred Prufrock"]. Know what? I'll bet if the thing were printed, someone would analyze it.

Here the writer is dishonest. The passage is more than meaningless sounds and pictures. In his play he must have had in mind tension between the fresh wind in the cornfields and the stale breakfast table conversation. It's a delightful and valid statement which makes its point in a sidelong manner. If incorporated into a larger context, it might become the most powerful paragraph of a paper. What a writer says unconsciously may carry more meaning than what he plans meticulously.

Much of Lewis Carroll's writing about Alice is sense rather than nonsense. Playful sense. Before you tighten your belt, purse your lips, and dry out your throat in preparation for impressing your audience, consider speaking playfully and seriously at once. Do you see no virtue in writing lightly? Remember that the persons you write to can avoid your writing more easily than your speaking.

Lewis Carroll is making sense in *Through the Looking Glass* when he has Humpty Dumpty say:

> "they gave it me—for an unbirthday present."

Alice and he go on:

> "I beg your pardon?" Alice said with a puzzled air.
>
> "I am not offended," said Humpty Dumpty.
>
> "I mean, what *is* an unbirthday present?"
>
> "A present given when it isn't your birthday, of course."
>
> Alice considered a little. "I like birthday presents best," she said at last.
>
> "You don't know what you're talking about!" cried Humpty Dumpty. "How many days are there in a year!"
>
> "Three hundred and sixty five," said Alice . . .
>
> ". . . that shows that there are three hundred and sixty-four days when you might get unbirthday presents—"

In the same book Lewis Carroll is apparently not making much sense in the first stanza of "Jabberwocky":

'Twas brillig, and the slithy toves
    Did gyre and gimble in the wabe:
All mimsy were the borogoves,
    And the mome raths outgrabe.

Millions of persons have taken those non-words to their hearts. They like nonsense. What they don't like is nonsense written by persons who think they are writing sense. In "Jabberwocky," Lewis Carroll was making a kind of sense. In the later stanzas he plainly tells a satirical story of a Jabberwocky (dragon) being slain by a brave young knight. Lewis Carroll is making fun of pompously heroic knights. The hero becomes ridiculous as he takes

. . . his vorpal sword in hand:
    Long time the manxome foe he sought—
So rested he by the Tumtum tree,
    And stood awhile in thought.

After that puncture of the knight's armor, the reader can see that the first stanza is a setting of the physical scene for this knight's encounter with the dragon. It was a brillig day, and the toves and borogoves were out there in the wabe.

You can write so persons will enjoy reading your words. Why not do that? Something sinful about enjoyment? You landed with the Mayflower? Wear a wide-brimmed tall black hat? Put on a fool's colors and be wise for fun.

WRITING FIFTEEN: Write for twenty to thirty minutes. Start on something or someone you are fond of or despise. Say anything. Describe. Give your opinions. Say what others have said of this person or thing. As you write, listen to your words. Before you begin, read these examples of word play and use any of the methods that appeal to you.

(a) In Samuel Butler's novel *The Way of All Flesh,* Ernest Pontifex's tyrannical father says to him:

> "I must insist on two things: firstly, that this new iron in the fire does not distract your attention from your Latin and Greek"—("They aren't mine," thought Ernest, "and never have been.").

(b) "Do you think it's going to rain?"
Tweedledum spread a large umbrella over himself and his brother, and looked up into it. "No, I don't think it is," he said; "at least—not under *here*. Nohow."

"But it may rain *outside?*"

"It may—if it chooses," said Tweedledee; "We've no objection. Contrariwise."

One difference between all this word play and much of the humor that we hear every day in conversation and on television is that it's making a point. It's not gag-humor, like these statements:

My Uncle George reminds me of a rabbit. He has a hareless head.

We have a cow that never udders a word.

Sometimes a play on words may be clever and pointed but inappropriate to the occasion, to the subject being played with, or to the writer. For example, in a magazine advertisement a chemical-plastics company once depicted a room divider made of plastic cane, above a line of type reading "It's cane . . . and it's able." This is a play on Cain and Abel in the Bible, but as used here, it's all wrong. Those two names conjure up the great tragic story of brother killing brother. No reader wants to connect it with an industry merchandising its wares, especially when the two-page full-color spread showed two sophisticated couples lounging in a sumptuous room decorated with expensive furniture and a large Oriental painting.

As I was writing this chapter on word play, I was called to a bedroom to kiss goodnight a six-year-old girl and her visiting stepbrother, five, who was for the first time sleeping in the same room.

"It's pretty nice, isn't it," I said, "to have a big brother to sleep in the same room with you?"

"Yes," she said, "but it's nice to have a sister, too."

"Everything's nice in life," I said.

"Yeah, except liver," she said.

"And going to war."

"Yeah."

"That's another bad thing, like falling in the lake from a rope up in a tree."

"Or falling in love."

METAPHOR

Deep comparisons are only extended metaphors, one thing seen in terms of another. Ring Lardner, the American short story writer, wrote of a young boy observing a girl:

He give her a look you could have poured on a waffle.

When a comparison is hooked together by the words *like* or *as* it is called a simile, as in these lines from the poet Henry Vaughan:

I saw eternity the other night,
Like a great ring of pure and endless light.

but the difference between metaphor (where one thing is directly said to be something else, as in Samuel Butler's metaphor, "Evaporation is an unseen heavenward waterfall") and simile is not as valuable to learn as how to make good comparisons, whatever they are called.

Some metaphors and similes:

(a) Angus (speaking of Macbeth): Now does he feel
His secret murders sticking on his hands;
Now minutely revolts upbraid his faith-breach.
Those he commands move only in command,
Nothing in love. Now does he feel his title
Hang loose about him, like a giant's robe
Upon a dwarfish thief.

WILLIAM SHAKESPEARE

(b) . . . beyond him, one white sycamore straight as diving.

REYNOLDS PRICE

(c) A tree in spring is a double-barreled shot gun exploding.

FIFTH-GRADE CHILD

Comparisons like these may seem so remarkable to you that you can't believe they would visit you. But that's what good metaphors usually do. They come to the writer; she doesn't manufacture them at will. They come to all persons, at all ages. Frequently they come most perfectly in fast, free writing, as they did to the girl who wrote this quick description:

> **I saw Chicago once. The heat *stood still* between walls formed by dirty *heaped-up buildings squeezed* tightly together. People walked under the "L" with greasy faces, not just white ones, but black and brown and yellowish-brown, eyes slanting up or down or straight across with lines fanning from the corners as they squinted. Even the hair piled high up on women's heads *escaped* in frizzy ringlets on the back of their bare necks. Children didn't hop on one foot or chase *fleeting* candy wrappers down the sidewalk, but walked *like grandfathers,* in order not to be *strangled* by the heat and soot. Red shirts and red dresses *stood out,* but everything else was grey, light grey or dark or dirty white, and everybody was too close to somebody or something. But at the end of the street the wind *purred* gently under the open sky and the sun *smiled down* on the *green face* of the lake.**

Most of the comparisons in this passage consist of simple personification of inanimate objects: candy wrappers are fleeting; hair escapes. Nothing remarkable about these, but four of the comparisons—

> Children . . . *walked like grandfathers* . . . the wind *purred* gently under the open sky and the *sun smiled* down on the *green face* of the lake.

strike with power. The first—children walked like grandfathers—gains power from freshness, originality. But the three metaphors which close the passage are not unusual. They gain force from smooth, pleasant sound and from the contrast the writer has built between their pleasant connotations and the unpleasantness of preceding words like *squeezed, frizzy, soot, heat, dirty white.* As always in writing, a word finds its meaning and charge more from the words that have preceded and followed it than from any one meaning ascribed to it in a dictionary.

Because all words on a page carry latent sound, most metaphors gain from sound as well as from the comparison they state. Shakespeare had his Prince Hal say:

> Falstaff sweats to death and lards the lean earth as he walks along.

So much is working in that sentence: the great metaphor of the fat man larding the *lean* earth would be enough of an achievement but Shakespeare creates a fine sound effect by filling the sentences with "l" sounds. Count them.

David Jones, the beginning writer who created the following comparison, also controlled the sound of his words skillfully:

> **With dawn come the ducks. You aim at the first one flying by and shoot . . . and watch him fly away. You missed because you forgot to lead the duck. When shooting ducks you don't aim where they are; you aim where they will be. You must lead ducks just the way a quarterback leads an end. He doesn't throw the ball at the end; he throws it over his head or in front of the end and if it is properly thrown, the ball and the end meet at the same spot.**

In this passage, the segments of sentences rock back and forth in even lengths and then join *football* and *end* suddenly and finally with the words "at the same spot." *Spot* ends the passage with an explosive sound that echoes *shot.*

Beginning writers often shy away from figurative language, afraid they'll fall on their faces with it. And they often do, because they make up metaphors and similes outside their experience. To find your metaphors and similes, look to your own life, what you know well. When you are moving through the everyday world and are arrested by a piece of cellophane tape plastered on the broken pair of glasses on your friend's nose, consider why it strikes you. And record in a notebook a precise description of what it looked like and what meaning it carried for you. Perhaps the tape looked dirty and ragged on an expensive pair of glasses. Then when you need a metaphor, the comparison may come to you with all the freshness of its particularity.

> *Falstaff to Prince Hal: Thou hast the most unsavory similes, and art indeed the most comparative, rascalliest, sweet young prince.*
>
> WILLIAM SHAKESPEARE

WRITING SIXTEEN: Record five sensory observations that strike you vividly and that you might use as comparisons at some later date. Don't choose what you think will impress others. Choose what hits your senses and holds you, for whatever reasons.

In a sense all language is metaphorical, stands for something else. The river runs. She smiles sweetly. The river is personified. Her smile is compared to sugar. As a writer you should become aware of the dead metaphor in language so you can exploit it. In *Walden,* Thoreau began writing this sentence,

> We meet at meals three times a day, and give each other a new taste

and he remembered the metaphor in the word *taste.* Because he did not allow the word to become abstract in his mind, he was able to finish the sentence in this way:

> of that old musty cheese that we are.

You can do this, too. Suppose you say that

> Aunt Helen was a plain woman,

Get on that word *plain.* If Grandmother was hard but exciting, you might continue your sentence this way:

> but Grandmother was the Rocky Mountains.

When you forget the dead and hidden metaphors in the language you may compose foolish sentences. For example:

> Changing the course of a fast, deep river would normally be a lost cause, but this is one cause the North High family cannot afford to lose hold of.

This is a metaphor used by a student editor to ask others to help him reform the school newspaper. In it, he forgets what he's saying and asks the readers to keep hold of a river. He should remember that water is impossible to grasp.

Here's an excerpt from a paint company's directions for using artists' colors:

> Where very thin glazes are desired, Liquitex colors mixed with the Medium may be quickly and lightly rubbed over the surface with fingers and thumb in the manner of oil glazes. On the other hand, unwanted color or glaze may be wiped off.

The writer committed a blooper in using the phrase "On the other hand." She forgot its dead metaphor. Just before that she's talking about literal fingers and thumb. Like a thousand other phrases in everyday language, "on the other hand" was once a brilliant metaphor. Now people use it so unconsciously they need to be jogged with the vaudeville gag: "On the other hand—she had a wart."

WRITING SEVENTEEN: Write two 10- to 20-minute free writings in which you talk of things you love. Let yourself describe them in metaphor and simile that come from your deepest knowledge about objects or processes or occupations. Don't be satisfied with simple, brief metaphors: "His face was like a sunny day." Develop a metaphor, let its parts speak to each other and create new and continuing comparisons, as this beginning writer did:

> **When I think of barnacles I laugh because if they were attached to my bottom I'd feel important—like the Queen Mary. Maybe I ought to think like this when I take a bath and slide across the porcelain ocean at the end of a narrow day.**

> *Alice didn't dare to argue the point, but went on: "And I thought I'd try and find my way to the top of that hill—"*
>
> *"When you say 'hill,' " the Queen interrupted, "*I *could show you hills in comparison with which you'd call that a valley."*
>
> *"No, I shouldn't," said Alice, surprised into contradicting her at last: "a hill* can't *be a valley, you know. That would be nonsense—"*
>
> *The Red Queen shook her head. "You may call it 'nonsense,' if you like," she said, "but* I've *heard nonsense compared with which that would be as sensible as a dictionary!"*
>
> LEWIS CARROLL

Do not hunt for subjects, let them choose you, not you them. Only do that which insists upon being done and runs right up against you, hitting you in the eye until you do it. This calls you and you had better attend to it, and do it as well as you can. But till called in this way do nothing.

SAMUEL BUTLER

chapter 15 your subject choosing you

BY NOW A PERSON in the circle has probably said that once when she or he was writing, everything flowed together—the choice of events and ideas, the form in which to put them, and the sound of the words. This is what is meant by inspiration. Maybe it has happened for you. Then writing becomes effortless. That may sound romantic, but it's a fact in the life of working writers. Not all the time, but often enough that you would be foolish not to try to set up conditions which welcome this spirit, or Muse.

If you did your free writing truly and freely at the beginning of this course, you surprised yourself by what you wrote. Most persons need about three tries before they produce a strong passage. If you didn't amaze yourself in free writing, go back and try some more. It's a guaranteed activity: if you write fast—without thinking of spelling, grammar, punctuation, or form, and try to tell truths—sooner or later you will write something that moves you and others. Then you'll become more confident, begin to treat your own experience with respect, realize that it's different from every other person's in the world—the ultimate source of your power as a writer.

Once you know in your bones where your power is, you can take Samuel Butler's advice, given at the opening of this chapter, and run with it. Write with it. Butler says that if you aren't called by a subject, do nothing. School often says you must follow the assignment whether you feel called or not. In the circle you'll usually have more options than school customarily offers you. For example, you may be allowed to write three papers and turn in only one. But even if you're assigned a general topic, within that you can let a more specific topic choose you. This chapter will show you how to do that.

Here's a story by a student:

NEAT

The lake with unbroken waves had a flexible quality like a sheet of plastic food wrap. The moon was partially obscured by the leaves. Sparks and heat rising from the fire intertwined in the leaves, making them strain upward like a bobber pulling against the weight on a fishing line.

As I lay in my sleeping bag I watched the other kids walking around the camp. Their loud whispers were muffled by the crackling fire. I watched the jagged flames which made chaotic shadows dance on the distant trees. I heard an animal climbing a tree. Probably a coon, I thought.

A red light glided across the water. Lights on the other side of the bay were soothing as they flickered erratically.

The other kid's expressions changed from serenity to fright. A bright light shone on Bill and Lynn.

I pivoted on my elbow to face four lights. Two on each side of what I figured to be a car. I lay there for what seemed minutes, watching the lights rumble closer. More lights came. I tried to stand up and run, but fell. I was still in my sleeping bag. I struggled in a frenzy to unzip the bag, and fell a few times more. Finally I was free. The lights were terrifyingly close, and they hadn't slowed down. I took a couple leaps out of the path of the cars. The others were running toward the lake and swamp to get out of the way.

Someone seemed to have said, "Is he mad?" but I realized it was in my head.

The cars swerved to a scraping halt, ripping sod with their sliding wheels. Insignias on the car doors read "WEAVER COUNTY SHERIFF." A husky man jumped from one car and glared at me. In that familiar tone of authority he hurriedly asked, "What are ya tryin' to run for?"

I looked at my sleeping bag. Across the middle was one neat, fresh tread mark.

DENNIS R. WATSON

That story embodies the eight fundamentals of good writing. It is intensely dramatic, it moves from the quiet of the lake with unbroken waves to a tread mark that signifies the near death of the narrator. A sheriff's mind-set told him kids at a beach who run are guilty of something. This little incident, told with power, speaks to one of the current issues of the day: the attitude and manner of legal officers toward citizens. It's persuasive because it puts readers in the situation, makes them feel the wrongness of a sheriff's actions rather than moralizes about them.

When Dennis Watson recorded that incident in his life he probably didn't think he was writing a paper on one of the national issues of the day, but that's what he did. Once finished, his paper pointed the way for other students in the class. Another student decided to write about his encounter with a sheriff:

BIG SMILE

I woke up with a sick feeling in my stomach. I glanced out the rear window of the car: flying luggage. I yelled.

The car screamed to a halt. My brain started to function. I remember hearing my uncle swearing. It took awhile for me to understand what had happened. The luggage rack had fallen apart. We looked at the contents scattered half a mile down the road. My uncie and I started to walk along, picking up things as we went. One of the suitcases was broken. The collection took about forty minutes. In front of us sat three suitcases, a grill, and a water container—and the broken luggage rack.

Where to put it all? We were on vacation in Tennessee and the station wagon was full. Six people and our camping equipment took up most of the room. We decided that the rack could be fixed if we had some wire.

At that moment a county sheriff's car pulled up. A fat man with glasses and a wide-brimmed hat got out. He said in a Southern drawl, "Anything I can do to help youall?"

We informed him of our problem. I was surprised to see a big smile break out across his face. He told us that he had some wire at his house. My three cousins helped load the bags into the car. We jammed in, but it was a tight fit.

As we followed the sheriff's car I began to wonder if we were ever going to make it to Memphis.

We drove a mile down the road. Then we followed the sheriff into a narrow driveway. The house was old but looked nice enough. He mentioned that we could go around to the back and he would be right out. I sat down on the grass still tired. I dozed a little.

When I woke about five minutes later the picnic table in front of me was covered with melons. There were muskmelons and watermelons. The sheriff had a big carving knife in his hand. The blade was curved and looked about a foot long. He was busy cutting melons into pieces. We were wondering why he was being so generous but decided he must be just showing Southern hospitality.

Then the sheriff took the knife and lifted it shoulder high. He started to come at me, slowly at first, but then fast. The knife seemed to get bigger as he approached. He kept coming. When he was about five feet away I panicked and ran for the car.

I jumped in, locked the doors, and waited. Nobody came. Thoughts of bloody knife wounds were going through my head.

Fifteen minutes later my uncle came back, followed by the rest of the family. I stayed in the car. The next thing I saw was the sheriff right behind them. As I met his gaze he gave me a cold hard look. The rest of them were smiling and dripping melon from their mouths. My uncle and the sheriff took some wire and tied the luggage rack securely. They then shook hands.

Everyone piled into the car. We drove a few miles. I couldn't stand it any longer. I asked if they weren't a little upset over what just happened. I was told that the whole thing was a joke. He was trying to scare me. I tried to laugh. All that came out was a cracked, broken sound.

MICHAEL ELLIAS

In "Big Smile," the writer stands off from the distant event and sees himself more objectively then he did at the time. He writes with the detail that puts him and the reader in the experience. He sees his own prejudice against Southerners and sheriffs, and in the act of writing about it so objectively, shows that it is now dissipating.

Think of your writing as possibly useful to yourself and others. In this class it isn't simply an exercise to be done for teacher's grade. If a number of your fellow students write about law enforcement officers, they can take the class beyond the stock responses of "cops are good" or "cops are bad." Their writings may be sent to a social science class that is discussing the citizen and the law. If their accounts are honest and full of accurately observed details, they constitute evidence in one of the central debates of our time.

If your teacher knows a teacher in another part of the city, state, or country who is using this book, perhaps she or he can arrange to exchange papers with another class. Then you can see if the perceptions of law enforcement officers evidenced in your class echo those of young people elsewhere. Again, a step toward objectivity.

Powerful writing is often dangerous. When it compels and convinces, readers usually conclude it is telling truth. And truth about things that count in our lives has a way of spreading rapidly. For example, if you were a law enforcement officer and suspected that some young people were writing truly and vividly about encounters with law officers, you would be curious to see what they had to say. Or if you heard that law enforcement officers were making public reports of how the young people in your town conducted themselves on weekends, you would be curious to see what they had to say. So when you write about your experiences that touch national issues, you may expect some of your words to get around, even if they aren't formally published. That's one of the reasons it's wise to try in your class to encourage accounts that show both positive and negative views of law officers, or whatever institutional representatives you are writing about. Not positive just to be nice, not "A police officer once kicked me in the stomach but most police officers are really very kind," but fully realized and felt experiences.

Before a writing on a national issue or any other topic can become useful, it must be read. If it's poorly done or half done, it needs to be rewritten or extended. For example, the following journal entry about a policeman is merely the bones of a good story:

> **The policeman that pulled me over was a really great guy. We were talking about school and he mentioned how much I'd grown in the last two years. He eyed my driver's li-**

> **cense. I was overwhelmed when he told me he was going to give me a break this time. He only wrote the ticket for ten instead of fifteen m.p.h. over.**

This paragraph needs to be a longer story. It could easily and naturally be extended by presenting the conversation between the policeman and the driver. Then the oppositions and the surprise would develop and build, as they did for the driver in the actual incident. The eight fundamentals of writing given in Chapter 3 need to be put into practice. As short as the statement is, it still wastes words. The words "really" and "only" are not needed. And the opening sentence is a *giveaway* which tells readers what to expect and prevents them from experiencing the facts and developing the tension the driver felt.

Writing like this is private rather than public. It doesn't communicate to others. It's personal but it refuses to let the public know enough to judge the writer's judgment.

Samuel Butler said, "Let your subject choose you." He did that himself, as many professional writers do, because he wanted to put himself into the flow of words and experience and ideas that sometimes come to a writer free. You can do that and still be writing about a national or local issue. Think of the society you live in. Right now it's testing all its institutions. Thoughtful priests are leaving the church and getting married; thoughtful teachers are leaving established schools and setting up free schools; thoughtful men and women are living together without being officially married. And thoughtful priests are staying in the church and praising its conventional ways; thoughtful women and men are speaking up for traditional marriage; and thoughtful teachers are warning against the dangers of too much freedom in education. These are controversial times. You can't have avoided experiences which touch some of the changes in church, law, race, school, marriage, the relationships between parents and children, government, the armed forces, war, bureaucracy, business, natural resources, narcotics, welfare, old age—the list is almost endless.

The experiences you write of do not have to be extreme: you don't have to have witnessed a murder or committed a crime. Perhaps you attended a wedding recently that took place in a pine woods and included rituals written by a bride and groom dressed in blue jeans. You were present at the breaking of centuries-old traditions. A report of what you saw is evidence in a national controversy. You need only tell what took place. If you wish, you can include your own feelings, but that's not necessary. This isn't the conventional school assignment which requires you to make "a concluding judgment at the end of the paper expressed in not more than twenty-five words."

For example, here's a factual piece of writing which touches upon the relationships of children and parents. You may want more than the writer gives you, but what he gives is solid evidence, something to ponder before coming up with suggestions for parents or children looking for ways to live with each other.

STRENGTH

A little man parks his car in the shade of the tree in front of our house. He walks toward me studying the house and its surroundings. The lawn, the trees, the bushes. He kicks at a weed sprouting up from a crack in the sidewalk. I remain in the porch chair as he comes closer.

He wears a gray pin-striped suit. In his hands is a briefcase and *The Wall Street Journal.* A thin red tie rolls down his fat stomach. His neck hangs out over the starched button-down collar of his Arrow shirt. His pants are baggy at the bottom; at the top he's poured into them. The belt buckle is in the last hole.

"Hello Ron."

"Hi Dad."

"Where's your mother?"

"Makin' dinner."

"Did you get that faucet fixed?"

"Yes."

"Did it need a new washer?"

"Uh-huh."

"Good, better come in and wash up."

As he enters the house, the screen door squeaks. He opens and closes it, searching for the insignificant noise. Again I feel it coming.

"After dinner better find the squeak and oil it."

"O.K."

"Where there's a squeak, there's friction and where there's friction, there's wear. Some day this thing'll fall right off."

You've just met my father. Age 52. Roman Catholic, married thirty years with six kids—three girls and three boys. Employed by a big corporation as a systems analyst with thirty years seniority. Lives in a fine house in a suburb of Cleveland and owns two cars, a two-car garage, a trailer, and an oil well.

After high school he held three part-time jobs, one as

an assistant manager in a grocery store while attending night school.

His father lived in the taverns and his mother, seeking only the companionship and love of her husband, followed him everywhere. They both died alcoholics.

My dad's theory is simple: work for the body, strict rules for the mind. Every Saturday he carried with him a list of chores we were to do. If we didn't get the work done, we had to do it on Sunday after church. Many times I stayed up Saturday night and worked on the car till 12:00 or 1:00 in the morning so I could watch the football games on Sunday. We fixed our own cars, made our own wine, reshingled our house, painted our station wagons, laid our own carpeting, repaired own own washing machines, dryers, TV sets, and radios. For three weeks we worked in our basement to finish it off besides doing our regular chores. By himself my father has put in our basement bathroom, wired up our television antenna, and on one summer day shoveled a ton of topsoil from our driveway to the backyard. I remember once he had to drill through glass but didn't want to buy an expensive diamond-tip drill. He used his fountain-pen, which had a diamond head, as a drill bit to fix a crystal chandelier.

Two summers ago a couple of cars smashed together on our corner and one of my friends came over and said, "O.K., you guys, fix these cars." It was meant as a joke, but still our reputation had made him think of it. Many of our friends hated to come over because my father either sent them home or put them to work. He wouldn't allow my older sister to wear blue jeans when girls started wearing them. About five years ago my brother lost his brand new hat, so my father made him wear a girl's scarf to church. He may have played catch with me about five times.

We couldn't listen to our radio or stereo on Sunday. Nor did we receive weekly allowances. He let my mother give us a nickel a week to put in the church collection. If our grades weren't good, A's and B's, we were not allowed to watch television during the week. In fact he moved the television set downstairs so it wouldn't interfere with our studying.

Up until two years ago I still had a bed time. Two summers ago I took Driver's Training and needed the family car to pass the final test. But he wouldn't let me use it.

Within four months I got a job, bought a car, insurance, and a license just in time to pass the test. What had made me mad was that he had let my older sisters use the car not only for the test but for other things too. When I became seventeen he started charging me $20.00 a week for room and board.

My father had precedence over the lounge chairs which are both upstairs and downstairs, the newspaper, the *TV Guide*, and even the shower. If he and another person happen to be getting ready to take a bath or a shower at the same time, he gets it first because he pays the water bills.

I believe he hates city life. We travel a lot. We've been in every state in the U.S. but two, Alaska and Hawaii, even traveled all over Canada and Mexico. Yet he still doesn't change, whether at home or away from home.

One time my brothers, my father, and I hiked seventeen miles to the bottom of the Grand Canyon, a trip which would take two days. During the entire time he acted like John Wayne in his movies.

"All right, you guys, take five," or "Let's go, get a move on."

He rationed out the food and water. We got back at him though because for the last few miles he was gasping for air and saying, "Wait up, you guys." He didn't have that commanding tone in his voice any more.

Many times my mother has threatened to walk out and I remember how my brother and I would make plans to run away from home. We'd wait until everyone was asleep and then my brother would come over into my bed and we'd plan our escape. Get the suitcase down from the closet and pack up and sneak out to catch a bus for Texas. We loved Texas because that's where all the cowboys were. Pretty soon we'd just fall asleep, too tired to go anywhere.

My father had one weakness—cigars. Three years ago he was smoking eight cigars a day until his doctor told him to quit. Now he has gained at least forty pounds, which are endangering his health as well as aggravating his bad back and heart. Age is catching up with him now and he's beginning to loosen up. But there are things I'll never forget. I can't forget.

I love him.

RON B. RICHARDS

What do you think of that statement about a father? Chances are some of your fellow students will disagree with you. It isn't a paper that comes to neat conclusions but it speaks from such depths of feeling that it can't be quickly waved aside. You may remember it for several months. It will probably make you think of your relationship with your father or mother and help you see it more objectively. Those are not small accomplishments for a paper written in school.

Here's another view of parents and child encountering each other. Again it tells truth so faithfully that it demonstrates how both parents and child can view a matter with totally different perceptions.

BIG SWALLOWS

It was Saturday night. We were driving around deciding when we should go home. Hank and Ken were sitting in front of my car with Hank at the wheel. Both were drunk. I was sitting in the back with a couple of bottles of wine. One was almost empty. I finished it and tossed it out.

We had just left a party. Well, I think you would call it a party. It was more like a place to sit and drink or smoke. We only knew a few of the people. That was one of the reasons we left.

I sat in the back holding the other bottle of wine. It was hard to decide if I should drink it. I was seventeen and had been drinking for about two years but usually one bottle of wine was as much as I could handle. After glancing at my watch and seeing it was only ten-thirty I unscrewed the top—tilting the bottle, I felt the cold wine meet my lips. It turned into a warm glow the minute it hit my stomach. Taking big swallows, I finished drinking in about fifteen minutes. Suddenly my head was spinning and I was in a state of semi-consciousness.

The next thing I remember is being in our garage. Hank woke me up and told me he would walk home. He asked if I was all right and said we could ride around a little longer. I told him to go ahead home even though it was only twelve o'clock. We both got out of the car and walked to the side of the house. I was planning on using the back door. As Hank walked down the sidewalk he didn't see me fall into the bushes. I was out cold.

I came around what must have been about forty-five minutes later. My mind was jumbled. I glanced up and saw some lights were on. Numb and dazed I got up and walked

into the house. Both of my parents were standing in the kitchen as I stumbled in, making a commotion. All I can remember is my mother yelling at me. They told me later that I just walked in and passed out on the couch. They had never seen me drunk before. I'm sure my mother thought I was tripping.

The next day I woke up at about noon. My stomach was upset and my head was still spinning. Staying in bed seemed like the best thing to do. I couldn't face my parents. They don't even drink. I kept thinking about what a wonderful relationship we had up until now.

After sleeping two more hours I began to feel better. I had to go out and see what my mother had to say. She was the only one home. I felt like a piece of petrified wood. The sickness in my stomach had turned to a nervous quivering.

I was standing at the faucet in the kitchen. I turned around quickly. My glance caught her standing behind me. I almost dropped my glass. Her stare was icy as I heard her say, "Is this going to be the type of thing we should expect from now on?" That was the extent of the conversation.

I watched the television for a while but couldn't seem to get interested. Then I tried to go back to sleep again. I managed to sleep about fifteen minutes. Time dragged by.

That night when my father came home we sat around the living room and talked. "What did you drink and where did you get it?"

My mother said, "Do you plan on doing this again?"

I said, "Probably."

She seemed near tears. "Just because everyone else drinks do you think you should?"

"Sure," I said. "It's no big deal."

Then my father cut in. "What about drinking and driving?"

I replied. "I try not to. Hank was driving last night."

The same thing never happened again. Not that I didn't get drunk. It was just that I made sure they didn't see me.

JOHN R. SENDER

Most of the writings, including the one above, in this chapter are printed with pseudonyms to protect the writer and others who might be injured if their real names were used. Writing truths is an act with consequences, usually good. But school has a way of getting you to go at things backwards. It becomes hung up on authoritative statements beause it wants to promulgate the Truth. And since authorities often speak the last word, that word is apt to be stated generally. Therefore a student feels pressed to make general statements. If asked to write a paper about Women's Liberation, for example, a boy writes, "After many centuries of enduring male chauvinism, women in America have finally begun to liberate themselves." That's his statement of the general idea he's read in many articles. Or a girl writes, "In the future, women will find themselves hired for jobs at the same pay as men, and in general will be accorded the same rights and privileges." And so on. Nothing there anyone wants to read at this stage in the movement. "But how could I write any other way about women's rights?" says a student. "I haven't read any books on the subject. I'm not an expert."

But every man or boy in the country has daily experiences that touch women's rights, which are being pursued in ways that are changing the sexual roles of Americans. His father lives in relation to the movement—he increasingly accepts and brings about changes or he resists them, or he moves back and forth between the two positions. His mother likewise. Every time the student—male or female—encounters the other sex, the experience is touching this subject. Examine yourself. If you're a man, are you treating women like sex objects? If you're a woman, by your behavior are you asking to be treated like a sex object? We need to have a current history of dating behavior in this country, small accounts of this date or that date, or the coming together of young people outside the custom of dating. How do young people act toward each other through sexual roles? Differently from the way older people act toward them? First we should not generalize but begin writing the record, putting down the evidence. Dozens and hundreds and thousands of little accounts of the behavior—including the talk—of persons of the opposite sex together, working, playing, studying, meeting, sharing, or retreating from each other. These stories are in your past experience and all around you. For example, when I recently attended the National Boys and Junior Tennis Championships, I overheard one of the waiting players—who looked to be seventeen or sixteen—say to one of his fellows:

"I'm not afraid to sit down next to any girl around here and put my arm around her."

"You aren't? Aw, come on."

"No, bet you a dollar I'll do it."

Just then a beautiful girl, who looked twelve, sat down on a bench far enough away that she couldn't hear the boys. She sat there silently, engrossed in the game before her, her clothes and hair perfectly groomed.

"See that girl? I'll do it for a buck."

She was the perfect target, fulfilled the stereotype of an American beauty.

"For how long?—thirty seconds? a minute?"

"No. That's too long. She'd leave. What would you do if you were her and somebody came up and did that? You'd be scared. You'd get up and leave. Just the arm around her—for a buck, O.K.?"

The talk went on. Later the girl left, unmolested.

That little incident, told simply and directly, is a full statement on the general topic of women's rights and more valuable than some long generalizing papers that summarize or quote what a number of experts have argued on the matter. The tennis player unknowingly turned the act on himself. He admitted that any normal human being would feel attacked by what he proposed to do to a girl he didn't know. He wanted to use this girl, any girl, to show off his maleness to his fellow players.

All around you are stories as good as that or better on the subject of women's rights. When you decide to write about a social controversy, maybe you'll do better simply to examine your experience for an incident or relationship that has made you feel uncomfortable, released, excited, especially happy, and then ask it it's not material for a case-history that bears upon one of the central issues of the day. For example, here's an account from a student's journal written about the smallest of matters, a little animal.

DON'T FEEL BAD

I am sitting in the kitchen—facing the bathroom door. It's open just a crack, enough for some of the darkness from that room to pour into this one. It's early and no sounds are up yet. There is a tiny scratching though. It seems to be creeping into the silence like a genteel, soft joke. I know what it is—but I sit here still because I might scare it away or it might push the door open and run over my toes—I just watch the crack, wondering where did it come from. Is it really there? I plugged up the hole under the sink. It's probably just sitting there, nestled deep in the purple shag of the rug, peering at the other side of the same crack I am peering at. I wonder if it's pissed about the De-Con and all the holes I have blocked up, like the two in the living-room by the fireplace. That's silly—it doesn't have to be mad about that tall glass vase or the bookend. All it has to do is

push a little, suck in, and it should be easy for it to squeeze by them.

It's probably not mad at all. It's probably just sitting in the bathroom trying to figure out a way to make it back to wherever it came from. Because I got up, came into the kitchen and turned on the light, it feels trapped in the purple shag. It doesn't have to feel bad, because I feel trapped by that crack. What if the door just slowly eased open? I'd probably be figuring out a way to get back where I came from, too. I wonder why I don't just go over there, break the crack by pulling the door open, and snap on the light. It's probably praying that I won't do just that, the same as I am praying it won't push the crack toward me.

Don't we both feel uncomfortable? I wonder if it snuggled in deeper at the thought because I just put my feet up on the rungs of the chair because of the same thought. Here we are—it and me—caught in the silence of a morning's yawn. We are sharing a time and a feeling and we are from different races of life. Maybe I should just turn off the light and go back to bed. It and I can't be suspended long in this unique understanding because this morning is about ready to sneeze her eyes open and then it and I will have to regress to hating and fearing each other simply because our understanding will be gone with the coming of the noise.

ANNE LAYTON

Trivial? The way a small animal's sounds affected this girl? Or sentimental because it gives animals the attributes of human beings? Maybe so to many persons, but right now there are many Americans who have begun studying and trying to follow Oriental philosophers who say that human beings, animals, rocks, and trees are one, together existing in this world, and they can get in touch with each other. Many of us on a walk in the woods at times have felt close communion with trees or animals. Is it possible that Oriental persons recognized the facts of existence better than we more practical Westerners? Anne Layton's story suggests she possessed Oriental sympathies. The point here is that she didn't read and summarize a number of books or articles on this "subject." She wrote down her own experience, about which she could speak more authoritatively than anyone else. Her story is a piece of evidence on which the controversy can be resolved or discussed with enlightenment. Hers is not the only evidence. Much more would be needed before a person should speak a final word on the kinship of animals and human beings. But not always do we need to speak final words, as school so often forces us to do. Often it's enough, and sometimes more truthful, to speak a word of experience that opens to other people new possibilities of living.

Never underestimate the record that is trying to be truthful to individual human experience. Frequently it's more convincing than a page full of statistics. At this moment in American publishing, magazine and book editors are increasingly printing thoughtful histories of individual experience. Seldom do they publish essays of ideas or summaries of trends unless they are accompanied by little stories or case-histories to give their ideas life and authenticity. Usually we are more persuaded by the record of a life than by a sermon, and the best ministers fill their sermons with little stories, as Jesus Christ did. And Buddha. And Mohammed.

WRITING EIGHTEEN: Write an account of the kind discussed in this chapter. You may get to it either way—by thinking of a moving experience in your life and seeing whether it touches one of the central issues of the day, or by thinking of a central issue and asking what experience you have had that touches it.

If you and your teacher wish, you may then write another account on a different issue. And another. The possibilities for writing innumerable papers are before you. With this method alone you can find topics for a dozen papers, enough to fill up the work of a whole semester.

Look sharply after your thoughts. They come unlooked for, like a new bird seen on your trees, and, if you turn to your usual task, disappear; and you shall never find that perception again; never, I say—but perhaps years, ages, and I know not what events and worlds may lie between you and its return!

RALPH WALDO EMERSON

chapter 16 keeping a journal

MOST PERSONS write notes to themselves (Get Kleenex and catsup. "I saw a rhinusahorus at the zoo"—Timmy's report at dinner, which should be forwarded in next letter to Grandma) and each spring they wish they had a note from last year telling when they first saw blossoms on the lilac bush. But they lose the notes, which are written on torn bits of paper, the backs of laundry slips, or the flyleaves of books.

An old cigar box will not do, because not enough of the notes get put in there, and those that do are difficult to consult: one must riffle through all of them to find one.

The answer is a journal instead of a box, a bound ruled book in which to make instant and permanent entries. Many professional writers keep one.

WRITING NINETEEN: Try keeping a journal for a week. You may not be the journal kind of person—maybe you have a photographic memory or an aversion to recording anything you feel has not been polished like a gem. But try keeping a journal for a week and see. Here's a day from one of Henry Thoreau's journals:

Dec. 5, 1856. Clear, cold winter weather. What a contrast between this week and last, when I talked of setting out apple trees!

P.M.—Walked over the Hill.

The Indians have at length got a regular load of wood. It is odd to see a pile of good wood beside their thin cotton tents in the snow, the wood-pile which is to be burnt within is so much more substantial than the house. Yet they do not appear to mind the cold, though one side of the tent is partly open, and all are flapping in the wind, and there is a sick child in one. The children play in the snow in front, as before more substantial houses.

The river is well skimmed over in most places, though it will not bear,—wherever there is least current, as in broad places, or where there is least wind, as by the bridges. The ice trap was sprung last night.

As I walk along the side of the Hill, a pair of nuthatches flit by toward a walnut, flying low in mid-course and then ascending to the tree. I hear one's faint *tut tut* or *gnah gnah*—no doubt heard a good way by its mate now flown into the next tree—as it is ascending the trunk or branch of a walnut in a zigzag manner, hitching along; prying into the crevices of the bark; and now it has found a savory morsel, which it pauses to devour, then flits to a new bough. It is a chubby bird, white, slate-color, and black.

It is a perfectly cloudless and simple winter sky. A white moon, half full, in the pale or dull blue heaven and a whiteness like the reflection of the snow, extending up from the horizon all around a quarter the way up to the zenith. I can imagine that I see it shooting up like an aurora. This is at 4 P.M. About the sun it is only whiter than elsewhere, or there is only the faintest possible tinge of yellow there.

There are a great many walnuts on the trees, seen black against the sky, and the wind has scattered many over the snow-crust. It would be easier gathering them now than ever.

The johnswort and the larger pinweed are conspicuous above the snow. Some fine straw-colored grasses, as delicate as the down on a young man's cheek, still rise above this crusted snow, and even a recess is melted around them, so gently has it been deposited.

The sun goes down and leaves not a blush in the sky . . .

My themes shall not be far-fetched. I will tell of homely

every-day phenomena and adventures. Friends! Society! It seems to me that I have an abundance of it, there is so much that I rejoice and sympathize with, and men, too, that I never speak to but only know and think of. What you call bareness and poverty is to me simplicity. God could not be unkind to me if he should try. I love the winter, with its imprisonment and its cold, for it compels the prisoner to try new fields and resources. I love to have the river closed up for a season and a pause put to my boating, to be obliged to get my boat in. I shall launch it again this spring with so much more pleasure. This is an advantage in point of abstinence and moderation compared with the seaside boating, where the boat ever lies on the shore. I love best to have each thing in its season only, and enjoy doing without it at all other times. It is the greatest of all advantages to enjoy no advantage at all. I find it invariably true, the poorer I am, the richer I am. What you consider my disadvantage, I consider my advantage. While you are pleased to get knowledge and culture in many ways, I am delighted to think that I am getting rid of them. I have never got over my surprise that I should have been born into the most estimable place in all the world, and in the very nick of time, too.

A day's record of observations and thoughts, from a journal which ran into several thousand printed pages. From these pages Thoreau put together several books, including *Walden,* a classic statement of the joys of self-reliant living which has been read for more than a hundred years in all parts of the world.

If a writer will go on the principle of stopping everywhere and anywhere to put down his notes, as the true painter will stop anywhere and everywhere to sketch, he will be able to cut down his works liberally. He will become prodigal not of writing—any fool can be this—but of omission. You become brief because you have more things to say than time to say them in.

SAMUEL BUTLER

Thoreau's entry for December 5, 1856 contained his usual miscellany of writing: simple notes of facts to mark the record of the year, observations of nature and men, thoughts. In your journal put down whatever strikes you. Think of it at once as private and public. You may be showing it or parts of it to others. If you find yourself recording such intimate secrets that you do not want them revealed, you can keep them in the book and copy out only those you want to show to others. The possibilities for entries are endless, as the following statement by Dorothy Lambert shows:

WHAT IS A JOURNAL?

Though a journal may be many things—a treasury, a storehouse, a jewelry box, a laboratory, a drafting board, a collector's cabinet, a snapshot album, a history, a travelogue, a religious exercise, a letter to oneself—it has some definable characteristics. It is a record, an entry-book, kept regularly, though not necessarily daily. Invariably some entries will be scrawled on the backs of ice cream wrappers, envelopes, paper bags, or programs, whatever blank surface is available at the moment. Some will be nearly illegible, written in the dark in the middle of the night. These entries can be recopied, pasted in, or dated and kept loose in the rear of the journal, but they are part of it; inspiration settles on one at the most awkward moments, not necessarily as one sits down to write with clean page, sharpened pencil, and open mind.

It is a record kept for oneself. As such, it is fragmentary, allusive, disjointed, uneven in quality. Nor should it be polished and unified; then it would be a collection of essays. What matters is the one entry in ten which sparkles, ready to be set in the ring of an essay or story or poem or letter.

Not only is it a record for oneself, but of oneself. Every memorable journal, any successful journal, is honest. Nothing sham, phoney, false. Who is there to kid? Yet euphemism, the word which hides the fact, is so much a part of the world; to break through the euphemistic mold of thought to honesty is very difficult. A journal need not be a confession, or a psychoanalyst's couch, however. Honesty lies in observing undeceived what lies about, not necessarily what lies within.

Finally, a journal is a place to fail. That is, a place to try, experiment, test one's wings. For the moment, judgment, criticism, evaluation are suspended; what matters is the attempt, not the success of the attempt. In a journal one practices the lines before going onstage.

A journal may be all gems, or all logs, or all plans and

blueprints, or all test tubes, or all confession, or all collections of oddments—or it may be a marvelous hodgepodge of the old-fashioned general store. What follows are some ways of seeing, of thinking of a journal, and some suggestions of what to do with it. You may follow one suggestion consistently, or try all, or none. At least you will become aware of what is possible.

1. Think of your journal as a treasury, a jewelry box for gems and gold nuggets, for quotes (others' or/and yours), pithy ideas, epigrams, turns of phrase, insights, analogies, puns, aphorisms, nutshell wisdom. You will write little, but think much.

2. Think of your journal as a storehouse into which you pack canned goods (others' ideas), fresh fruit, nuts, corn, string, straw, K-rations—almost anything edible and useful, in preparation for a rainy day, when you can browse through you storehouse with delight and constant amazement at what is there. Like a pack-rat or the Collier brothers, don't stop to be discriminatory in your salvaging and collecting.

3. Think of your journal as a collector's cabinet in which you place or mount butterflies and moths, or glass figurines, or . . . What will you collect? salt and pepper shakers? stamps? model ships in bottles? oddments, little ironic quirks of life? Do you collect for others to see, or just to have?

4. Think of your journal as a snapshot album and you a roving photographer clicking a shutter on life. Light and dark contrasts, color, texture, angles and circles, portraits, landscapes: what will you photograph? Steichen chose faces and hands; Ansel Adams chose the Sierras. See life through a lens, telescopic, microscopic, or wide-angle, but a lens. In focus.

5. Think of your journal as a laboratory for experiments, blank pages waiting to be tried. Dissect. See what the insides are like, how it runs, how it's put together. Examine minutely; see with a microscope. Mix test-tubes. Weigh. Trace patterns; fix laws. Ask questions and set about to find answers.

6. Think of your journal as a giant wardrobe which you can step into and try on marvelous clothes. Put on others' styles, look in the mirror, see and feel how they fit. Wear what you like; change with the seasons; try on 49 hats and

buy none. Be Parisian, Ethiopian, or Hindi: experiment, experiment. Even poetry, though by phrases, not rhymes.

7. Think of your journal as a drafting board. Blank pages will become blueprints, plans for a house to live in. Or are you drafting just window sills, or a whole cathedral? Accuracy, careful detail, sharp lines, no smudges on the pages. If you are an idea-person, what will you build? Watch your idea-house grow, as you add on bedrooms for the birth of new thoughts.

8. Think of your journal as a psychoanalyst's couch, a confession. Lie down, and talk, talk, talk. Ramble on about irrelevancies, or else list in order your sins. Repeat, go over and over as you peel away each layer of onion skin to the core. Explore your depths. Dreams, Fantasies, Truths.

9. Think of your journal as a tape recorder attached directly to your brain. Record your stream-of-consciousness, your associational thoughts. Don't fuss for words; write as fast as you think. Use dashes, dots, skip lines and spaces for "punctuation." Replay: can you find a coherence in your thoughts? Emphasize and clarify such associational leaps.

10. Think of your journal as a continuous but unmailed letter to a specific, real person. Preferably of the opposite sex, highly interested in you. Make every entry a love letter, every entry an act of love. Or choose to write to a close confidant. Or to your mother. Or possibly to your yet unborn children. What would you tell them? no moralizing, no mush.

11. Think of your journal as a letter to yourself. What would you have yourself know? Or remember ten years from now? Which self of your many selves will you choose to write to? Or yourself as you *were,* say, at ten? Or yourself as you will be? Will your other self/selves answer back? Turn your journal into a dialogue or triologue with yourself. Argue, debate, reconcile.

12. Think of your journal as a history—memoirs—and you as a VIP: the average citizen. Write for an extraterrestrial reader, or a terrestrial one of the 22nd Century. Let them know how we really lived and thought. Or else record the current world events, as filtered through your eyes, your consciousness, your concern. Record how history touches you.

13. Think of your journal as a travelogue, even though you may travel only through tunnels from dorm to class, like an underground man. See afresh, as if you were born yesterday, or recently distilled from another planet. Record the quaint customs, lore, folkways, speech patterns, superstitions, magic, and miraculous sights of the local terrain. Be Livingstone, Margaret Mead. Or be Magellan; chart the unknown; fill in the map of your world.

14. Think of your journal as a religious exercise, one which might lead to a religious experience, or religious insight. Write it as a letter to God. A dialogue? Follow St. Ignatius' meditative methods: application of the senses; composition of scene. But write it down. Become all tongue, all eyeball, all nose; only hands; the world's ear. Be at the place, fly back to the time. Put yourself in other's feet; especially try those you can't stand, those who seem foreign to you. Use these meditative principles in areas not considered religious; meditate on the secular. Write prayers, personal prayers; write litany; write secular prayers, secular litany. Search for metaphors, new metaphors, for the ineffable, the wordless, the inexpressible. Reach out into the void, reach down, reach up, to find ways of telling others what you believe.

Mrs. Lambert's essay on journals is not a map, merely suggestions. Take one, take several, as you wish.

The great journal keepers have always distrusted their memories. When an idea strikes them for a piece of writing, they write it down even though it is only an idea, so far without the materials to give it body. Samuel Butler, whose published *Note-Books* are widely quoted, made such notes for writing he hoped to do some day. Here are three out of a long list:

1. Tracts for Children, warning them against the virtues of their elders.
2. Family Prayers: A series of perfectly plain and sensible ones asking for what people really do want without any kind of humbug.
3. The Sense of Touch: An essay showing that all the senses resolve themselves ultimately into a sense of touch, and that eating is touch carried to the bitter end. So there is but one sense— touch —and the amoeba has it. When I look upon the foraminifera I look upon myself.

If you are aware of the fabulous quality of reality, your notebook is bound to be exciting reading in spots. Here are excerpts from a number of student notebooks:

1

Mom to three-year-old: "Mary Jane, get out of your Coke!"

2

I have drained six cartons of lemonade and twelve glasses of tap water since this afternoon, and two quarts of milk. I have a fever but am on my feet, slushing off to class —reading, writing, and I get paid today.

3

My seven-year-old sister at a birthday party: "Oh, Momma, my feet went to sleep. It feels like salt and pepper mixed."

4

One of the salesmen at Sears absent-mindedly wore to work one shoe and one bedroom slipper. He didn't have time to go home to change, so he developed a limp for the day.

5

A white-haired old woman scooped up spilled dry oatmeal from a busy intersection after the bottom of her grocery bag had burst. She explained to one honking motorist that she didn't want to waste the oatmeal—she would take it home to her ducks.

6

My sister celebrated her sixteenth birthday yesterday. Her boy friend surprised her with a beautiful heart necklace. Later, a strange man surprised her at an intersection by pulling out in front of her car, and she rammed his car with hers, cutting her forhead, nose, and mouth. One scar under her chin is heart-shaped.

7

Last week I saw two guys walking down Western Avenue carrying on a conversation ten feet apart. I even

walked between them. Interpersonal relationships are growing less personal but this was too much almost to believe. One of them, I suppose, had determined to assert himself, keep his pace and have the other come up to him. The other probably determined the opposite, so they walked along, making fools of themselves.

8

Charlie came home on leave today after eight weeks of basic training. He learned to kill.

My Uncle was gassed in the First World War and when I knew him he sat in a chair watching television all day and talked in a hesitating manner.

9

On the corner of a parking lot on Rose Street, a mailman stopped at the mailbox, unlocked it, opened the front, took the mail out, and sat down inside the mailbox while he sorted the letters.

10

It's the first day of school. It seems so empty. Oh, there's lots of things to do, but there is something missing. There is no one older. When we were sophomores and juniors there was always the big seniors. Now there is no one left. We're seniors, last year of high school. Is it really the fact that we're as big as we will get? Hard to say what's missing. It's lonely here.

In writing journal entries you should begin by concentrating on what you say rather than how you say it. Entry 10 is carelessly written. The expression *there is* appears to often. Twice it led the writer to use a singular verb with a plural subject ("there's lots," which says in reverse "lots is"; and "there was . . . the big seniors" which says in reverse "seniors was"). But the writer put her finger on why high school students sometimes feel lost at the beginning of their last year. Since she solved that puzzle, she shouldn't have said, "Hard to say what's missing." If she wants to publish the statement more widely, she should omit that sentence and improve the verbs throughout. If you look at your journal entries some time after you wrote them and find them in need of revision, you might cross out words and make changes for practice, but you don't need to. A journal is personal. If a teacher or someone else can talk you into publishing some of your journal entries, fine; but you shouldn't allow your journal to be graded.

Here are some more journal entries:

11

I hate that sand dune. It looked down at me. I felt small. It seemed to be laughing at me as the wind from the lake blew over it. I hated it even more. I began to run up the side. The sand, like wet cardboard, under my feet. Heat. I could feel it conquer my throat. It was steep. Bushes and fallen tree branches served as handles. My legs were aching. Made me go faster. I fell. Made me feel like a dog crawling on all fours. I went on. The laughter got louder as the wind blew harder. Just kept running. Panting, until I found myself standing on the top of it. The lake and beach below looked so small. And the sand dune. Now that it was under me, it didn't seem so big either. My turn to laugh. Felt like God.

12

Moved. Just like that. She moved. I had known her for a long time. She had thick, curly eyelashes, long. Envied. Lise always grew her nails long, too. It was sort of awesome to look at them sometimes. They were curved and filed into a fine oval. No one at school said anything about it. No teachers. They didn't say anything. It's different now. Lise moved. She went to Grand Rapids. The nuns there were different. Strict. Scary. Lise was in typing. The nun said to trim the nails by the next weekend. She didn't. The nun wasn't to be ignored. Up to the desk. Lise had to cut off all her finger nails. Right then. Right there. It's too bad she moved.

When you write in a journal, keep your sense of a reader. That reader may be no one else but you, but so much later in time that he or she needs to be spoken to fully, to be put there. The writer of Entry 13 chose an incident involving deep feeling and wrote strong sentences, but she held back a little too much.

13

We went to the funeral and afterwards his grandpa asked me to go out to the house with all the other people. I did, and everybody ignored me. I think Kent did because after

> **we went to the cemetery and the minister said the last words underneath the tent, Kent went over and sat in one of the limousines, leaving the door open, perhaps so I could come and say a kind word or pat him on the hand. I didn't want to. I lowered my eyes and walked right by him. I think he even said my name.**

Benjamin Franklin tells in his *Autobiography* how he read and studied a pasage of writing he admired, wrote down "short Hints of the Sentiment in each Sentence," and then several days later tried to reproduce the passage. Almost all professional writers have learned fundamentals in this way before developing their own style. No surprise here: long ball hitters have learned from imitating the best long ball hitters. Painters have learned from imitating painters they have admired.

Good writers never plagiarize from other writers, but they borrow and build on what another writer has said. When E. E. Cummings wrote his great line "pity this busy monster, manunkind," discussed in Chapter 14, he may have got the notion of playing with *man* and *unkind* from Thoreau's lines in *A Week on the Concord and Merrimack Rivers:*

> I love man—kind, but I hate the institutions of the dead unkind. Men execute nothing so faithfully as the wills of the dead, to the last codicil and letter. *They* rule this world, and the living are but their executors.

When Thoreau wrote in "Walking":

> Any man can stop a hole to keep the wind away, but no other man could serve so rare a use as the author of this illustration did.

he was clearly alluding to lines Shakespeare gave to Hamlet:

> Imperious Caesar, dead and turned to clay,
> Might stop a hole to keep the wind away.

although he did not mention *Hamlet.* These two writers didn't steal from Thoreau and Shakespeare. Cummings pushed further a word play of Thoreau—if he borrowed at all; and Thoreau turned a phrase of Shakespeare into half of a neat compliment to him.

All people must borrow from those who have gone before, but they should understand what constitutes stealing from the printed page, however difficult that act is to define. Writers don't always have to use quotation marks. All men are created equal—the reader recognizes the source. Writers can give the wise reader a hint that they are borrowing, as Thoreau did when he borrowed from Hamlet. But they shouldn't take a series of words—say more than seven—from another writer when they are distinctive and valuable in style or message, and allow the reader to believe the words are their own.

Student term papers often abound in such plagiarism. Speaking in the most obviously alien voices, students write stolen sentences like this:

> The nugatory effect of the prolix discussion was that the Treaty of Rackham was forever doomed.

This is calculated imposture, in writing called *plagiarism.* The most responsible way to borrow is immediately to acknowledge indebtedness, not by footnote or quotation marks (although they are frequently helpful), but by naming the source:

> Burke said that . . .

WRITING TWENTY: After keeping a journal for a week, stop for a week and then go back to its pages. Choose the entry which most moves you, and work it up or cut it down until you have produced a small piece of writing whole and satisfying to you.

WRITING TWENTY-ONE: After one week's respite from journal writing, begin your journal again and make a daily entry or two for two weeks. Choose an object, a place, a person that interests you, and note it each weekday for two weeks—include weekends if possible. Observe it daily. You'll see it in different lights because the weather has changed, the time of the day, the weather inside you. Write in your journal what it looks like and what it makes you feel, on at least ten different days.

Maybe you'll find yourself writing a long description one day and only a word or phrase on another day. Ask other persons who have a chance to know this thing well, or to observe it frequently, how it looks to them and makes them feel. Record the best answers you get.

After all that looking and listening, put together from your best journal entries a piece of writing about that thing. It may be several pages long or a few compact lines of prose or poetry.

• • •

A recent development is what's called the Double-Entry Journal. You take a sheet of paper (might be from a loose-leaf notebook, but doesn't have to be) and draw a line down the center so there are two columns. In the left-hand column you write journal entries and then pass the page on to someone else. That person then writes comments or responses to your entries right opposite them in the right-hand column. That other person gives you a similar page, with entries in the left-hand column and you respond in the same way.

Double-Entry journals can be used for many purposes. When you're reading something in school, you can take out passages that you especially like or disagree with and write them in the left-hand column. Then in the right column you can record your reactions to those passages.

Some teachers have used Double-Entry Journals to keep in touch with their students' thoughts and feelings that can't easily be part of class discussion. They ask students to write two or three short entries every day for a few weeks or a whole semester, and they respond briefly in the right-hand column. Double-Entry journals are conversations in writing. They provide some of the advantages of being a writer rather than a talker—the chance for reflection before comment, the producing of a record that stands through time and can be referred to again and again.

Nor use too swelling, or ill-sounding words.
BEN JONSON

chapter 17 writing second-hand

BELOW is printed a book review by Anatole Broyard, a reviewer for the daily *New York Times*. Remember what Mr. Singwich, the English teacher in junior high, used to tell you about book reports? "Summarize the plot, name and describe the leading characters or principal theme of the book, tell the purpose in one sentence." If Singwich felt daring that day he might have said, "You may make your own judgment of the book, but reserve that until the end, and do not use the word 'I' anywhere else in your report." He was telling you to use no firsthand experience, and to be *scholarly*, as he understood the word.

Since the *Times* is the newspaper of historical record in the United States, you might expect Mr. Broyard's review to be dull and impersonal like a book report written for Mr. Singwich. Here it is:

> THE OBSTETRICS OF THE SOUL
>
> *DEATH AS A FACT OF LIFE*
> *By David Hendin, 255 pages. Norton. $7.50*
>
> "I don't understand what I'm supposed to do," Tolstoy said on his deathbed—and neither do most of us. The conspiracy of silence with which we surround the subject of dying led Geoffrey Gorer, the British anthropologist, to coin the phrase "the pornography of death." But a "good death" is an indispensable end to a good life—so crucial, in fact, that a

German writer called it the "obstetrics of the soul." To die with dignity is important not only to the dying person, but also to his or her survivors, who will always be able to remember the one they loved in this light.

According to David Hendin in his "Death as a Fact of Life," dying today is often rendered obscene by technology. Many patients are kept alive when they are no longer human beings, but simple circulatory systems, breathing but otherwise unresponsive tissue. Under these circumstances, life may sometimes be more terrifying than death. The dying person's relatives and friends are elbowed away from him by machines. And since these machines interfere with the natural course of decline, no one knows exactly when death will come and the patient often expires with only technology for company. In this connection, the author quotes Theodore Fox's famous remark: "We shall have to learn to refrain from doing things merely because we know how to do them."

Mr. Hendin quotes surveys to show that most dying people would prefer to talk about it, and are greatly relieved when the silence is broken. I know that as I read his book, I felt my own anxieties about death first articulated, and partially assuaged. It *is* therapeutic to bring that immemorial enemy of ours out into the light. As the author points out, for some of us the threat of death can have an integrative rather than a disruptive function. It can make us see our life as a coherent whole and give us an opportunity to sum it up emotionally and intellectually—to deny the fashionable charge of "meaninglessness or absurdity."

Accepting death is not necessarily a form of resignation, of giving up: it may be a positive reorientation. We can look *back* over our life as well as forward to its end. We can congratulate ourselves on what we have done and reverse the old saw that "you can't take it with you." By renouncing the terrible duty of pretending, Mr. Hendin says, we can take the bandages off our fears and our feelings and die with love instead of lies as the last thing we hear.

The author has done a brilliant and highly sensitive job of bringing together the literature of death—from the need for revising our legal, medical and psychological criteria to the fact that the dead are forcing the living into an ever-decreasing space. He discusses the science of cryonics, or freezing the body in the hope of future resuscitation (cost

$20,000); the case for and against euthanasia; the need to train doctors to *face* death as well as fight it; the "hospices" being built for dying people, so that they can spend their last days in as homelike an atmosphere as their medical needs permit; the advantages of cremation and its relative unpopularity in the United States, and much more.

I found the chapter on "Children and Death" especially moving. Mr. Hendin knows how to evoke a feeling as well as most novelists and he is never, as far as I can remember, guilty of mere sentimentality in dealing with the most highly charged subject in our emotional repertory. Warning us against feeding inane euphemisms to children, he cites the case of a little boy who was told that his dead mother "went up into the sky." Shortly afterwards, the boy was taken on a visit by airplane and was very sad and disappointed because he had looked on every cloud but had not seen his mother. Informed that his infant brother had been picked up by God and taken to heaven, another child kept his windows locked, refused to cross open spaces and played only in the shade of trees for fear the same thing would happen to him.

Unacknowledged death haunts us far more effectively than the ghosts of our childhood. The author feels that the more fully it is faced, the sooner we are likely to recover from the shock of someone's death. If we do not make peace with them and separate ourselves from the dead through appropriate periods of mourning and grief, we may find it difficult to attach ourselves to anyone who might help replace them afterwards.

Though there is not a superfluous page in "Death as a Fact of Life," I found myself—emotionally, not morbidly—drawn to those passages dealing with the dying person. When Mr. Hendin speaks of the indignity of deterioration, I remember the humiliation I saw in my own father's face when he was a Rube Goldberg tangle of tubes and life-coercing machines. His difficulties were increased by his "stiff upper lip" philosophy that locked both of us in the anguish of all that we wanted to, and could not say. A terrible loneliness lurked in his eyes, but it was too late for him to learn or change.

What the author does not say because it may be beyond the scope of his intent is that our entire life is a preparation for our death, and we may expect to die well or badly depending on how we have lived. Freud told a story of visiting

William James at the time when the American psychologist and philospher had a brush with death in the form of a heart attack. He could not refrain from asking James afterward how he had felt about the prospect. James replied that he had lived his life and done his work. Death held no terrors for him. Edmund Bergier, the psychiatrist, remarks in one of his many books that, after a satisfying sexual experience with someone we love, it is natural to feel sleepy. I mention these two remarks because I feel that, somewhere between them, we may find the answer to one of life's most intimidating questions.

The New York Times, January 25, 1973

Maybe Singwich would give Mr. Broyard a C for that effort. He started his book report with secondhand comments by Tolstoy and Geoffrey Gorer, and you can't tell whether they had appeared in Mr. Hendin's book or Mr. Broyard had swiped them from somewhere else. Then he tells about his "own anxieties about death" and at the crucial point, just before the end of the review, talks about his own father's death. He's constantly butting in on the author with his own ideas and feelings about death.

That's what Singwich might think, but many readers of this book review who have sat down and discussed their reactions have felt otherwise. They were moved by Mr. Broyard's report of how he was moved by David Hendin's book. They wanted to read it. And right away, before they could get the book in their hands, they discussed the way people face dying.

Like most good writing, Mr. Broyard's review fulfilled the eight points presented at the end of Chapter 3. It didn't waste words. It put the reader there, gave him a full example (about the boy told that his mother "went up into the sky") as well as a summary in paragraph 5 of what the book covered. It made things happen for the reader as they happened for Mr. Broyard when he read the book. It brought up some of Mr. Hendin's surprises: for example, the simple statement about not prolonging painful life: "We shall have to learn to refrain from doing things merely because we know how to do them." And the notion that death can be integrative rather than disruptive when we at that moment look at our life as a coherent whole. And Broyard went beyond Hendin to say surprisingly that "we may expect to die well or badly depending on how we have lived."

Mr. Broyard did not forget to judge the book: he pointed out that like a novelist Hendin evokes feeling, he is not sentimental, he does not waste words ("there is not a superfluous page"). But Broyard wove these judgments and the paragraph sketching the content of the book back and forth with his own response to it. He allowed himself to present some of his own experience on which his response was based. This weaving of the *objective* (description of what's in the object, the book) and the *subjective* (Broyard's own feelings and knowledge) provides a tension, and therefore a relief, for the reader. The review is not all the same, not all impersonal or egotistically personal. And it provided the fundamental of all good reviewing or criticism: enough evidence so the reader could begin to judge the reviewer's judgment.

Can you write like that? It's hard to do once you've learned how like an Engfish to swim in the dry water of school. Actually Mr. Broyard did his job naturally. He read a book, was moved by it, let his readers know how and why. Then he disciplined himself enough to sketch the book's contents so a reader would know what it presented beyond Mr. Broyard's special interests.

There are your readers out there—the rest of the class and the teacher. When you write secondhand, remember you yourself are always responding partly on the basis of your own experience, and your readers will be responding partly on theirs. So it's a secondhand experience, but also a firsthand one, and if you think of your readers, you'll remember they have hands too.

SHOWING WHY A WRITING AFFECTS YOU

WRITING TWENTY-TWO: Choose a piece of writing (book, magazine article, story, editorial, play, poem—makes no difference whether you read it in school or out) which moved you so much that you might naturally talk to a friend or classmate about it. Maybe you love it, maybe you hate it, maybe you have mixed feelings. But it hit you hard. Write a paper showing why and how it hit you. Let your reader see what in your experience or thinking made you excited by the writing. And in so doing, tell enough about the writing that another person who has never read that writing will see what hit you. This is not a book report. Don't try to summarize what you read. Don't try to cover everything in it.

Here's an example of such a paper, written by a college senior:

1

When I read *In Cold Blood*, our house was empty. One small reading light shone in the blackness of my musty den. It was late in the evening and the occasional creaking of the floors was the only sound. I swore I wouldn't read it again. It was a story of two men who committed four mur-

ders. This was what Truman Capote wished to show us, in the most factual language possible in a novel. The results were horrifying. They were not simply two characters. Capote let me know these men slowly, detail by detail, until I felt comfortable on a first-name basis.

I had never met two men who had shot four people in the head. They were men not unlike many students at this school. True, they had idiosyncrasies that were brought out, but they probably drank beer, brushed their teeth, and wore T-shirts just like I do. By the end of the book I actually felt sorry for them. They were human beings and capable of error.

How many eligible Perrys and Hickocks are in the dorm or my classes? If I point a pistol at a girl's head I am stupid, careless, and unsafe. If I move my right index finger one quarter of an inch, I become a maniac. One quarter of an inch is the measure of a madman. How many of us do not have one split second of weakness, one moment of unconsciousness when we do something completely irrational?

"I don't know why I did it. I guess I just wasn't thinking."

I believe that a man, any man, at the right place, at the right time, and with the right apparatus, will kill for no apparent reason. We are all capable.

This book scared me, bothered me, made me sick. I do not even know whether I liked it, but I know I'll read it again.

TIM SWEENEY

Here's the first draft of another such paper, written by a high school student. Its materials could be clarified and polished, but the critic and the work both come alive and encounter each other at a surprising point.

2

I've watched dirty little brats get up at 7:00 in the morning and play outside all day by themselves. Their mother works and so she can't watch them. They walk the streets by themselves looking for something to do. Anything that interests them they play with. You always read about kids playing in old refrigerators and getting suffocated. Their mothers didn't pay any attention to them.

I always swore I'd never be that kind of a mother. My kids are going to be happy playing in the yard so I can watch them. Kids aren't happy when they're neglected all day.

I read about Ulysses in *The Human Comedy* by William Saroyan. He walked around and amused himself all day. When he waved at the black man on the train, he marveled at life. This man was friendly. If he had been in his own yard, he would have missed the black man and missed his singing.

Ulysses would never have seen the boys steal the green apricots from Mr. Henderson's apricot tree. Ulysses would never have known that it isn't a sin for little boys to steal apricots. He would never have met Big Chris because he got caught in a bear trap.

I wanted to deprive my children of a childhood. My Ulysses would never know my love and he would never grow to be a man. His older brother would never reach manhood by delivering telegrams at night. I don't suppose I would ever wait up silently every night just in case my son wanted to talk. Delivering death messages isn't easy, and maybe he wouldn't even feel like talking. I'd deprive my children of life.

Now, if I could choose my future, I'd be poor. I'd work all day and my children would explore the city by themselves. At night I would come home and they would tell me what they saw. When my oldest son dies in war, my middle son will tear the telegram and I will invite a soldier who knew my son into my house.

The first time you try a criticism like this you'll probably fail to give enough of the work or of your own experience. In the following paper, the writer showed a fine understanding of the spirit of Huckleberry Finn, but she needs to include a few examples of how Huck "did such a neat job" of running away. And she needs to say a little more about why and how in her own life "Everything has to be proper and formal."

3

Cam told me *Huckleberry Finn* was the only book he enjoyed reading this year. Isn't it the truth? Everybody tries to make more out of a story and ruins it. But the adventure and fun in this book are real. I've always been sort of a tom-

boy. So, I know what it's like to run off and enjoy the outdoors. Wouldn't it be exciting to go down a river on a raft? I love to be around water anyway. And there would be lots of camping, too. It makes you feel clean and healthy. Why didn't Huck run away sooner? That's not so important. It just seems like he did such a neat job of doing it, though. But something like a lot of blood and a mess would upset my parents too much. I would have to run away without mess. That's the trouble with our society today, though. Everything has to be proper and formal. It would be more fun if I could relax and be messy. How about running away tonight?

The following paper is an original and compelling comment on death. All it needs to be a great paper is a little more about how death appears in the novel.

4

***On the Beach,* by Nevil Shute, is a stimulating look at death with a touch of the feeling of people near the end.**

This book comes to mind in this time because of life passing so quickly. As everyone would eventually die in *On the Beach,* so will everyone die in our world. The difference is in the cause. And in the time. Here during the past couple of days I have noticed a closer relationship between teacher and student. The way of the gatherings of classes is deeper. I have seen a teacher touch a student, me, when she doesn't ever touch anyone. Feelings are here now. They are open and my mind sees it. People will realize for a time that life is short and one must see every thing that one can. It's hard. Now it's doubly hard and very tense. But these people are closer. The librarian scolded me for talking and ten minutes later she came by and patted me on the shoulder. I am sensitive and in the air the eyes see the human feelings reaching out toward each other to hold for a while because there may not be a tomorrow for this person. In a time it will all pass away again and people will scowl at other people and strike out with whipped tongues and I will shudder at the sight of it and think of the memory of silence.

I will watch and be wary and then my day will come.

JAN OKEMURA

Like a number of writings by beginners printed in this book, Paper 4 needs grammatical polishing. The pronoun *it* is several times inaccurately or confusingly used. But the paper communicates feeling with subtlety.

Paper 5 more fully brings alive both the book and the writer's experience which intersects with it; but it, too, could be strengthened with more examples. Try to write a paper which achieves balance. And remember that what makes these papers provocative is their honesty.

5

Fleabags and flophouses, burleyque gals and bloody buckets. Strange words to those unaware of Skid Row, U.S.A. There's one in almost every city.

Sara Harris went to a Skid Row. She interviewed some of its inhabitants—prostitutes, drunks, addicts, and madmen; and in her book, *Skid Row, U.S.A.* reveals by a series of dialogues the people and the life they live.

Until I read this book five years ago, I hadn't even heard the words "flophouse" and "fleabags." I wasn't even aware that such fantastic people existed. People who live in 25¢ a night rooms. A Ph.D. who wore a Phi Beta Kappa key drank liquid black shoe polish as a substitute for expensive liquor. The utter abandonment of themselves so bluntly presented in this book shocked me and I didn't really believe it. But I asked a teacher about it and of course he affirmed that Skid Row was a serious problem. This made me want to take a better look at other people around me. I asked Mom to drive to the sections of town that would be considered something like Skid Row. She didn't want to, so I sneaked out and walked through town to the bars and dumpy hotels. A few men passed me, dirty and messy. Women in sloppy clothes shuffled by. One woman had on spiked heels that clicked and wobbled when she walked. I glanced quickly at their faces. The woman was a mask of wrinkles and stringy hair, of red eyes and orange lips, and I only stayed a few minutes.

This writer made his knowledge come home.

All of the five papers are presented here in their first drafts. You can probably see a number of ways to polish them. In Paper 5, for example, the third sentence gives away the conclusion and should be omitted, so the reader will accompany the writer on his journey and share his discovery. The next to last sentence should precede the one that now comes before it.

When you write of something secondhand you should expect to find more Engfish than usual in your first draft. Maybe the true words came truly to you in a pleasurable flow, and there is little to be done to improve them. But be wary. Before you read that first draft to anyone or have it read aloud, study the next three pages and then go back to your work.

Mr. Broyard and the five student writers presented speak in voices that ring true and strike the ear hard. Not any ear, but the ear of an audience tired of the thick, pulpy language which we call Engfish. You hear it from teachers in classrooms; you read it in the paragraphs of second-rate scholars; you see it in the writing of high school and college students who have imitated what was too much around them. When Lareen Morgan realizes she is being interviewed for "Senior Portraits," the high school newspaper column, she shifts into pedantic gear and says:

> High school has encompassed many memorable, yet trying times.

You may have the urge to reply, "So has working in the fertilizer plant." The word *encompassed* sounds impressive at first but on second consideration the reader realizes that it's so inflated it's about to pop in Lareen's face.

When a college professor was asked to write an article for a learned journal, he too shifted into Engfish and said:

> Unquestionably the textbook has played a very important role in the development of American schools—and I believe it will continue to play an important role.

You may have the urge here to say, "So have spitballs." The professor goes on:

> The need for textbooks has been established through many experiments. It is not necessary to consider these experiments but, in general, they have shown that when instruction without textbooks has been tried by schools, the virtually unanimous result has been to go back to the use of textbooks. I believe too, that there is considerable evidence to indicate that the textbook has been, and is, a major factor in guiding teachers' instruction and in determining the curriculum. And I don't think that either role for the textbook is necessarily bad.

The professor begins his statement with the weasel word *unquestionably.* The very point he is going to try to make in the paragraph he calls unquestionable before he starts. From then on he throws (*lobs* would be a better word; nothing has force in this paragraph) a bunch of dull generalizations in his reader's face. Something has played a *role* in the *development* of something. How many times have you heard that vague line? What role? An *important* role. What does that mean? What kind and rate of development? How did the schools develop as a result of the textbook? What a mishmash of educational language: "need established . . . many experiments . . . virtually unanimous result . . . considerable evidence . . . major factor." These are Weasel Words. They don't say anything for sure yet they keep insisting they are certain and unquestionable. The professor talks about impressive experiments but never mentions one. He doesn't think it is "necessary to consider these experiments" yet he employs them as the only evidence for his argument. Note his last sentence:

> And I don't think that either role for the textbook is necessarily bad.

That's the only possibly exciting sentence in the paragraph. Someone has apparently said that using a textbook to guide teachers' instruction or determine the curriculum is bad. Who said that? Why? The writer needs to say, but he isn't fixing to say anything for sure. He won't give the reader anything to examine and be sure about. He's just talking through his weasel nose.

Every writer talks weaselry at times. This language is hard to see because it is so common.

> It was *sort of* a flop.
> He was *kind of* a hero to me.
> That, *incidentally,* is four fouls.
> Going through the weeds there was *almost* like walking in a swamp.
> His father, *by the way,* is a crook.

> *"I've got a sort of idea but I don't suppose it's a very good one."*
> *Winnie the Pooh,* A.A. MILNE

In hurried conversation such weaselries should be forgiven, but not in writing, where the author has a chance to revise and tighten. The weakness of *sort of* and *kind of* is that they don't tell whether the writer thought "it" was a "flop" or "he" was a "hero." If the writer wanted to communicate that the play was not completely a flop but a failure only in the first act, she should have said so. If she wanted to say that "he" was a hero in one way, but not in another, she should have told in what way. Otherwise, she should have simply said: "It was a flop" and "He was a hero to me. Usually *sort of* and *kind of* take the punch out of the words they precede. They lessen rather than increase meaning. If you scatter them throughout your writing, your reader will eventually suspect you don't mean anything you say. Note these weasel words:

> The *final* conclusions of the workshop.
> There is a *limited amount* of seating space.
> Throwing mud in her face wasn't *too* nice.
> Falling down the stairs isn't *exactly* fun.
> But being in that wreck was an *especially* devastating experience.
> Mary was a *remarkably* lovely queen.

Other words frequently used in weasel fashion are *relative, particular,* and *various.*

> This is a *relatively* minor matter and need not concern us long here.

If the readers don't know relative *to what,* they can't extract much meaning from *relatively.*

> This is a *particularly* fine example of social organization.

Fine already tells the reader the example is above ordinary. *Particularly* steals attention from *fine.*

> In his travels around the world, the captain has encountered many diseases in *various* countries and *various* environments.

This is straight cornmeal mush. Most readers would like it better fried crisp and served with hot syrup. If the writer wants to make his point with power, he should say "about two thousand diseases in fifty-six countries and in environments ranging from ice floes to tropical rain forests."

Most academic writing is loaded with weasel words and phrases; for scholars are taught to be cautious, to qualify. But there are times to be cautious and times to be bold. Watch this pedantic phrase weasel its way into an otherwise straightforward sentence:

> Last week the world was contained in a blue plastic egg filled with jelly beans and a set of rabbit teeth—*at least it was* for five-year-old Jack.

The author doesn't really mean to hint that anyone else's world beside Jack's was filled with that bunch of jelly beans and set of rabbit teeth, but she heard a weasel squeal somewhere and echoes it in her sentence.

As I write this chapter warning others of weaseling, I remember that when I was writing another text, an editor pointed out that almost always when I used the words *in fact,* I followed them with an unsupported personal opinion. Frequently writers try to make up for weak opinions by introducing them with one of the following expresions:

indeed	surely	honestly
obviously	certainly	frankly
of course	needless to say	sincerely

The most dishonest man I ever knew constantly prefaced his remarks with the expression, "I would be less than candid if I did not say—."

Writers are often dishonest with themselves: they speak apologetically, defensively, pompously, or condescendingly when they do not feel apologetic, defensive, pompous, or condescending. A teacher who once submitted a poem to an editor of a magazine, hoping for publication, referred to her manuscript in her covering letter as "This bit of fluff, modeled after "The Children's Hour.' " Her comment sounds like the introductory remarks many persons make before they speak in a group meeting: "Now I don't claim to be an expert in this subject and what I have to say probably isn't worth much . . ." Then they make a fifteen-minute speech. One is tempted to say to the teacher: "If you think your manuscript is fluff, don't send it to the magazine"; and to the apologetic speaker: "If you don't think you're qualified to speak, don't speak. Or if you are qualified, don't waste our time telling us you aren't."

Whether a word is weaseling or not depends upon its context. If writers bring most of their sentences alive with verbs crammed full of meaning, with details that speak to all of their readers' senses, then they can afford to use some of the paler, emptier words in the language. At times their readers may crave relief from lines bursting with life. If, for example, you're writing a remembrance of childhood, you might well say:

> At any rate, something important happened in town and I sang at the ceremony.

because you don't remember the event. *Important* is usually a weak word. *At any rate* is vague and almost meaningless. And *something* frequently shows a writer's failure to investigate thoroughly. But here all the words are acceptable. If you can't remember why or how an event stood out for the townspeople, you're justified in using the vague word *important* to describe it. To be vague in one sentence in a story that is otherwise precise and specific is not sinful. Your readers will understand. Good writers learn what words and phrases lead them often into poor communication, but they don't try to achieve an absolutely pure diction. A sparing use of conversational tags like *very* or *too much* or *particularly fine* won't wreck an otherwise vigorous piece of writing. Nor will a little unnecessary repetition.

> *"What do you know about this business?" the King said to Alice.*
>
> *"Nothing," said Alice.*
>
> *"Nothing whatever?" persisted the King.*
>
> *"Nothing whatever," said Alice.*
>
> *"That's very important," the King said, turning to the jury. They were just beginning to write this down on their slates, when the White Rabbit interrupted:* "Un*important, your Majesty means, of course," he said, in a very respectful tone, but frowning and making faces at him, as he spoke.*
>
> "Un*important, of course, I meant," the King hastily said, and went on to himself in an undertone, "important—unimportant—unimportant—important—" as if he were trying which word sounded best.*
>
> *Some of the jury wrote it down "important," and some "unimportant." Alice could see this, as she was near enough to look over their slates; "but it doesn't matter a bit," she thought to herself.*
>
> LEWIS CARROLL

How much the readers know about a subject should affect the writer's decisions about cutting down sentences. Samuel Butler, a strong advocate of tightening writing, said that diffuseness "sometimes helps, as for instance, when the subject is hard; words that may be, strictly speaking, unnecessary will make things easier for the reader by giving him more time to master the thought while his eye is running over the verbiage."

Nevertheless, most writers need to develop more ruthlessness toward their writing as John Ciardi, poetry editor of *Saturday Review,* said. It is theirs. They must initially love it. Finally, though, they must see it for what it is and remember that their readers are busy persons, and human beings, who are easily irritated by writing which does not get a satisfactory mileage with its words.

The ways of being untruthful about the world and dishonest with oneself are legion. But the effort to tell the truth is so exacting that once seriously undertaken, it becomes a habit. And one truth breeds another.

Not everyone who uses weasel words is a weasel at heart. If you read well the writings you examine and retain your essential honesty, you will use these expressions so seldom that your readers won't notice them. Don't strive for absolute purity; every person is born with an ego which at times drags him into a weasel's hole. The surest way to reduce weaselry in your writing to a forgiveable amount is to know what you're writing about and to find something to say you believe in. As you have seen, surprises then begin to appear.

WRITING TWENTY-THREE: Throughout this book, you've had available to you models of actual writings done by persons who've gone through a program like this before you. Now see what you can do without them. Maybe you'll feel lost, or maybe you'll feel freed to do something that only you are able to do, and you'll write something different from what models "tell" you to do. Something powerful because it's original, because it comes out of your unique experience.

Read aloud a short story and keep a watch on that part of you which may be saying, "This character in the story reminds me of. . . ." Or "This character is just the opposite of some person or event in my experience."

Don't force the comparison. Let the feeling come to you. If it doesn't, read another short story, and if necessary, several others, until you hear such an echo as you read.

What you're being asked to do here is follow the method of the best thinkers and writers. It's both simple and difficult. You must discipline yourself to carry out all the steps, not just one or two. Here's the procedure:

1. When you've finished reading the story in which you found a character that reminded you of someone in your own experience, write

several pages in which you picture your person in action for a reader who knows nothing about him or her. Make the person come alive on the page. Later you're going to compare your person with the one in the story, so you need to present that her or him in the same kind of detail the writer of the story presented a person. If the character or event in the story was a minor one, you won't have to write more than a few paragraphs or pages, but if major, then you'll probably have to write something much longer. That's your first paper.

2. *Likenesses.* In the second paper, point out how the person you've presented from your own experience is like the person in the short story. Or, if the person in the short story caught you because she or he seemed the opposite of someone in your experience, point out the *differences.*

3. *Differences.* In the third paper go one step further. Ask yourself if there are likenesses within the differences. Suppose you're saying that Aunt Sarah in the short story reminds you of your grandmother because she has many friends. Perhaps your grandmother, like Aunt Sarah, has many friends, but knows some of them very well, while Aunt Sarah knows her friends only superficially. She chats with them on the telephone, but neither she nor they share any of their deepest feelings or interests. It's all "Isn't it a nice day," and "Wasn't the food at the church supper unusually beautiful last night?"

4. *Likenesses?* In your fourth paper, try to go still further. Point out, if you can, likenesses between those differing knowings of friends by Grandmother and Aunt Sarah. This is the payoff question, the one that takes you beyond what most people do when they analyze a character in a writing or in their own experience. Perhaps you find that although your grandmother and Aunt Sarah both have many friends, and one knows some of them deeply and the other doesn't know any of them deeply, they both are kind to these friends (or both are occasionally mean or cruel to them).

So here's the pattern of what to look for in this in depth analysis of someone:

likenesses
differences within those likenesses
likenesses within those differences

or

differences
likenesses within those differences
differences within those likenesses.

If necessary, say, for example, "Well, Grandmother knows her friend Janie Stapleton very well and Aunt Sarah in the story doesn't know her friend Sue Andes very well. (Unlike). They both treat those friends mean some times. (Alike). And now I'm hoping to find a difference in the way they are mean to these friends, but I don't. They both make fun of their friends, insult them over the phone, in much the same way." (Alike). Don't twist the facts to fit the pattern. If you can't find a difference within a likeness, record that fact. The value of this procedure is that you ask the questions: you look for likenesses within differences, or vice versa, and that act helps you see more richly the people involved.

Write down examples of the way Grandmother and Aunt Sarah talk to their friends. You need evidence for your judgments, and so do your readers. Always in this comparative thinking and writing, try to give your readers enough of the action, speech, or thoughts of the people so the readers can judge your judgment of the people you're writing about. Not only will that help your readers, but it will help you in your analysis. As you put down the evidence for your judgments, the words on the paper may surprise you and lead you to new judgments, new understandings.

What's the point of all this comparison? Just *an exercise* in thinking? No. It's more than that. If you compare a character (or event) in a short story (or a piece of non-fiction, like a newspaper report or a magazine article or a book) with someone in your experience, the process will reveal things you never realized before; so that you'll not only understand better what you've read, but you'll understand better your Grandmother (or whatever you're examining in your own experience).

You can use this method with any two ideas, objects, or events, as well as persons. Whether you start with likenesses or differences, you should move to the opposite and keep going.

This method is the habit of good thinkers. You can apply it to your reading of anything—science, history, social science, psychology, whatever.

. . . the crudest honest sentence is a re-sounding of experience. Have you heard a bright child describe an airplane crash? Have you heard a returned soldier describe his once-more-slept-in bed, at home? Sentences resound when experience is comprehendingly relived.

SIDNEY COX

chapter 18 controlling sound

WRITING APPEARS a soundless enterprise: the pen slides quietly across the page. And reading appears a silent act:

"Where's John?"

"He's curled up on the porch reading. I haven't heard a sound out of him all afternoon."

But one writer says of another writer, "He hasn't any ear," and she means the most damning criticism. For one of the chief resources of writers is control over the sound of their sentences.

Scanning the printed page, most readers hear in their unconscious ear the sentences sounding against the echoing memory of all the words they have heard in conversation.

The following passage utilizes sound skillfully:

I COULDN'T STAY

I couldn't stay in the library with the rain pecking at its windows. The blackness outside invited me to lose myself in its depth. So I walked into it, letting the sharp spray tingle my forehead and tangle my hair. I walked slowly until my coat was damp and heavy and my knee socks slid around my ankles, making them itch. It was night and nobody saw how the rain treated me. When I got to the room,

I listened to water splattering under the wheels of cars and rinsing the stained sides of the brick buildings. I wanted to sleep through the night and wake up washed like the world on a new day.

SUE SMILTNECK

The girl who wrote this passage didn't know how well she had used sound effects. Most writers don't consciously create all of their best sound effects. They write thinking of meaning, and their sensitive ear helps them select words that strike other ears significantly. In "I Couldn't Stay," note these sound effects:

rain pecking
*sh*arp *sp*ray *tingle* my forehead and *tangle* my hair
wa*ter* splat*ter*ing
r*in*sing the staine*d* si*d*es of the *b*r*i*ck *b*u*ilding*s
*W*hen . . . *w*ater . . . *w*heels . . . *w*anted *to* . . . *w*ake up
*w*ashed . . . *w*orld

It was a hard rain: the reader can hear it pecking and splattering. Rhythms are set up by the repetition of consonant sounds (*tingle, tangle,* etc.) in what is called *alliteration* and in the repetition of vowel sounds (*rinsing, brick, buildings*) in what is called *assonance.* Human beings like repetitions. They sense strength in the *repeat-and-vary* pattern. All persons employ sound skillfully without being taught. In a speech given to American teachers in 1966, Edmond Wright, a British schoolteacher, pointed out that under extreme emotional stress all persons speak in strong rhythm and often with alliteration.

Rich, you're a rotten, raunchy rat!

He told students to write down what persons at home said under stress: they found considerable alliteration. One student complained that he didn't hear any, so Mr. Wright suggested he go home and pour a glass of milk over his brother's head and then listen to his father. He did. He heard considerable alliteration.

Knocking around in your head are the sounds of your native language: spoken or muted echoes of what you've read, perhaps the lullabies your mother sang to you, the rich cursing of men hunting or playing games, the formal rhythms of a trained voice reading in church or synagogue, the skip rope song, the hurried swallowed phrases of other children singing the "Star Spangled Banner" or chanting the "Gettysburg Address," the taunts they sang in the street:

> Simpy Sam is a stupid old man!

Without trying, most persons can write rapidly such sound effects as these by a high school girl:

> **I like to go fishing. But I don't like to touch worms or slippery, slimy fish. They wiggle. I went with Anne three years ago. That was fun until she broke her promise and made me take the fish off. Then it swallowed the hook. It was terrible. It wriggled and writhed in the bottom of the boat. Then it just lay there. Dead.**

This isn't an exceptional piece of writing. The seventh sentence suffers from It-ache. In the sixth, *it* refers to the fish; then suddenly *it* refers to the whole struggle of the fish with the hook. But in sound, the passage is strong. *Slippery* and *slimy* and *wriggled* and *writhed* alliterate with force and their sounds echo the sense of what they say. The last two sentences allow the record to run down appropriately, and *Dead* stands by itself, final—in its position, its shortness, and its two hard *d's*.

In the phrase "bottom of the boat," the writer has repeated the *b* sound skillfully. You may say that she didn't mean to hit that sound hard and that it adds nothing to the passage because the *b* sound doesn't suggest *boat* or *bottom* as the *sl* sound in *slippery* and *slimy* suggests the squirming fish. True, but one of the marks of strong writers is that their sentences from time to time carry an occasional repetition of sound that gives the words a strength like the "bone" in spaghetti cooked not too soft by an Italian chef. Note the pattern of sound repetition in these next passages when you read them aloud. The authors were probably not trying for any effects, but they achieved them nevertheless.

> Men are *h*orri*b*ly *ted*ious *wh*en *th*ey are goo*d* *h*us*b*an*d*s an*d* a*b*omina*b*ly concei*t*ed *wh*en *th*ey are not.
>
> OSCAR WILDE

> **It's like *wh*en you break up with a girl and you've explained all your reasons to her *wh*y. And *sh*e says, "I *s*till don't *s*ee *wh*y it *w*on't *w*ork." And you've *s*een i*t* ou*t* and you've hi*t* *th*e *bl*ank har*d* col*d* *w*all of *s*oli*d* no*th*ing.**
>
> HIGH SCHOOL STUDENT WRITING FREELY

These passages get their bone from repeating consonant sounds. Vowel sounds also work their spell:

> These were s*o*ftw*oo*ded trees, p*o*plars, t*u*lip trees, c*o*tt*o*n-w*oo*ds. There were fences ar*ou*nd *o*ne *or* tw*o* of the h*ou*ses, but mainly the yards ran into each *o*ther with *o*nly n*o*w and then a l*o*w hedge that wasn't d*o*ing very well. There were few g*oo*d friends am*o*ng the gr*o*wn people, and they were n*o*t p*oo*r en*ou*gh f*o*r the *o*ther s*o*rt *o*f intimate acquaintance . . .
>
> JAMES AGEE

Here a highly skillful writer was trying to evoke the spirit of low-key joy felt by a small boy on summer nights. He did this partly by employing many variations of *o* sounds, and the *schwa* ("uh") sound that all the vowels take in certain words. Many American-English words carry with them a sound that supports the meaning they signify, as in this passage:

> **The door squeaked, then shrieked, and I felt my nerves frazzle once again, ragged nerves unraveled like the shattered end of the shoestring I couldn't get into the eyelet of my tennis shoe when I was a boy.**

Much academic writing suffers so from its empty abstract words that the reader never comes to the point of appreciating its repetitions of sound. For example:

> But besides these immediate practical advantages, important as they are, your membership in the Council enables you to function more effectively as a member of the English teaching profession. It does this by affiliating you with one of the most influential professional organizations for teachers . . .

Some bone of sound exists in that passage but no reader wants to hear once more together the tired words "function . . . effectively . . . affiliating . . . influential . . . professional." The above passage addressed to teachers may carry too many *f* sounds in too brief a space. Too frequent repetition of a sound may render a passage ridiculous. "Peter Piper picked a peck of pickled peppers" makes a funny tongue twister, but it will always tickle readers with its little explosions rather than impress them with its meaning.

In the first place, certain sounds—the voiceless s, for example—possess a range of potential *suggestibility, rather than a fixed or single capability. Thus, a prominence of s's is capable of suggesting certain classes of natural sounds (rustling, hissing, sighing, whispering) but not other classes (booming, humming, hammering, or groaning).*

In the second place, this power of suggesting natural sounds or other qualities is relatively weak—too weak to operate unsupported by meaning—and because of its range, is only latent.

KARL SHAPIRO AND ROBERT BEUM

The following passage, written by a college girl, not only reveals an ear for sound that fits meaning but suggests in its overall rhythm the way a little girl talks:

Ugly dorm food! Thick chili and dry crackers make a pasty lump. I used to eat some soda crackers plain when I was little. In our backyard we made mud pies and ate crackers. It was heroic action to eat four in a row without taking a drink from the hose.

At my sixth birthday party we had to chew and swallow five crackers and then whistle to win a prize. Marlene Davis and I were the best. She had a big mouth and when she talked, white bubbles of spit came out of the corners. Naturally curly blonde hair kinked all over her head and dribbled down to her blue bug eyes. She was skinny, with scabby elbows.

We started eating crackers at the same time. Cramming them in was easy, but gagging them down hurt. Marlene had a head start with all that spit in her mouth. She won, so I called her "skinny bug-eyes" and made her cry. Then I opened my presents.

JUDY SMOLIK

This description of Marlene utilizes another major sound device used by professional writers: the quick ending sentence, the short punch that surprises. A short sentence after a number of longer sentences varies the rhythm of a passage. Rhythm is a device involving sound, a beat or lack of beat, sensed in the ear, not comprehended intellectually.

Parallel construction often creates sentences or parts of sentences of equal length and thus sets up rhythm that becomes powerful when controlled and occasionally varied. Read aloud the following excerpt from a meditation written by John Donne, Dean of St. Paul's Cathedral in London in 1624, and listen for the equal and answering beat of parts of sentences following upon each other:

> Who casts not up his Eie to the Sunne when it rises? but who takes off his Eie from a Comet when that breakes out? . . . No man is an Iland, intire of it selfe; every man is a peece of the Continent, a part of the maine . . .

Part of the power of Donne's meditation arises not from the sound of its syllables but from the formality of its language. If you read aloud the following paraphrase of a part of Donne's meditation and then Donne's lines, you will hear the informal language of conversation and then the sonorous language of the cathedral:

> The death bell rings for anyone who thinks it is ringing for him, and even if it quits ringing for a while, its effect upon him brings him to God. Everyone looks at the sun when it comes up. And no one quits looking at a comet when it flashes. Everyone listens to bells everywhere. But no one could possibly stop listening to his own death bell. No man can live separately by himself. Every person is a bit of the whole world and if any little part of that world disappears, he is affected by its disappearance, just as he would be by the destruction of a friend's house or his own house. Because he is part of mankind. Don't ask whom the bell is ringing for. It's ringing for you.

That version swings in places, for example: "Don't ask whom the bell is ringing for. It's ringing for you." But it lacks the majesty of Donne's original. Listen to him toll the bell:

> The Bell doth toll for him that thinkes it doth; and though it intermit againe, yet from that minute, that that occasion wrought upon him, hee is united to God. Who casts not up his Eie to the Sunne when it rises? but who takes off his Eie from a Comet when that breakes out? Who bends not his eare to any bell, which upon any occasion rings? but who can remove it from that bell, which is passing a peece of himselfe out of this world? No man is an Iland, intire of it selfe; every man is a peece of the Continent, a part of the maine; if a Clod bee washed away by the Sea, Europe is the lesse, as well

> as if a Promontorie were, as well as if a Mannor of thy friends or of thine owne were; any mans death diminishes me, because I am involved in mankinde; And therefore never send to know for whom the bell tolls; It tolls for thee.

Donne ends comment upon the bell with a short powerful statement: "It tolls for thee." It gains its power from the long rolling statements which precede it. You may employ this device. Let yourself—or some character you're giving words to—get wound up and go on and on, and then stop suddenly with a clincher.

Note how Ralph Waldo Emerson does this in a paragraph from his essay "Self-Reliance." He gains further emphasis by shifting from Elevated to Kitchen Language (a device which will be discussed in Chapter 19).

> I have no churlish objection to the circumnavigation of the globe for the purposes of art, of study, and benevolence, so that the man is first domesticated, or does not go abroad with the hope of finding somewhat greater than he knows. He who travels to be amused, or to get somewhat which he does not carry, travels away from himself, and grows old even in youth among old things. In Thebes, in Palmyra, his will and mind have become old and dilapidated as they. He carries ruins to ruins.

These endings punch hard partly because of their meanings. If what you say in an ending line is obvious and dull, it will not be made impressive by being stated shortly. However, the reader may be grateful even for a dull short sentence if all the preceding sentences were long. Just as professional writers learn to create flow in their sentences—so they don't have to think consciously about it—they learn to vary the length of their sentences. If a great many are long, they habitually throw in a short one. And vice versa. They aren't afraid to drop in a piece of a sentence, a phrase, a single word; and let it stand as a sentence. As they write, they hear the sound of sentences as well as the sound of words.

Another way to create faithful and exciting sound in your writing is to try to put down what you hear. The sound of a bullfrog? In *Walden,* Thoreau calls it a *trump* and puts it down *tr-r-r-oonk!* In his *Journals* he describes the pigeon woodpecker's "whimsical ah-week ah-week." In *The Field Book of Ponds and Streams,* Anne Haven Morgan writes the American toad's call as "wheep."

When she heard the sound of traffic on a nearby street, a mother working in a beginning writers' course remembered her children's youth through sound:

HOME

At noon, traffic on Stadium transmits an even, steady sound, the passing of many cars blending together in a deep, harmonious hum. At two o'clock in the morning, a single car creates a gradual crescendo as it approaches, a diminuendo as it moves into the distance.

One car at night carries a lonesome, nostalgic sound. I am reminded of times I've lain awake waiting for teenagers to return. In the deep quiet of the country night I can hear the first faint sound of a car coming down the highway a quarter of a mile away, slowing down to turn the corner onto the gravel of our country road, the gradual increasing of sound as the car approaches; then a momentary lowering as it slows for the bump of the little bridge; an increasing again for the rise of the little hill where our house stood. I can remember lying tense and breathing lightly, waiting for the moment when the noise of the car would continue on past the house into the distance. Or—it would pause, diminishing abruptly as the driver pressed the brake and the car coasted with its own momentum into our driveway. I heard the final beat of the motor, the quick staccato of young feet, first on the porch steps, then on the stairs. Soon the hall light, always left on for the last one in, was snapped off.

My child was back under my roof again.

GERTRUDE ANDRESEN

Here the writer not only remembers sounds but evokes some of them by her choice of words and building of sentence rhythms. The statement

> then a momentary lowering of sound as it slows for the bump of the little bridge

employs the word *bump* perfectly—a short word with a little burst and closure in it, coming in the middle of the statement so that it sounds exactly like what the writer is describing. Maybe *bump* was the only word that came to the writer's mind, luckily right in sound for her purposes. Maybe she also thought of saying *slight rise in the road, ripple,* or *protuberance,* and discarded them because they didn't contribute anything in sound. Often a writer doesn't know how she achieved her good sound effects. Sometimes she doesn't hear them until a reader points them out. Yet they are there and she has a right to take credit for them.

You may train your ear by reading aloud good writing. Then when you read aloud your own writing you are more likely to hear skillful sounds. In reading a second or third draft you can change a word here or there.

To write fully, you must use all your senses. Remember how places and objects smell, the taste of the back of your hand, the touch of concrete, the sound of a laugh—an American's laugh, a Southerner's laugh, a Northerner's. Such variety.

The representation of sounds in words can become conventional and even trite—"bang!" "screech," "eek!" Here's a writer recording sounds in fresh words:

> **I like the quiet crackling of root beer foam; the swish, then flap of the net as the basketball passes through . . . squeaky popcorn; slept-on mattress . . . moccasins treading soft sand, crisp as toasted linen; steel door weightlessly slammed shut; secret roar of sea shell; whirr of a movie reel; the ps-s-s-t of freshly opened coffee . . . whirr and buzz of the WALK signal; a Band-Aid coming off . . . creaky wicker chairs . . .**
>
> SISTER MARY LOIS GLONEK

WRITING TWENTY-FOUR: Put down in words a page of sounds you like and dislike. Study the passage above by Sister Mary Lois. Note her accuracy and restraint. She avoided the obvious and conventional representations of loud sounds. You may follow her direction or others. Like all symbolizing of experience through words, the representation of sounds is complex and subtle. Sometimes it's almost a precise rendering of actual sound; sometimes a satirical conventionalization, as in the *Batman* series—"Zowie! Blat! Pow! Bam!"

The most significant sound in life is that of other voices. The best writers seem born with an ear's memory for the way a person speaks, and if they write down the conversations of a dozen persons in one story, all speak recognizably differently. Maybe this is a natural gift, not to be learned. But you may try, at least, to see whether you have it.

Few, if any, professional writers put down conversation that is absolutely and completely accurate in manner and extent; for it would be boring. Most of us talk dully a great deal of the time. But the skillful writer captures enough of the real tones and rhythms and dialect of his character in writing to make them sound authentic. Consider this passage from the first chapter of *Huckleberry Finn.* Mark Twain varied the length of his sentences, the repetitions of sounds within words, and the word patterns of a rural uneducated boy from Missouri:

> Her sister, Miss Watson, a tolerable slim old maid, with goggles on, had just come to live with her, and took a set at me now with a spelling-book. She worked me middling hard for about an hour, and then the widow made her ease up. I couldn't stood it much longer. Then for an hour it was deadly dull, and I was fidgety. Miss Watson would say, "Don't put your feet up there, Huckleberry"; and "don't scrunch up like that, Huckleberry—set up straight"; and pretty soon she would say, "Don't gap and stretch like that, Huckleberry—why don't you try to behave?" Then she told me all about the bad place, and I said I wished I was there. She got mad then, but I didn't mean no harm. All I wanted was to go somewheres; all I wanted was a change. I warn't particular. She said it was wicked to say what I said; said she wouldn't say it for the whole world; *she* was going to live so as to go to the good place. Well, I couldn't see no advantage in going where she was going, so I made up my mind I wouldn't try for it. But I never said so, because it would only make trouble, and wouldn't do no good.
>
> Now she had got a start, and she went on and told me all about the good place. She said all a body would have to do there was to go around all day long with a harp and sing, forever and ever. So I didn't think much of it. But I never said so. I asked her if she reckoned Tom Sawyer would go there, and, she said, not by a considerable sight. I was glad about that, because I wanted him and me to be together.

The forty-year-old man who was writing this book spoke in the voice of a boy. At times, he used adult words that Huck would never have spoken, but he captured a youth's language in enough of the lines to establish Huck's authentic voice and make it immortal.

Do you often say, "I'll take my chances"? Or do you more often say, "I just want to know what to expect"? Is what you ask from life each day your chance? Or is it certainty?

SIDNEY COX

chapter 19 writing reports

THE LIVE CORE

MOST PERSONS expect two out of three lectures, reports, sermons, editorials, and presentation to bore them. So when they are told to write a report, they produce another boring piece of writing. They forget that one out of three reports they have read was entertaining, surprising, or exciting, like this encyclopedia entry on Davy Crockett, taken from *The Oxford Companion to American Literature,* 1965:

> CROCKETT, DAVY (David) (1786–1836), born in Tennessee, spent a shiftless youth until his political career began (*c.* 1816) with his appointment as justice of the peace. He boasted that none of his decisions was ever reversed, because of his dependence on 'natural-born sense instead of law learning.' After being twice elected to the state legislature, he accepted a humorous proposal that he run for Congress, and to his surprise was elected, serving from 1827 to 1831, and again from 1833 to 1835. Because of his opposition to Jackson, the Whigs adopted him as a convenient tool through whom to draw the backwoods democracy to its standard. Davy was soon turned by skilful politicians into a frontier hero, whose picturesque eccentricities, backwoods humor, tall tales, shrewd native intelligence, and lusty pio-

> neer spirit were all aggrandized. Whig journalists were soon at work, and in short order turned out such books, attributed to Davy, as *Sketches and Eccentricities of Col. David Crockett* (1833), *An Account of Col. Crockett's Tour to the North and Down East* (1835), *The Life of Martin Van Buren* (1835), and *Col. Crockett's Exploits and Adventures in Texas* (1836). With the exception of the last, which is posthumous, he may have had a hand in all these works, and he gladly claimed the *Tour* and life of Van Buren. Swallowing the Whig bait, he enjoyed his sudden rise to fame, and was glad to aid in propagating the myth, which, however, removed him from office, since his constituents would not tolerate his desertion of Democratic principles. Piqued, he left Tennessee to participate in the war for Texan independence, and a few months later died in the heroic defense of the Alamo, adding a final dramatic chapter to his career. *A Narrative of the Life of David Crockett, of the State of Tennessee* (1834) passes as his autobiography, although the claim has often been disputed. In any case the book has the robust manner attributed to Crockett, and contains fine examples of the farce and exaggeration of the tall tale.

This report includes a great number of specific facts—dates, offices held, political parties, names of books—encompassing a lifetime, and yet told in less than 350 words. Although James D. Hart, the editor, was writing a reference book, he didn't present simply a collection of facts about Davy Crockett. He wrote the article with an angle: Here is Davy Crockett, who became an American hero celebrated in folk song and story. How did that happen? Did his life merit the myth that has arisen about him?

Remembering his audience of educated Americans, Mr. Hart didn't begin the article by saying Crockett is a famous backwoods hero. He expected his audience to know that, and he got right down to telling how Crockett became famous. He omitted many facts about Crockett's life, partly because he had to save words (he was writing an 888-page reference work which names and describes thousands of persons, books, newspapers, and places), and partly because he didn't want to divert the reader with facts not critical to his angle.

Mr. Hart didn't think he was "letting the facts speak for themselves." He knew that all facts take on meaning because of their setting. He made his judgment about Crockett and chose facts which bore upon it. He presented Crockett as a man who rode luck to fame, allowed himself to be used by politicians, permitted his name to be connected to books that were in large measure not written by him, and deserved his fame as a skillful teller of tall tales.

> *Even the reporting of pure physical research findings, to cite an extreme example, is not unbiased. It is biased in favor of revealing the findings. In recent years the practical import and responsibility of such a bias has been felt deeply by atomic scientists. The question is not whether a communication is biased. The question is:* toward what value system is the communication biased?
>
> GERHART WIEBE

To write this report, Mr. Hart had to know a great deal about Davy Crockett. If he had known less, he wouldn't have been able to find so many facts which touched his angle. Like all good pieces of writing, this report sounds authoritative partly because it implies the writer knew more facts than he employed—the iceberg structure, as Ernest Hemingway called it.

When you write a report, know your subject. If it's a book you're writing from, you may need to read it several times, compare it with other books, and see what other persons think of it. Most of all, you need to test it in some way—does its experience or theory ring true to your experience, to your learning? Such questions will help you see more clearly what the book is saying. If you're writing a report from direct observation, you may need to ask questions to see how others see the subject. Talking with other persons about a book you've read or an event you've witnessed usually helps you see more than you saw on your own.

> *. . . I always try to write on the principle of the iceberg. There is seven-eighths of it underwater for every part that shows. Anything you know you can eliminate and it only strengthens your iceberg. It is the part that doesn't show. If a writer omits something because he does not know it then there is a hole in the story.*
>
> ERNEST HEMINGWAY

You should write a report with an iceberg of facts available to you, and you should choose and shape the critical facts to appear as the ice above the water. The professional report writer doesn't start writing until he has a large iceberg. He learns to sense when he has a sufficient core of materials and he learns quick, efficient ways of getting that core. For example, many sportswriters have available to them a running record of a basketball game, which looks like this:

UNIVERSITY OF TOLEDO VS. SAN FRANCISCO STATE

SECOND HALF

TOLEDO		SAN FRANCISCO STATE
TIME LEFT		
20:00	29	23
19:29		25 Williams jumper center of keyhole
18:46		27 Williams laid in set up
18:28 Lewis made layup	31	
17:43 Lewis one-hand jumper beyond key	33	
16:06		29 Caranica drove for layup
15:56 Jones jumper side of circle	35	
15:14 Galicki personal foul		Brown missed personal foul
15:03 Galicki laid in Jones' pass	37	
14:43 Lewis' jumper side of circle	39	
14:28 Pawlak personal foul		31 Caranica laid in setup Caranica missed free throw

This part of the game record shows only five minutes and thirty-two seconds of the action. An assistant or a representative of the teams may keep such a record, but the writer knows it will be available and he uses it. You may make a similar log of the activities you cover. Be prepared with whatever instruments you need to collect materials—notebook, tape recorder, 3 x 5 cards, camera. Gather whatever printed information is available—an agenda outlining the order of items in a meeting, lists of officers or speakers, minutes of last meeting, programs. Double-check all names for spelling. Learn as much as possible about the event before you go to it.

The writer who goes underwater and discovers the whole iceberg gives himself a chance to make the report fascinating to readers. He can discard the dull, the partially relevant, the tedious, and present only the bright, snowy peaks. Here's a report of a baseball game by Robert Lipsyte (*The New York Times,* August 5, 1966). Think of how many notes and records Mr. Lipsyte must have consulted while writing this story. His angle was not hard to find: the New York Mets (in ninth place) had beaten the San Francisco Giants (tied for first) while the Giants were using their star pitcher Juan Marichal. Lipsyte chose to tell his story concentrating on the relatively unknown Ron Swoboda, the Met who hit the winning home run, and to bring in the famous Marichal as his antagonist.

METS BEAT GIANTS 8–6, ON SWOBODA'S HOMER IN 9TH

Ron Swoboda, who won it in the ninth inning with a three-run pinch-hit home run, said: "It was a story-book game. Holy Cow!" And it was just that.

Most of the crowd of 41,038 at Shea Stadium sat stunned yesterday long after the Mets had beaten the Giants, 8–6. Swoboda's drive cleared the leftfield fence and the 22-year-old outfielder jogged around the bases in a mood he later described as "elation . . . the epitome . . . my greatest thrill!"

More than 24,000 in the crowd had bought their tickets just before gametime because the great Juan Marichal was starting for the Giants. For almost six innings they got what they paid for—perfection from Marichal and something less than perfection from the Mets.

The 27-year-old Dominican righthander, out of action recently because of a sore finger, had registered his 17th victory Tuesday night, by the official scorer's decision, after retiring the last four Mets. Yesterday, kicking high on a dusty mound, he retired the first 17 Mets.

3 OUTS ON 6 PITCHES

In the second inning, with six pitches, he put out the side so quickly that he had to wave his sleepy outfielders back to the dugout. In the third, facing Dennis Ribant, the busy little Met starter, he was worked for his first full count before Ribant lined out to Willie Mays, a well-hit ball that Mays had to hustle to catch and gave a few plaintive voices reason to holler, "Let's go Mets."

In the sixth, Ribant bounced one over Marichal's head

for a single, and the crowd prepared to console itself with a brilliant one-hitter instead of a perfect game.

The Giants, meanwhile, were doing what was expected of a team that started the sunny afternoon game leading the National League and fresh from having beaten the Mets three times in a row. They scored a run in the fourth on Willie McCovey's 21st homer of the year, a run in the fifth on Marichal's double and Jim Davenport's single and a run in the sixth on Jim Hart's 24th homer.

GIANTS GAIN 5–0 LEAD

In the seventh, San Francisco made the score 5-0. Tito Fuentes drove one of Ribant's pitches into the leftfield corner. Larry Elliot dropped it in foul territory and examined it, apparently thinking the ball was foul, while Fuentes went to third, credited with a double. Ossie Virgil, who had replaced Davenport at third base, then singled and McCovey walked.

With the bases loaded, Darrell Sutherland replaced Ribant, and Mays singled home two runs.

In the last of the seventh, the Mets began to move at last. They needed three singles and a throwing error by Marichal to get one run. The people who had come to see at least a shutout went home.

Tom Haller hit a homer for the Giants in the eighth, making the score 6–1, but it was a wasted gesture. In the bottom of the eighth, the Mets charged.

Jerry Grote reached second on a two-base throwing error by Virgil, and John Stephenson, a 25-year-old catcher pinch-hitting for Dallas Green, the third Met pitcher, blasted his first homer of the season. Singles by Chuck Hiller, Al Luplow and Larry Elliot made the score 6–4.

In disbelief, the crowd froze.

HAMILTON IS VICTOR

Jack Hamilton, the winning pitcher, put out the Giants in the ninth. Then Marichal strolled back to the mound. He demanded that it be dampened because he was kicking dust into his own face. A little man with a green sprinkling can scurried out and dampened the mound.

Satisfied, baseball's best righthander pitched two balls and a strike to Ken Boyer. Boyer hit the fourth pitch over the fence for his 11th homer of the season, and Marichal was pulled out for some showering of his own.

"Let's go Mets." There was no plaintiveness now, no whine. There was hope.

Ed Bressoud, who had been playing an erratic shortstop for the injured Roy McMillan, singled to left. Ron Hunt, pinchhitting for Grote, bunted, forcing Bressoud at second. Stephenson, hero of the eighth inning, hit a wrong-field single to right. There was one out, two men on base, and the score was 6–5.

The roar was swelling now as Bill Henry, a left-hander, replaced Lindy McDaniel, a right-hander. The next scheduled batter, Chuck Hiller, was called back for a right-handed hitting replacement and Manager Wes Westrum said to Swoboda, "Get a bat."

Swoboda later admitted he was excited because "that's it, when everybody's relying on you." He kept telling himself to "stay loose" and he forgot that the last time Marichal had started against the Mets, on May 20, Swoboda had won the game with a tenth-inning homer against the same Bill Henry.

The first pitch was high; it would have been a ball if Swoboda, overanxious, hadn't swung and missed. The second was a ball, low and inside. The third, waist-high and fast, was thrown with the stuff that dreams are made on.

Although Mr. Lipsyte, the reporter, tells the outcome of the game in the second paragraph, 8–6, he then begins a story in which he builds tension: How and when did Swoboda do it? What was happening to the marvelous Marichal? How did the pinch hitter outshine the star? Frequently writers of reports build their story around such tension between two poles. A report of a laboratory experiment can be a suspense story: Will the scientist find the answer or won't he? Will his newly improvised piece of equipment work?

Mr. Lipsyte was writing a story of surprise, an upset. So he put the reader at the game, watching the expected happen: Marichal pitching a one-hit game for six innings. Thus he built tension for the Mets' rally. He could have provided many details about other Giants' players than the pitcher, but his angle made him present little individualizing details about Marichal, who was the Giant.

In the second inning, with six pitches, he put out the side so quickly that he had to wave his sleepy outfielders back to the dugout.

Like all good writers, Mr. Lipsyte doesn't forget what he has said. He makes facts and words speak to each other. In the fourth paragraph, he shows how well Marichal was pitching:

> Yesterday, kicking high on a dusty mound, he retired the first 17 Mets.

In the fourteenth paragraph, remembering the dusty mound, he says that Marichal

> . . . demanded that it be dampened because he was kicking dust into his own face.

This is the great Marichal demanding. Mr. Lipsyte says:

> A little man with a green sprinkling can scurried out and dampened the mound.

Later, Mr. Lipsyte says

> . . . Marichal was pulled out for some showering of his own.

Dust, dampening, showering: the words speak to each other. In the last paragraph, Mr. Lipyste says:

> The third, waist-high and fast, was thrown with the stuff that dreams are made on.

For Mr. Lipsyte, the comeback of the Mets was so great that it deserved an echo of Shakespeare's lines in *The Tempest* (IV, i.):

> We are such stuff
> As dreams are made on, and our little life
> Is rounded with a sleep.

The speaker is Prospero, a magician who commands the air and earth. Mr. Swoboda was a magician at Shea Stadium.

Here's an Associated Press record of the same game as presented in *The Kalamazoo Gazette* for August 5, 1966. Probably only part of the original wire-service report was used, for the account was printed in a roundup article including games of other teams. You can see how the extra space available to Mr. Lipsyte allowed him to bring alive the scene. His report in many respects is fresher and more dramatic than the AP account.

METS SHOCK GIANTS WITH SWOBODA'S PINCH HOMER

Ron Swoboda, unlike lightning, has struck twice in the same place, and Bill Henry has been left smoking.

Just two weeks ago, Swoboda flashed off the New York Mets' bench and jolted fireman Henry by slamming the veteran reliever for a ninth-inning homer that gave the Mets a 3–2 victory over the San Francisco Giants.

Thursday, the 22-year-old right-handed hitter reduced lefty Henry to ashes, again coming off the bench in the ninth with a crackling three-run clout that carried the Mets to an 8–6 triumph over the Giants.

"It was just like a fairy tale," said Swoboda, relegated to pinch hitting this season when the opposition starts a right-hander.

The earlier belt kept the Giants out of a virtual tie for the first place in the National League. This one dropped them into second place, two percentage points behind Pittsburgh, which hammered Los Angeles 8–1.

The Mets trailed 6–4 entering the ninth when Ken Boyer started the Mets' thunder with a homer off Juan Marichal, seeking his 18th victory. Lindy McDaniel, who took the loss, relieved and gave up singles to Ed Bressoud and John Stephenson. Then Henry entered and moments later Swoboda struck.

Marichal, who had beaten the Mets 17 times in his career without a loss and retired the first 17 hitters Thursday, thus managed to slip off the hook.

Willie McCovey, Jim Hart and Tom Haller homered for the Giants and Johnny Stephenson also connected for the Mets.

In this report, Mike Recht of the Associated Press achieved some style by using the metaphor of lightning throughout—"unlike lightning, has struck twice . . . flashed . . . reduced lefty Henry to ashes . . . a crackling three-run clout . . . the Mets' thunder . . . Swoboda struck." His angle was that Swoboda again homered against Henry. But in the paragraphs printed by the *Kalamazoo Gazette* Mr. Recht's story doesn't take on the excitement of Mr. Lipsyte's, which led up to a suspenseful last paragraph.

Readers expect more life from columns of opinion than reports of events. But a column or short piece of opinion or comment on passing events doesn't become strong simply because it exhibits more personal judgment and opinion than reports and other more objective writings. It may easily be boring, flat, and without significance to readers. Here's a discussion of happiness published in a school newspaper.

HAPPINESS

There are many different kinds of happiness. The meaning of happiness can be defined according to a person, his environment and his heredity.

Let's narrow this word down to what happiness is to high school teenagers. To one teenager, happiness might be a set of "wheels," a "weed," and plenty of "petro."

This person seems to think that in order to be happy, all he needs is a showy sports car, cigarettes and gasoline. Why would he think this way? He might live in a shabby house, not have much in the way of good clothes or property, so he wants something more than the normal teenager, something he thinks he can be proud of and show off.

Another teen might decide happiness would be a good education and a bright future. This person has most of the "flashy" comforts of life handed to him on a silver tray. What he really wants is to make his own future, the chance to prove himself.

Is either opinion wrong? Happiness depends on the person. Two extremes were taken in this case, to try and define what happiness really is. It all points out that to gain happiness there must be a certain amount of discipline along with the desire. If the desire is great enough, this thing happiness, in any definition, can be obtained.

The point of this passage is defensible. Not everyone needs to strive for the same kind of happiness. An old idea, though, and of little value or interest to a reader unless brought alive with telling examples. This writer seems not to have found an iceberg. She says that driving a showy sports car may be a legitimate kind of happiness, but she doesn't reveal enough knowledge of what it's like to drive a sports car to convince a reader. Why did she pick this example? Perhaps because she just came back from an exhilarating ride in a car. If so, she should have taken the reader on the ride. If not, she has chosen a wrong example. If she has not talked to a young person who wants to "make his own future" and a chance "to prove himself," she shouldn't use him as an example. If she has, she should reveal what he has done, what he hopes to do, how his aspirations and achievements make him impressive. If she doesn't know such a boy, why is she talking about persons who value a good education and look toward their future?

Most professional columnists write out of consuming interest in particular events, ideas, persons. They are given a regular space to fill each month or week or day because they write compellingly.

Here's a report that might well be the first of a series on the writer's summer trip to the Soviet Union. It could be printed in the school paper as a weekly column entitled "Foreign Correspondent":

A LITTLE SPOT

At 8:30 on a cool June morning we left our hotel, feeling full of eggs, dark bread, sweet rolls, cucumbers, and fruit juice, and started walking toward the mausoleum. Nine Americans, going to see a thing sacred to Russians. We had heard the rumors before, but still several members of the group took turns bringing them up. "You know it *could* just be a wax dummy."

"Yeah, I heard only his head and hands were saved—the rest is fake."

What'd they do with Stalin? He used to be in there, too, ya know."

"They moved him underground, out of sight somewhere. Down to the dungeon with you, old man."

"Someone told me that the head and hands look *most* like wax. I bet the whole body is wax and everyone's getting excited and religious about a hunk of wax. What a joke!"

"But I know someone who saw him six years ago and again two years ago. She said she thought Lenin was smaller the second time. That means it's really a dead body; it also means Lenin's shrinking."

"Oh come on! How could it be a real dead body in there? He'd look a lot worse than just smaller by now."

"Naw, they got ways to preserve bodies—but maybe they aren't foolproof. A friend of mine was here last summer. He said there's a little rotting spot behind Lenin's left ear. He asked me to look for it."

As we turned the corner, we were in sight of Lenin's final resting place—a low red-brown marble building. There were hundreds of people milling about in the rain. They formed a sort-of line, dangling haphazardly over the red cobble stones of Red Square. Toward the front, the line was distinct, while near the end it looked as if people were standing behind other people, assuming whoever was in front was in line. This part of the line was a city block of

crowd, connected to the main line in many places, spreading fan-like. Our guide left us at what seemed to be the end of the line, and went ahead. A fellow-American said, "Man, can you believe this crowd? I thought we'd be the first ones out here, especially since it's raining."

I knew it would be crowded—I've heard it always is, even if it's below zero."

In a few minutes Nina, our guide, returned and moved us up in the line, up to where it was a distinct two-by-two line. We were visitors, and fast finding out the strong Slavic custom to push visitors to the front—to see Lenin, to see a parade, to get into a museum or restaurant sooner. As we were walking through patiently waiting Russians "We don't deserve it" flickered through my head. We took our new position, in twos, behind a family of Soviet citizens. The man was wearing a baggy grey suit, which reminded me of the late movies on T.V.; his wife wore a loose fitting print dress, which extended below her knees. Each had a hand on the shoulder of one of the children standing directly in front. The mother leaned over, crossed her arms on the far side of her daughter's neck, and gently whispered something in her ear. As she straighted up, they all looked back and smiled. The marble building was in full view now, wet and shining. Huge slabs of dark stone jutted out from the main building on both sides of the door and two guards, with guns, stood erect near the black granite. The closer we got, the quieter the crowd. I watched the family enter, and I followed them into the marble cave in a spirit of reverence. We were moving all the time, shuffling around Lenin, filing through, and out the door on the other side. Two guards stood at Lenin's head and all three had the same expression, stiff, unfeeling, with pursed lips. Lenin lay under a glass dome, slumbering peacefully on lush cushions. There were flowers under the dome with him, there were flowers outside the dome. A light from somewhere shone on his face. He looked waxy, pale, dead. I looked again; he looked asleep. He was tiny, no more than 4½ feet tall. The hair on his head was invisible, the same color as his skin, but on his face it showed ruddy-grey under his nose and from his ears to his chin. He wore dark clothing, dark shoes. His hands rested gently on his thighs—at any moment they might flop to his side. We approached the outstretched

man from his right side, walked the length of his body next to the velvet guard rail, up shallow marble stairs, around his feet, down the stairs, along the left side of his body, and up to his head again. Not a sound but the echo and re-echo of our footsteps, a silent cough, and my own awed heart beat. I felt myself leaning slightly toward the rail, sneaking a peek behind his left ear. It was there, a small darker spot which could have been a shadow, could have been a mole, but something was there. Across the room near the entrance several women were crying, a few even crossed themselves. Did anyone else see them? I glanced back at the rest of my group as they passed Lenin's head for the last time and gazed intently at his left ear. We eased out the exit door. I looked over my shoulder at the endless, continuous double line of people, flowing through the entrance, and around Lenin. Outside the drizzle had let up and the line fell apart, quietly. Silence ended when someone in my group asked, "Did you look? Did you see it? What do you think—was it really *him*?"

"I don't know. I don't know that it matters."

KATE MACK

Most professional columnists are good writers to study because they often write of matters that other persons make boring. Kate Mack wrote professionally of her visit to Lenin's tomb; she shaped her experience into a solid personal-public piece of writing.

THE ALTERNATING CURRENT

Kate's column is lively because it employs most of the eight fundamentals of good writing, maybe all of them. And one other strategy of professional writers: the Alternating Current. Like James D. Hart and Robert Lipsyte, Kate shifts back and forth from a lowly to a bookish vocabulary, what might be called Kitchen and Elevated language. When we're talking informally in the kitchen with friends or relatives, most of us do not use the word *haphazardly* or such a phrase as *slumbering peacefully on lush cushions.* We don't talk about an *awed heart beat.* We don't speak in formal metaphor, saying that we *followed them into a marble cave in a spirit of reverence.* We simply say, "We went into the mausoleum after them." Instead of *gazed intently* we say "looked hard." Most of Kate's sentences are stated in Kitchen language: *to see a parade, to get into a museum or restaurant sooner . . . sneaking a peek behind his left ear.* So like most exciting writers, she uses elevated and Kitchen language in the same piece of writing. This alternation keeps readers awake, makes them sense a tension in the language. Bad preachers don't use the Alternating Current. They drone on in an unrelieved elevated vocabulary. Bad editorial writers do the same. They have no sense of the lightness that can be achieved in a writing that discusses a solemn subject in sober setting.

> We hold these truths to be self-evident . . .

This statement from the Declaration of Independence would be spoken by few persons in their kitchens, but

> all men are created equal

might well be there. Speaking of King George III, the writers of the Declaration said:

> He has plundered our seas, ravaged our coasts

in language again not of the kitchen, but the rest of the sentence might have been said there:

> burnt our towns, and destroyed the lives of our people.

You may understandably say that no one could keep up Elevated language through a piece of writing. But some persons try. In a good part of her column on "Happiness" the writer spoke in a voice foreign to the kitchen:

> There are many different kinds of happiness. The meaning of happiness can be defined according to a person, his environment and his heredity . . . Happiness depends on the person. Two extremes were taken in this case, to try and define what happiness really is. It all points out that to gain happiness there must be a certain amount of discipline along with the desire. If the desire is great enough, this thing happiness, in any definition, can be obtained.

"To try and define what happiness really is" is a statement that might be said in the kitchen. But it's not used consciously as a contrast to the more elevated language of the first part of the sentence. Note the alternation of language in Robert Lipsyte's baseball article:

Kitchen	*Elevated*
they got what they paid for	perfection from Marichal
hustle to catch	plaintive voices
The people who had come to see at least a shutout went home	a wasted gesture
Marichal was pulled out	In disbelief
he was kicking dust into his own face	an erratic shortstop
There was one out, two men on base and the score was 6-5	The roar was swelling now

Elevated language is usually more precise than Kitchen language and comes to us trailing associations different from those carried by Kitchen language. In many ways it is superior as a vehicle of expression, but no one wants to hear it steadily throughout a lecture or a column. The ordinary speech of ordinary people is our anchor, and no good writer forgets it. Even a writer composing articles for a reference book remembers the value of alternating between these two languages—James D. Hart wrote his article on Davy Crockett largely in Elevated language but he saves it from dead levelness by the word *shiftless* in the first sentence and by quoting the vernacular employed by Davy:

natural-born sense instead of law learning.

The rest of the article is filled with Elevated: *picturesque eccentricities, aggrandized, propagating, constituents, etc.* Mr. Hart uses an occasional Kitchen expression like "were soon at work" or "Swallowing the Whig bait." Quoting a statement in Kitchen language is a good strategy for writers who feel bound to maintain a sober, dignified style, and sometimes they may through quotation point out a surprising variation in the style spoken by one of the persons they are reporting. For example, Mr. Lipsyte quoted the Kitchen language of Ron Swoboda:

"It was a story-book game. Holy Cow!"

and then revealed him using Elevated language in describing his mood:

"Elation . . . the epitome . . ."

Sometimes writers make a whole column or report out of what others have said. Good reporters are on the lookout for strong remarks from the persons they interview. They don't use the dull statements that are made to them. For example, here's part of a column in a school newspaper, "Is Your Spirit Dead?" A dangerous subject—more space has been wasted in school papers trying to stir up spirit in a student body than on any other subject. And this column begins with two obvious and dead quotations:

> **School spirit is "a desire, a wanting" to make a school great, according to Varsity cheerleader, Betty Uvan. "No one else can improve school spirit except the individual himself," she said.**
>
> **"I guess school spirit," explained junior Dave Mark, "could be defined as a feeling of pride or respect in all of the representative units of the school and a willingness to assume the responsibilities of citizenship at school."**

What these students say is old stuff and the manner in which they say it is flat.

The Alternating Current isn't difficult to turn on in your writing. The secret lies in the genuineness of its juice, the speech you already have in your unconscious memory. If you remember your native dialect—the language you learned at Mother's knee—and alternate that with the language of writing you've picked up through reading and listening to teachers in classrooms, you'll find the current naturally coursing through your prose. Finding it is again a matter of honesty. What is your voice? Do you hear how you speak when you're not thinking of your language? Listen to the country, the Kitchen, the ball game, the streetcorner talk in your life. Introduce it sparingly into your writing. At the same time you'll find yourself varying the length of your sentences, and that's another form of Alternating. You often talk in shorter sentences than those written in books.

The Alternating Current flows in this quick piece of writing: rich, full descriptions and then short crisp sentences.

> **I used to hunt with Gramp. He didn't hunt like my father. We would walk along the cramped, hollowed-out cowpath. The bushes and weeds would push out at us from both sides. I always walked behind. It led along the murk-filled brown-greenness of the channel that connects his two lakes. I would wait for something to break. He taught me never to kill anything unless I was going to eat it. He**

helped my brother shoot a pigeon once. He would have eaten it if it had not smelled so much.

When the hunting was poor, we would go down by the lake and shoot beer bottles that some ass had left behind. There were always some there. Gramp would sit on a rotten stump and remember. He used to shoot pickerel as they pulled their heavy egg-filled bodies up the narrow channel. He said that they would spawn near the roots of the silver-gray pussy-willow trees. They're gone now; so are the pickerel. He would sit and laugh. And tell how the warden had chased him for two miles up to his slate-gray house. He had hid in the barn until he had left and then fried the warm fresh pickerel on the old black stove that was the heart of the house on a cold misty morning. We all learned something from him although he never taught us anything. I never knew it until he left. Tomorrow is never the same.

TOM CRONK

This is the way writers keep their writing alive. Tom Cronk may not have known that he was following an age-old tradition, but he was. Lively writers create tension in their sentences in many ways. They employ the Alternating Current, or move between the general and the particular, the long and short sentence, the expected and the unexpected. By reading their work aloud to themselves and to others, they train their ear so that they write with variety. They don't write half the work in Kitchen language and half in Elevated, but rather continually alternate them. They write to please themselves and be good to their topic. Off and on, they think of their audience, especially in their second draft. If they're writing a satire, they usually don't alternate their style. When they're purposely taking on the voice of a pompous fool, they need to stay with it. In some writings they can't afford to vary their language, or they will break a spell, a mood.

WRITING TWENTY-FIVE: Write a report of a place, a person, or an event, maybe a short sketch of your grandfather modeled on the Davy Crockett article. Or a report of an event you know a certain group of readers would like to hear about. Find an angle, cram in the critical facts, keep the narrative alive with Alternating Current.

WRITING TWENTY-SIX: Write an editorial or a paper of opinion. Find an iceberg of fact on which to base what you present to the reader. No matter how lofty your thoughts, you can base them. You'll do better, probably, to begin with the core of experience and let yourself earn the idea or opinion. Remember how the column "Happiness" suffered from lack of underpinnings. Note how this little essay grows out of experience:

OLD CREEPY DEATH

It's rainy and cool outside and we waded through too many ankle-deep puddles before getting back to the dorm. Now my feet are cold. But that's nothing new. They'll stay cold until I fall asleep and can't feel them anymore. I wonder what it would be like to go to sleep with warm feet? Even on recent warm nights they've been carefully smothered under layers of blankets and quilts that have been folded down to the end of the bunk. It would be fine if you could ignore them, but I never can. You're all warm and comfortable except for those two awful extremities. They ache cold. And though they seem to be separate from the rest of me, they are persistent in keeping me awake.

I once knew a girl who wore sleep socks. They were regular wool socks except they had felt faces on the soles of them. One was a woman's face with cute little bow lips and long eyelashes. She offered to let me wear them and I tried to. But I couldn't stand it. I kept thinking of those faces on the bottom of my feet and of how I had one male foot and one female foot. I didn't like the idea of the two of them being alone together down there, especially on my feet. It was no way to get my feet warm. Besides, I felt bad when I had to make a trip to the john and walked on their happy-go-lucky faces. I don't like the idea of socks, anyway. Even if they would work. My feet feel bound and too restricted. So, maybe I've chosen cold feet.

But what makes me so conscious of them is what the cold feels like. I've always thought that their kind of cold must be how death feels. Like poems have told me how death and coldness creep up on you until you're completely cold and completely dead. So every night I thrash my feet around to make sure the cold isn't creeping up my legs. When I think of me dying I think of dying in bed while I'm sleeping so I won't know about it. And I can't help but think that I'll most likely die the night that I can't keep the cold limited only to my feet. That's why I hate them the most, the pleasant thoughts that accompany them. I put off sleep for a while each night to make sure

that the rest of me is staying warm. But then, I've probably got it figured all wrong. Death will probably play a trick and the cold will work its way from top to bottom. But that wouldn't really be so bad, to have your nice, warm, cozy tootsies be the last to go. Because as long as my feet are warm I can feel warm all over and I could ignore old creepy death.

LOIS BERG

. . . The lucky listen to those who have fun when they talk, to born mimics and story-tellers, to those whose words, literate or not, play with the people that they talk with, and keep, somehow, in play with the motion of their hearers' minds.

SIDNEY COX

The Alternating Current is usually more appropriate to opinion papers than to reports, but you saw at the beginning of this chapter how it gave texture to a report on Davy Crockett. Nevertheless, many reports call for a less attention-getting style. A business executive may ask an engineer or consultant to visit a plant and report on the efficiency of its operations. A scientist may have to report on the behavior of fish used in an experiment. Often their reports should he highly objective, keeping the observer out of the sentences as much as possible. However, those who write and read such reports should never forget that any human report is a product of an individual's perceptions.

Poetry is a response to the daily necessity of getting the world right.

WALLACE STEVENS

chapter 20 writing poems

POETRY—ugh. "My heart is plunged in misery." Or, "Methinks I have seen your visage before."

Many people hate poems, would never think of writing one. Understandable. Too often teachers have assigned poems that speak in voices which sound pretentious and phony to readers unaccustomed to the language of another time. Meter—a regular beat to the lines—and rhyme make poems sound unlike ordinary talk, and therefore artificial.

Like bad poets in the past, many present-day students who write for the school literary magazine think that rhyme and meter alone make a poem. The result is "Sorrow, My True Story," that awful wail printed in Chapter 5, and many other creations printed in school magazines that are seldom read except by their writers.

The core of a good poem is made up of something other than these traditional poetic techniques, as is suggested in this paper written by a student:

POEMS

I grew up with a boy named Johnny. His nickname was Junior. He didn't wear clean clothes or shined shoes everyday. He didn't have his hair cut twice a month or even twice a year.

He left Stadium High School at the end of the third quarter of his sophomore year. He came back his senior year, about the fourth week of school, but I never really felt

Junior was that interested in the school life. He and I were in the same English class.

One day our English teacher gave the class a small assignment. It was to be at least a half page long and was to be in a poem's form, and the topic was to be college, and it was supposed to be read at the end of the period.

This was the last period of the day, and she said after everyone read his paper the class could leave. Junior and I always sat in the back of her class. We were the only Blacks so we never wanted to participate in class discussions.

There were a lot of poems read, which said a lot about nothing and, just like always, we were last. I read mine first. I knew basically what this teacher liked. She liked those nothing poems, the type that made the world all pretty. I needed at least a "B" in the class to keep my grade up to standard so that was the type of poem I wrote. The class dug it.

Junior wasn't like that. He didn't care what a teacher thought about his writing. He wrote as he felt. His poem went:

> **I think I'll go to college**
> **And mess with the broads and learn big words.**
>
> **Should I go to college**
> **And learn things my brother never heard?**
>
> **Should I go to college**
> **And wear thick glasses and never say "Hi"?**
>
> **Naw, I won't go to college.**
> **I'll just sit on the corner**
>
> **Drinking wine 'til the day I die.**

Everybody in the class laughed but us. Everything we did in that class was funny. A month later, Junior dropped out of school. I wonder—was that funny?

EDWARD RANSOM

In 1800 the British poet William Wordsworth had the same notion as Ed Ransom. He got so sick of phony poetry that he wrote an essay condemning poetic diction and said that a poet should be "a man speaking to men." (Today we would say, "a person talking to people" to avoid the suggestion that men are the only sex that counts in the world.) He added that poetry "takes its origin from emotion recollected in tranquillity." I would guess that if he were living today he might be disturbed by the lack of meter in the following poem written by a student, but he would say it fit his definition and would have some praise for it.

BUMPS

I knew a girl once
who had a '62 Falcon
with one headlight missing
and she believed that
you'd get less shock
from bumps
by driving over 'em fast.
So every afternoon
she'd pick me up after school
and we'd race off
looking for new bumps
to test her theory on
and she'd always be muttering
something about
cushions and suspensions.
And one Thursday
when we were finished
she dropped me off
at Tommy's Luncheonette, where
they had the best cheeseburgers,
and a bunch of guys
that were just hanging around
started making fun of her theory
and she got mad
and sped off . . .

And I never was exactly sure
how it happened
'cause I got the story
from a computer operator
who couldn't really be counted on
for correct facts
but they say
she was going
about 83 miles an hour or so

down Pleasant Street
when an old guy
in a Cadillac
pulled out
in front of her,
and he swore
on a Bible
that he never
saw her coming.

A simple way to define poetry is to say it is writing that uses all the strategies of prose but more fully and intensely. Most poets don't waste words. They employ more metaphors than prose writers. They control the sound of the words and the rhythm of sentences with more care. They try to wed sound and sense. They use symbols, flashbacks, flash-forwards, dialogue—all without Explainery and Insistery. They play with words, making them speak to each other closely or wildly. They know that punning can be a deep delight rather than a bad joke. Good prose writers know all these strategies too, but they don't use them as intensely. Poems are meant to be read aloud. Most prose would be better if its authors wrote it with the expectation that it would be read aloud also.

The principal difference between poetry and prose is compression. Most poems require readers to work hard. Often they are expected to consider A and B and guess C without being given it. That's why poems are put down differently on the page from prose, which is usually lined up on both left and right margins. The shape of a poem on the page is a signal to the readers to slow down, do more guessing, often read through it a second time.

Once you know what poems are, you can presume they are easier to write than you thought. Many prose passages are so short and compressed they seem to be wanting to become poems. Look at your writings, especially in journals. You may find such passages. Here's one in which a student was remembering childhood:

If I were to write a book, it would be about spongy rubber balls. Without a doubt, spongy rubber balls are the number one pastime for children.

You can ball them up and let them goosh out between the spaces of your fingers. You can play base-, basket-, and foot-ball inside. You can squish them up and cram them into your mouth, and then at the dinner table act like you're throwing up and poof—out comes the ball.

That passage could easily be made into a poem. Cut it a little. Arrange it like a poem:

SPONGY RUBBER BALLS

You can ball them up
and let them goosh out
between your fingers.
Play baseball with them
and football—inside!
At dinner table
squish them up
and cram them
into your mouth.
Act like you're throwing up,
and poof—
out comes the ball!

John Milton, author of one of the most successful long poems ever written, *Paradise Lost,* said that poetry is more "simple, sensuous, and passionate" than rhetoric. That's a pretty good working description of most moving poems. Here again are prose passages which were made into poems:

NAME

If he asks me
to say my name
in class
one more time,
I'm going
to make up
a new one.

SCHOOL LANDSCAPE

All
those
empty cars
in the parking lot
look
so
left
there.

Many of the best modern poems are *sensuous,* as Milton put it. They appeal to the senses. Their objects and actions are not abstracted but presented concretely, as in this love poem by a boy:

CHEEK

Her cheek
is as
smooth
and
cool
as the
other
side
of the
pillow.

That poem makes you feel the girl's cheek and the pillow. Another student wanted to say he often felt wanderlust. He followed Milton's advice when he wrote:

ABILENE

A lot
of times
I want to be
on the outskirts
of Abilene
and slap my pants
and make
big clouds
of
dust.

In fact he wrote that sentence as prose in his journal and here it has been arranged as a poem. To consider what is meant by being sensuous, think of how this poem might have been written if it were not simple, sensuous, and passionate but cold and abstract. The same thought might have been expressed like this: "Often I get the feeling that living here, going to school, is more than I can take. Then I wish I were far away in some of the places I have been at moments in my life when I felt really wonderful."

Wordsworth and Milton praised emotion and passion in poetry;

but they, like many good poets today, didn't exclude ideas from their poetry. Here's an idea poem by a student:

GREAT

Fifteen-cent
hamburgers and
guys carrying
around 6-transistor
radios listening
to the world
series do not
a great
nation
make.

Like good prose, good poetry carries surprise. Fifteen-cent hamburgers as a test of a great nation. Or maybe a common, ordinary feeling like the cars in the parking lot looking left there, but surprising that the writer would say that. No one else has said it before. "Sorrow, My True Story" in Chapter 5 cries out and shouts but doesn't surprise as much as this little poem:

BURN

May
the
flames
of
love
burn
your
heart
to
a
crisp.

More passion in that poem than in the wailing one. And so much more compressed. It carries a cliché, *burned to a crisp;* but it's saved by being used with such a high-flown phrase as *flames of love*. Still there's surprise in that short poem. Most beginning poets who write of love or boredom usually do nothing more than bore their readers. Here's a poem on lonesomeness which is simple but not sensuous. The passion which lies in it must have been recollected in tranquillity because it's expressed in a surprising way:

TWO

A jet
just divided
the sky
in two:
half for me
half for you.
I wonder
who you are.

The above poem controls its sound skillfully up until the last two lines. It repeats a *j* sound, emphasizes *i* sounds in *divided* and *sky,* rhymes *two* and *you,* repeats or parallels *half for me, half for you.* Most of the other preceding poems were made out of prose sentences or paragraphs and sound prosy. They do not control the rhythm of phrase, the interior sounds of words; they do not employ alliteration. The following poem carries a whole sound to it, as if the speaker felt so strongly she had to talk in rhythmic phrases and words that can be read aloud smoothly and softly:

MEETING

Love and I met today.
It was just a casual acquaintance,
not one of those candle lights in Rome,
Just a walk in the rain.
Maybe it was just the rain I was in love with,
But we made it through together
and if it was the rain
I hope it storms soon.

This isn't a sensuous poem. It doesn't make you feel or see the rain or the person walked with. But it surprises and it controls its sound. And happily, though it's slow, casual, and almost melancholy, it speaks humorously in the last line. One suggestion: drop the third use of the word *just.*

In all the poems presented here, Milton's suggestion that poetry is *simple* is evidenced. Nothing fancy. No parading of the writer's vocabulary, no insisting with adjectives and adverbs.

WRITING TWENTY-SEVEN: Try writing a short, simple poem. Maybe your journal carries a passage that wants to be a poem. Look to your experience and don't for a moment let the word *poem* make you forget truthtelling.

Nothing said here was meant to imply that writing within boundaries—like those imposed by meter and rhyme—is bad for a poet. Some of the most powerful poems have been written within tight conventions. But this chapter is meant for beginners and persons who do not consider themselves poets at all. If you wish to see what working within limits does for your expression, you might try writing the Japanese verse form of *haiku.* Here's a sample written by an American boy:

Afternoon sunlight
splattering through swaying tree-
tops, butters the ground.

TOM THAYER

The haiku is an old verse form in Japan. It consists of three lines of five syllables, seven syllables, and five syllables, without rhyme. Traditionally it presents a small happening, moment, or notion in the life of nature in which a simple thing is observed so closely or in such a juxtaposition with other natural events that it comes across newly, surprisingly. As you can see, it's another country's institutionalized form of a fabulous reality. Again, it has a sudden ending, usually requiring the reader to find its significance on his own. Here are two haiku by Japanese poets:

One man
and one fly
waiting in this huge room

ISSA

I sit like Buddha
but the mosquitoes
keep biting.

OEMARU

These poems don't follow the 5-7-5 pattern because they're translated and the translator cared more about the naturalness of phrasing and idiom in English than about the syllable pattern.

Here's another haiku by an American student, this time cheating on the form, giving only four syllables to the first line:

A fly circling
A half-filled glass of Kool-Aid—
His sweet, liquid grave.

MEGAN REESE

WRITING TWENTY-EIGHT: Write three haiku poems. If you wish, depart from natural subjects and write of man-made things or events.

You can go on to write rhymed, metric verse. Robert Frost is a fine model because he was able to find rhymes that don't sound corny. His lines are almost irresistible in sound. They don't slavishly follow the accented pattern and often they sound like relaxed conversation at the same time they are disciplined by a somewhat regular beat.

By now when you write anything, you'll probably think first of truthtelling. After that, when writing poems, think of compression. It helps you attain intensity, so essential to poems, as Milton hinted with his "simple, sensuous, and passionate." Intensity may also arise as it does in any good writing because the poet has talked of things which together surprise the reader but finally make sense to him. The skilled poet may press and press upon one point or feeling without being monotonous. Consider this poem by a student:

TAPS

1 plus 5 = 6
I am 6. Remember that.
8 plus 3 = nothing that I know of.
I am not eleven anything.
I skip that one. The teacher is mad.
Why don't you do your work?
She taps her red pen on my head. Hard.
I do not cry. I am a big girl. I go to school.
Do your work, says the cruel gleaming-teeth teacher.
She taps her red pen still more on my head.
One-two-three-four-five-six-seven-eight-nine-ten-eleven.
Now I know eleven. I do the problem, finish my work.
Now I understand eleven. I hate eleven.
I am a big girl. I will not cry.

PEGGY HOWARD

Peggy intensified her poem by pressing and pressing, on numbers. That's her subject. But she goes beyond citing addition problems and the number of times the teacher tapped on her head to say "I am not eleven anything." She uses short sentences, she repeats numbers, she builds the emotion (becomes passionate). She uses parallel construction in short hammering clauses: "Now I know eleven. I do the problem, finish my work." She repeats the word *eleven* strongly, not monotonously. It is a superb poem, employing the eight fundamentals of good writing. It makes the reader work. Only once does it come out and state its point: with the word *cruel.* Dropping that word would make the poem better, force the reader to see that the final hatred in the poem is directed not against the number eleven but against a tyrannical teacher.

If you have access to a word-processor, you can easily play with the shape of your poems by writing lines of different lengths and then pressing the "CENTER" key for each line. In the seventeenth century poets shaped their poems like wings, crosses, trees, and other objects they were writing about. You'll enjoy doing that, but don't let yourself think that the shape of a poem on the page is more essential than what you say in it.

Here's a poem by a high school junior that asks a great deal of the reader:

BOOKSTORE

I purchase a dream at the counter
of peeling linoleum,
of scarred wood,
place a dirty quarter
in the sweating clerk's hand,
politely hiding my repulsion at the touch
of his calloused palm . . .
and start down the aisle.

I edge past a smiling old man
engrossed in an illustrated calendar
from Sweden,
two teenage girls giggling over a confession magazine,
a fat woman reading an ad for reducing candy,
and a pimpled boy with a comic book.

They step aside for me,
not looking up to see my face,
to see my skin hidden by makeup,
to recognize our common reality.

Only the bell on the door
is obliged to say farewell, tinkling tinnily.

If you read that poem at the same rate as you read prose, you may have to try it again before you understand. That's part of the poetry contract; readers are expected to slow down when they see signs that the poem before them is put together like a puzzle. And they are not to feel ashamed or outraged if they have to read it twice. And two readers may find different meanings in it. If the difference is extreme (for example, if one reader believes that "Bookstore" says that old men who read girlie magazines are alien and disgusting and the other reader believes that the narrator is putting herself in the same class with him) then either the poem is written badly or one of the readers has read it badly.

"Bookstore" is subtle and surprising in its thought. It might be still better if the writer had not so frequently put an adjective before her nouns. Such a technique makes for monotony in expression; it creates sing-songy description. But "Bookstore" is so fully a poem—displaying many of the strategies open to poets—that it's a good one to discuss with your classmates. How do you read it? What do you get from it? What cues lead you to your meanings?

For centuries in China part of the test for bureaucratic officials to be admitted to office consisted of writing a poem. These officials were men. Most of the published poets in the Western world have been men. Yet most of the poems written in schools have been done by women. Same old story: women don't get the praise and the publicity. But in American schools boys usually are afraid to write poems because they may be thought effeminate. A wild circle of irony. It's time everyone started writing poems that demand truthtelling. We might have less Engfish in government, business, and organizations of all kinds—maybe less lying. The best poetry is often hard, lean, and muscular, like a good tight end or a middle linebacker.

Here's a poem by a high school boy. He wrote it the day after he had heard that three young people in his school had been killed the night before, two in one auto crash, one in another.

THREE DEATHS

What's the use when the kids are all gone?
Why the drawn faces for kids gone along?
I wanted to bang my head on the wall
and fight for more lives.

What are the steps for events such as these?
Trillium grows along the river
where birds beat deer to the water
and yesterday was such a nice sunset.

But when will I know of this death?
Breath of steam ices the cracking cold sunshine
where penguins wouldn't look too lost
and snowshoes walk among the trees.

I'm not sure if I'll take a walk today.
I'm sick of knowing only the knobby outdoors
when the state of these kids is dead,
and I know of no way to play with that.

MARK PATTULLO

Now two examples from a professional poet, William Carlos Williams, who writes strong sounding lines. The two poems differ from each other in sound. They move differently. That's one of the effects a writer can achieve by controlling sound.

THE DANCE

In Breughel's great picture, The Kermess,
the dancers go round, they go round and
around, the squeal and the blare and the
tweedle of bagpipes, a bugle and fiddles
tipping their bellies (round as the thick-
sided glasses whose wash they impound)
their hips and their bellies off balance
to turn them. Kicking and rolling about
the Fair Grounds, swinging their butts, those
shanks must be sound to bear up under such
rollicking measures, prance as they dance
in Breughel's great picture, The Kermess.

POEM

As the cat
climbed over
the top of

the jamcloset
first the right
forefoot

carefully
then the hind
stepped down

into the pit of
the empty
flowerpot

Dr. Williams' mastery of sound should come as no surprise to readers who know he was a poet. A practicing M.D., he wrote poems in his office in between seeing patients or on the way to visit them at home.

In "The Dance," Dr. Williams writes only two sentences, listing again and again a few nouns joined by prepositions, or a verb form ending in *-ing*. Once he says they go round and round, his parts of sentences repeat and repeat and thus go round and round themselves:

the squeal and the blare and the tweedle
a bugle and fiddles
their hips and their bellies

One way he gets the parts of sentences to swing is to join them with *and*, a word he uses six times.

Read aloud, the poem almost flies off the page, because Dr. Williams has employed so many sound effects—alliteration and assonance, the repetition of *ound* in *round, around, impound, Grounds, sound.*

Dr. Williams' second sentence is not actually a sentence but a jamming together of the parts of several sentences which do not keep straight their subjects and verbs. For example, the shanks are not "swinging their butts"; the dancers are. Dr. Williams knows what a sentence is, but here he deliberately violates grammar in order to increase the feeling that the speaker is himself breathlessly swinging around and around rather than reciting a carefully composed statement at a speaker's podium.

In the second poem about the cat, Dr. Williams has arranged his words to slow down the reader as he speaks the lines. Instead of the constant repetition of words ending in *-ing,* he uses many words ending in sounds that stop rather than prolong sound: the word *top* not a word like *new,* the word *jamcloset* not a word like *see.* Also many of his words begin with hard sounds: *cat climbed, flowerpot.* In "The Dance," he wanted beer-drinking peasants to swing in circles; in "Poem" he wanted a cat to step precisely and carefully. The sound of words is poets' business. They must be able to control it as pitchers control a curve.

Let yourself write with the feeling of swinging freely and hearing your words as you write. Then you'll get the parallel rhythms and alliteration and the right sounds of voices. You can always shorten, tighten, expand, change here and there. This love poem has the right sound for what it says:

LOVE POEM

Every hitchhiker
silhouetted on every freeway exit
suitcase shoulder-slung
leaving every city
is you.

"Pick me up, hey,
give me a lift, I'll go
anywhere."

I would send out fleets.

COLLEEN ANDERSON

This chapter has been designed to get you over any fear or animosity you might have had toward writing poems. It's an introduction and nothing more. Hundreds of other remarks could be made about the nature of poetry and its strategies.

WRITING TWENTY-NINE: In your journals look for short, concentrated passages that might be turned into poems. Or try your hand at writing a poem out of your experience. Look at the first version you have written. Then cut it and cut it. Leave not one word that an intelligent reader will not need. Here, for example, is the first draft of a poem:

Fiery red hot coals
glowing in an old fire
on a bland summer night
me
        staring
                wanting
to touch one
but the beautiful coals
that look so soft and orange
        would burn.

Consider what might be cut or rearranged. Be tough on your poem. Most poets write a poem and revise it, let it alone for a few days, and come back to it. They drop lines, stanzas, words. They rearrange. The revisions frequently number eleven or more. Here's a cutting and rearrangement of the above poem:

Fiery coals
glowing soft and orange
in an old fire
on a bland summer night
me
        staring
                wanting
to touch one.

Compress your poem. Intensify it. Make the reader work.

In both versions of this poem the poet makes a grammatical "error," saying *me* instead of *I,* probably on purpose, because it sounds better. Poets care a great deal about sound.

The clever questioner learns little.

LU PO HUA

chapter 21 "tell me something" interviews

ONCE I READ a batch of interviews done by students in a writing class. They were much alike. They asked three questions, "Where do you live?" "What's your hobby?" and "What do you intend to do after graduating?"

Most of the answers to those routine questions were themselves routine, very short, and not revealing. "I live over on Valley Road with my mother and little sister. After school I like to get a six-pack of beer and go to the playground with my buddies and shoot baskets. When I get out of school, I want to be an auto mechanic or go in the army." Little or nothing came out to show that these interviewed students were individuals different from each other. Most of them seemed boring.

This chapter will present a more positive kind of interview, easier to do, and more valuable for everyone concerned. Here's an interview by a student named Lois Rothrock, who chose to interview a friend who was a paraplegic. She didn't ask routine questions. (Barry is not this man's real name. I've changed it in case he no longer wants to make public these feelings.)

BARRY

When Barry Baker was 16, a truck ran into him while he was riding his motorcycle. Now he is a father, a successful insurance agent, and a paraplegic.

He agreed to talk to me about what he had done with his life.

I said to him, "You've been in a wheelchair for a long time. Have you ever looked back and relived your accident?"

"Not really," he said, "because I can't exactly remember what happened. One minute I was cruising along on my bike and the next thing I knew, I was in a hospital bed.

"My most vivid memory of that moment is the taste of onions. I know this may sound really gross, but I used to love liver and onions. Right before I took off that night, I had a big meal of them. After the accident, I must have been puking up liver and onions for hours. Hated 'em ever since. I still won't touch them.

"My first reaction when I woke up in the hospital was a whole bunch of things—disbelief, fear, bitterness, self-pity. It took me a while to get over all those feelings. A friend of mine came over and told me point blank that I'd never amount to anything if I didn't get my ass in gear and stop feeling sorry for myself. He really made me aware of what I was doing to everyone I really cared about, including myself.

"The members of my family were shocked about the accident, but they just took it as something 'God had planned.' It was a little harder to get used to me though, I guess. In the beginning they were too easy on me because they just didn't know what they were expected to do. Finally, I had to tell them that I *could* push my wheelchair and I *wanted* to do things by myself. They got the hint real fast. They've been more than supportive ever since.

"They had to get used to me. I get strange looks from people in stores but I don't know most of them, so I don't really care. I figure that if people like me, they'll like *all* of me, and my being in a wheelchair is part of the package.

"Of course, there are people who think I can't do anything for myself. I tend to disregard them. I can drive a car,

I can participate in wheelchair athletics, I still can do almost everything I want to. I like to prove all those people wrong. It's one of my big kicks.

"For one thing, I swim. I play wheelchair basketball, and I'm in wheelchair track. I run relays and throw the javelin and shotput. I've participated nationally in all these events. One year I took a first and second in swimming, and I got third place in both the javelin and shot put.

"Those were exciting moments, but they were just for fun. The big thrill was when I found out my wife was pregnant with my daughter. Because of my accident, I had never expected to have any children. The doctor told me I was sterile, and I sure proved him wrong. Some day I'd like to do the same thing by walking. Boy, I'd like to see his face if I took off across the floor on my legs."

This is a brief interview. It doesn't go into how Barry Baker carries out his job as an insurance agent, but for such a short piece of writing, it passes the apple test. It has a core—the way Barry refused to give up because he was a paraplegic, and flesh—experiences that make his struggle seem distinctive. And it's rounded off. We see Barry in action enough to be convinced. His indomitable spirit is not simply referred to. It comes alive through the experiences and thoughts he relates.

Here's how this interview was produced. The interviewer knew Barry well enough to realize he hadn't let his disability ruin his life. She admired him for that and decided to find out more about how he got to his present state. Like the students I mentioned earlier, she could have asked him where he lived, what were his hobbies, and what he intended to do in the future. But she focused on the questions her own curiosity had developed for her. She made an appointment to see Barry at his convenience, and recorded their words. In the final draft of her interview, she omitted her questions. I give some of them here so you can see what they were:

"Barry, you've been in a wheelchair for a long time. Have you ever looked back and relived your accident?" . . . "Is that your earliest memory, then, waking up in the hospital?" . . . "What do you mean by that?" . . . "I can understand why not. Do you remember what your initial reaction was when they told you about the effects of the accident?" . . . "What finally made you quit?" . . . "What was your family's attitude about what had happened to you?" "Have you found that, as a handicapped person, people do tend to treat you differently?"

You can see that some of Lois's questions got Barry talking so that he presented the flesh of the apple, not simply the skin: "Is that your earliest memory, then, waking up in the hospital?" "What made you finally quit [feeling bitter and sorry for himself]?" But one question was obvious and poorly chosen: "Have you found that, as a handicapped person, people do tend to treat you differently?" Barry's answer, "Of course—" suggests that it was an "of course question," one that readers of the interview don't want to spend their time reading. They want the answer, not the question. And that's true of so many questions asked in interviews: they're triggers and they're necessary, but when put down on the page they don't advance the stories being told.

Lois asked some good questions, for example, "What was your family's attitude?" Barry might not have thought to go into that subject. And she kept most of the questions open, saying, for example, "What do you mean by that?" rather than telling Barry that he must have meant this or that and eliciting a yes or no answer from him that said very little. "Open-ended" questions are usually best: "What happened then?" or "How do you feel about that?" Rather than "Did the man hit you then?" or "That made you feel awful, didn't it?"

On television we often see an interviewer trying to put someone on the spot, like a prosecutor cross-examining a defendant. That kind of questioning has its place, but it's a special one, usually pretty nasty, and it needn't be the model for all interviews.

When Lois wrote up her final draft of an interview, she dropped most of the questions she had recorded originally in her transcript. Many writers publish their interviews as question-and-answer sessions because that's what they think an interview is supposed to be. And some ask antagonistic questions only because they want to appear clever as interviewers. The show-off instinct again, fatal to good writing.

> *A battle of wits is made one by two halfwits.*
>
> LU PO HUA

If you're asking persons about something they do well, and that you admire, they will likely get rolling and give you a great deal of wonderful stuff about themselves without being asked many questions. When that happens, sit back and take notes fast, or attend to your tape recorder, and let the person go on. If she or he says too much, you can always cut some of it in your final draft. But watch out for asking too many questions. They may act as interruptions and shut off feelings building in the talker that often lead to new revelations for the speaker and for you.

Many newcomers to interviewing feel that every word said by both parties must be faithfully recorded and presented in the final draft or they're not being truthful. In fact, almost all professional interviewers drop much of what was said orally, add things, and change the speakers' language so as not to embarrass them. When conversationally spoken words get into writing, they often make a person sound foolish, because it's the nature of conversation to vanish instantly in the air. Words spoken are not words written, which once down on paper, can stare at you forever. So most interviewers and reporters take care to revise transcripts of spoken words. If a person departs from Standard English just once or twice during an interview, saying, for example, "The heat and humidity in the middle of that afternoon was too much for us," the interviewer changes the *was* to *were* to agree with the plural subject of *heat and humidity*. They don't want to imply that the speaker ordinarily is ungrammatical. But if the person speaks customarily in a dialect that departs from Standard English, the interviewer is likely to retain the language as spoken—"We wasn't gonna have nothin' to do with that machine. It was spittin' sparks like it was blowin' its nose."

A common habit we all share in speaking casually is to repeat words carelessly or weakly. If you tape record a conversation between yourself and a classmate, you'll probably be amazed to find how often you stammered, said "uh," or repeated a word that didn't contribute to your meaning. For example, in the interview above, in one paragraph Barry used the word *really* twice.

> . . . so I don't really care . . . I figure if people really like me . . .

In the finished draft, Lois dropped one of those uses of the word in order to make Barry look better as a speaker. You may say that's misrepresentation, but remember, once written down and published, this interview is a special statement from Barry. It's not simply words thrown away on the playground or in the halls. It stands as a presentation of him for others he knows and doesn't know.

Beyond that, there's the question of embarrassing the persons you interview by presenting things they said in a private conversation.

Every piece of writing—fiction or non-fiction—about a person is only a *representation* of that person, and then a partial one. You can't reproduce people in all their complexity in a piece of writing, not even in an 800-page novel. You can't ever give the whole truth. So consider the dangers of writing about any real person, but also be charitable with yourself—you can't do the impossible.

If in the interview above, Barry had said that his best friend had stopped seeing him regularly after the accident, that would be a dangerous statement to make public. It could injure that friend's reputation severely. If Barry felt that this friend had shown again and again that he had shunned him, he might want that to appear in the interview. Nevertheless, as interviewer, I would be reluctant to include that information. At the least, I would tell Barry that I wasn't going to give the *name* of that friend in the interview. In writing publicly about a person, you risk all sorts of injury. Suppose that the friend was just about to get over his overly-sensitive reaction to the way Barry looked as a paraplegic and next week was going to renew his close friendship. Your published interview might keep him from doing that. One way to protect persons you interview is to show your first or second draft to them before you write it up as a finished work. Even then, you may have disagreements about what should go into the final version. Interviewing is a delicate business. Think of how you would feel if everything you said as a person being interviewed were to be published in an interview someone did with you. The chances for harming people are many in interviewing. You may get someone to air her objections to her boss or to working conditions, and the word gets back and she is fired. These things happen. Newspaper reporters face such difficulties every day of their lives.

You'll find interviewing a challenge—you want to tell truths that count but in ways that are just and fair and sensitive to people's feelings and rights. That's seldom easy, but whoever said truthful and valuable writing is always easy?

Here are two interviews done in class (at least 20 minutes are necessary for the job, and 50 minutes are better). In the first one, Craig Smith interviewed Kirk Wheeler about something he does well—play baseball.

INTERVIEW WITH KIRK WHEELER

"I like baseball a lot better than football," said Kirk. "Basically because practice is more fun, and it's not as much work. And football takes up a lot of time. The baseball season is a lot shorter.

"There are really only a few things I don't like about baseball. One is that the season is during trout season, so I don't get to go fishing as much. You also have to work on the field a lot, no matter what the weather is like, to keep it in shape.

"I play centerfield, and I like that position. I like to play there on defense because I get to use my speed some to catch fly balls.

"I like to be challenged in all the games. Sure, it's fun when you're beating a team by five or six runs. But the win is sweeter when you win by only one run.

"I don't really remember when I started playing for a long time. I guess I was seven or eight when I first started on the little league team. I've played ever since. I've played varsity baseball since the tenth grade.

"The one game that really stands out in my mind is the first game we played against James River last year. The score was tied three-to-three. I hit a home run! The first one I ever hit, and probably the only one. That put us up four-to-three, and we won.

"It felt good just to know that I helped the team out. It surprised me a lot. It meant a whole lot more to me because we won the game.

"It's really hard not to get nervous when you're in a situation like that. Everybody's looking at you and expecting you to do really well. But all you can do is do your best. And if you don't get a hit or a run, all you can do is hope that the next guy does, or go out on defense and try to stop the other team.

"You can't get down on yourself. You're not going to have a great day every game. But it's important to remember not to break your concentration. You've got to concentrate on the ball, on the coach, on your stance, on every part of the game. You just have to concentrate on everything you do.

"Sometimes it's hard to concentrate on every pitch. Maybe a bird will fly by and you watch it instead of the ball. Or a silly girl will be sitting on the wall yelling something at you.

"I remember the game last year when we went down to New Castle. It was freezing. It started snowing when we were playing. You could hardly see the ball. Nobody really cared if we won or lost; we just wanted to get home. We didn't play really well that day either. We let the weather get in the way of our concentration. You've just got to learn to keep your mind off those things and on the game.

"Another important thing that goes along with concentration is that you've got to know what you're going to do with the ball on defense. You've got to be thinking one step ahead. One year I was playing in the state softball tournament in Petersburg. The other team had a runner on second that I knew was fast. I thought he would try to go if the batter got a base hit. The hitter put the ball through the infield right to me in centerfield. I threw the guy out at

home. You've got to be thinking ahead and concentrating. That's the secret."

Now that you know how some interviewers handle their material, you can guess that probably Craig probably started the interview by asking Kirk, "What do you like to do that you do well?" And "Why did you start playing?" Then when Kirk finished answering that question, Craig probably felt the need for some little stories that would bring Kirk's baseball career alive. At that point he might have said, "Tell me a game that stands out in your mind." And later, "If you had time to tell me just one thing you think is essential to playing good baseball, what would it be?" But simply putting down Kirk's answers, without Craig's questions, makes a clear, easy-to-follow interview. Kirk's mention of the need to ignore distractions leads into his final point about concentration being an absolute essential for playing good baseball.

You probably noticed that Kirk, like the rest of us, habitually repeats certain words and phrases when he's talking informally. You might consider which of those repetitions you would eliminate in the final draft of the interview.

Unlike many writers, Craig knows how to punctuate a series of paragraphs all spoken by one person. He put quotation marks at the beginning of each paragraph, but omitted them at the end of the paragraphs until he got to the last one. That's the conventional way of showing that only one person is speaking. In a conversation between two persons, the words of one person are marked off by quotation marks before the first word and after the last. Then the next statement, or paragraph, spoken by another person, is handled the same way.

Another interview in that same class shows how a good interviewer keeps looking for fascinating material. Vonda Nofsinger began interviewing Lori Gilliam about her ability to listen to other people talk about their troubles. When Lori suddenly began talking excitedly about her cat, Vonda urged her to say more, and before the half hour was up, Vonda had a pretty impressive interview about a cat, not about Lori's ability to listen to other people. After she wrote out a first draft, Vonda realized she needed still more about the cat and went back to Lori and asked her to tell some little stories about how the cat acted when he was doing one of his attacks on people. Here's the result:

THE INFAMOUS NERMAL

When Lori Gilliam talked to me about her ability to listen to other people's troubles, she kept mentioning her cat, so finally I just said to her, "Well, why don't you tell me about

yourself as a person who's good at putting up with a wild cat?" Here's what she said:

"Nermal could be described as fat. He's a long-haired, gray Persian. He's just tremendous! Once I weighed him. He weighed about twenty pounds.

"He's had more names. I was going to call him Dirt-ball when I first got him, because he looked like a little dirt ball. Then I wanted to call him. D.C., then Pooky. Now he's Nermal, or Hans-Nermal. He answers to German. His name came from the comic strip *Garfield.* But Mom won't let me call him that in front of her. She says it's stupid. She calls him "Damn Cat!"

"My cat is so mean. You know those 'Beware of Dog' signs. I was going to get one that said 'Beware: Attack Cat on Premises.'

"Sherrie Wheeler says he's possessed. She screams if he walks into the room. I think she feels that way because of all the stories that my Mom has told her.

"Once he hit my grandmother, and all she said was 'Lori Lynne, come over here and get this cat.' I'm the only one who can control him. One time, Mom told Nermal, 'I'd like to hit you with my fist.' He attacked her then, too. One night when he attacked Mom I had to pull him off her and throw him outside, and then he climbed the screen trying to get in. It got to where you couldn't walk outside without him jumping on you. He thinks he owns the place now. He even has his own chair. He won't let anyone sit in it, and it's the biggest chair we've got and the only one with a cushion. He thinks he's the dominant figure in the house, sitting there in his huge wicker throne.

"You can always tell when he's going to attack. He lays back his ears and meows. And he twitches his tail. Other times, he'll lick you, and then he'll bite.

"I think I'm the target of his frustration. He has taken a claw before and stuck it in my arm like a needle."

Lori then rolled up her sleeve to show me war wounds from that battle and other Nermal attacks.

"Another time I was lying on the floor crying. He jumped on my head and started pulling my hair. He grabbed on with his front feet and teeth, and he kicked me in the head with his hind feet. I picked him up and threw him across the room.

"If you run from him, he'll run after you. If he's picked you out, your number is up. He even chases dogs out of the yard.

"He's my man. He's cool."

Like any other good piece of writing, an interview needs a strong ending. As interviewer, it's your job to choose a spoken passage that has more meaning to it than others, that carries a clout, or that truly closes out the talk rather than lets it dribble away. Vonda found a perfect statement for ending her interview with Lori. In five words it explains the unexplainable—why Lori allows such an attacker as Nermal to live with her.

A small point: In the middle of the story Vonda refers to Sherrie Wheeler, and then never mentions her again. When professional writers introduce a new name into their writing, they usually identify the person in some way, for example, "My friend Sherrie Wheeler says . . ." or they drop the name and give only the identifying words, "A friend of mine says . . ." They're aware that suddenly introduced names of unidentified persons may puzzle their readers. They may think, "Who's this Sherrie? Did she come in before and I missed her?"

WRITING THIRTY: Interview one of your classmates and allow yourself to be interviewed by him or her. Remember the fundamentals of a "tell-me-something" interview: Ask the person to tell you about something she or he does well and likes to do. Don't ask questions that bring forth only "yes" or "no" answers. When the speaker bogs down in generalities, ask open-ended questions like, "Tell me about the first time you did it." Or, "Can you tell a little story about how you did it once when it was especially hard or easy?" Remember your job is not to show off your own knowledge or understanding of what the speaker is telling you about. It's to get that person talking on a roll. Try to capture the speaker's unique way of talking. After you've finished the interview and written it up in a first draft, go back to the speaker and ask for more little stories, or whatever's necessary to make everything clear in an interview that's filled with nuts and big hunks of fruit like a good Christmas cake.

Now here are two interviews with persons outside the class that Vonda and Craig attended.

For some time, Pam Robertson had admired Nancy Thornton, a woman she knew who worked in a florist's shop. So she went to her and asked Nancy why and how she did her work there so well and seemed to enjoy it so much.

INTERVIEW WITH NANCY THORNTON

In the flower shop I watched as Nancy Thornton picked out a basket, filled it with water and oasis, and placed it on the work table. Buckets of flowers surrounded her. She chose a rose, cut it to the proper length, and pushed it into the awaiting block of oasis. Then she began to speak.

"I started designing flowers about two and a half years ago. Before that, I had been a school teacher for sixteen years. When I moved to Buena Vista, there were no teaching positions available. I applied at a nearby florist's shop and began my training as a designer. I had previously been in many garden clubs, and I just naturally enjoy working with flowers.

"I prefer to work with fresh cut flowers, and I like to do special things like parties and weddings. I once did a special garden arrangement for a high school prom because at the last minute the centerpiece they had planned didn't work out and they decided on a gazebo in its place.

"A background in art is very helpful because a designer needs to have many creative skills. This allows the designer to be versatile in working with various arrangements as well as building a reputation for the designer. The most important characteristic a designer must have is that he must enjoy working with flowers."

Note that here the speaker is getting more and more formal in language. Her conversational tone is deserting her. In an interview, you ordinarily want the liveness of conversation, not the formality of a lecture or a sermon. We all tend to talk that way when we feel our words are being written down. If the person you're interviewing becomes overly formal in language, interrupt her or him with a request for a little story as an example, and then you'll find the language will loosen up. Note that Nancy Thornton's language changes back to informal when she gets down to details:

"Sometimes I work with flowers from ten to twelve hours a day. For the customer's as well as the shop's sake, the last piece I fix must be as nice as the first piece I fixed that day.

"And, oh, I could tell you some stories about people and the types of flower arrangements that they want. One time a lady brought me some old turkey feathers and wanted me to fix them into some sort of an arrangement. I

managed to do it, and I was shocked at how nice the arrangement turned out to look.

"One day a man walked into the shop and ordered his own funeral piece. He wrote his own cards and said that he knew he was going to die soon, and if he were to get the flowers he wanted, he had to order them himself.

"I also remember a touching experience when a man came in and ordered a dozen roses for his wife. He enclosed a poem he had written himself about his wife. There was something about each of the twelve months that pertained to his wife. He was really just a common laborer, and I could tell that he hadn't had much of a formal education, but the poem was lovely. I thought then how lucky his wife must be to have a husband like him."

Another snip, snip; a flower put into place, and the basket was finished. Nancy made a bow and attached the card. She placed it in the cooler to keep the flowers fresh until the person who had ordered the lovely basket came to the shop to pick it up.

Pam was lucky. She chose someone to interview who was good at telling little stories. When you have such luck, sit back and listen to the stories and put them down.

If you're fortunate, you may find people who speak with zing, who relish the sound of their words. Tracy Rudasill knew what he was doing when he decided to interview his friend Meg Carter about something she does well. Her speech is so lively that an interview with her on any subject would probably be enjoyable reading.

MEG CARTER SITTING BABIES

"I just finished babysitting with the cutest little girl named Virginia. She's such a cutie pie. She has long blonde hair, with little curlies in it, big blue eyes, and fat little cheeks. She's a dollbaby. Listen. She tells me when she wants to go to bed. She can count to ten, no eleven. She knows all her colors. Out of the blue she just said, 'You have brown eyes.' It about blew my mind. The best part is, she tells me when she needs to be changed. Can you believe that? And she's only one year old. I just love Ginia to pieces. That's how she pronounces her name—Ginia."

"You like to babysit. Tell me about it, Meg."

"Well, when you're a certain age, people just call you

up. I guess you could call it that *responsible age*. They knew my sister first, and then they just started asking me.

"Let me tell you about this one time. It was terrible, but it was funny. It was my first sitting job. It was at my best friend's house with her two little sisters. The parents left, and everything was fine until bath time. I'll never forget it. It was so funny. I was to give a bath to this one-year-old and this four-year-old. I was filling up the small tub for the one-year-old. I had it all filled up and had gotten her undressed when she peed on the floor. Well, the four-year-old started laughing so hard that she peed too. As I was cleaning up the four-year-old's mess, the little baby tipped over the tub of water. Water was all over the bathroom. It was a new bathroom and water was everywhere. The rug was soaked, the towels were everywhere. It was terrible. I then proceeded to give the four-year-old a bath. I filled up the tub and was ready to begin. The four-year-old hit the water faucet and the water was spraying everywhere. We sat in the bathroom in tears of laughter. The baby just had a big grin on her face. I didn't really want to tell the parents, but I did. They understood and got a laugh too. The irony of it all was that Laura, my good friend, and I used to give those kids baths all the time. No problem. Not until my first job did I soak the bathroom.

"You know, I really wasn't nervous the first time I babysat. I felt right at home. The only thing that ever scares me when I babysit is scary movies. I recall scary movies sometimes and scare myself. Then I get the kids together to keep me company."

"What do you like in a parent?"

"Ohhh, I'll tell you what I hate! I hate it when parents are late. They say they'll be in at a certain time, and they come in hours later. I can't stand that! Also, it's bad when parents don't leave a telephone number to call in case of an emergency. One time, I babysat for this doctor, and a patient must have called a hundred times. I didn't know what to do or where to reach him. I also hate when parents let the kids wear panties when they aren't potty-trained. I'm always cleaning up pee every five seconds. The biggest one is being on time. If parents aren't on time, it just shows their irresponsibility.

"I like parents that let me know about the child. What food it likes or dislikes; where the diapers are; if the child

has a special blanket; what satisfies or discourages the child; where the phone is; where the T.V. is; and so on. That's what I'm going to be like when I'm a parent.

"I hated this babysitter I had. She locked me in my room and talked to her boyfriend all the time.

"I like to make the kids laugh. I try to play games that interest them. More or less, I just try to think like a kid. I don't sit on the phone and talk."

"So you really like to babysit. I bet you can hardly wait until you have your own kids, huh?"

"Well, not really. Children are *great* responsibilities. I'll tell you something, though. They're a pain in the butt sometimes. I think I'll wait a while before I have kids of my own."

In the third from the last paragraph lies one of those short and telling statements that sum up a whole attitude: "More or less, I just try to think like a kid." I believe that Lois should have moved it to the end of the paragraph (a position of power) rather than left it buried in the middle.

In the fifth paragraph from the end of the above interview, the interviewer has used semicolons to set off the sentence elements—". . . What food they like or dislike; where the diapers are; if the child has a special blanket;. . ."etc. Commas would be conventional, for these elements couldn't stand as sentences themselves. Furthermore, in setting down conversation most professional writers don't use semicolons. They feel periods or commas suggest the rapid-fire voice of conversation more appropriately.

If you use a tape recorder for interviewing, you'll find that transcribing the words from the tape onto paper is slow and excruciating work. A great help is a small inexpensive pedal that you can buy at most electronic supply stores. It allows you to stop and start the tape recorder with your foot, leaving your hands free for typing or writing.

WRITING THIRTY-ONE: Conduct an interview with someone outside your class whom you admire for doing something well. Remember the opening interview in this chapter, with Barry Baker, the paraplegic. Go for surprises. Don't presuppose you know what the person you choose is going to say. If you do your job well, the person you interview will learn more about what she or he does well than ever before, and will come to surprising understandings in the bargain.

I am also convinced that the more you know about your craft, the freer you can be from it. My interpretation of freedom has nothing to do with sloppy or careless technique that is a caricature of freedom. To me real freedom arrives when the artist's creative instinct can function without limitation and without consciousness of technical means.

GABOR PETERDI

chapter 22 the order of words

A BOY OF SIX speaks as if he knew his meaning depends a great deal on word order. He wouldn't think of saying:

> Of wouldn't he think saying.

And he wouldn't mess up the agreement signals in this sentence by using words that signal oneness when they need to signal twoness:

> Johnny and Bill has his own bike.

And he wouldn't say:

> It was nice of they.

because in the American grammatical system words like *he, she,* or *they* preceded by prepositions signal their relationship by changing to the object form (*him, her,* or *them*). Kids show this by the time they're six or eight. But sometimes they run into an adult—maybe a teacher—who is so worried about someone saying,

> You and me should go to the show.

that they say,

> She didn't give it *to* you and *I*

when their unconscious and normal feeling for the signal would make them say,

> She didn't give it *to* you and *me.*

J.D. Salinger made his hero Holden Caulfield, in *The Catcher in the Rye,* talk in this highly self-conscious ungrammatical way:

> I think I probably woke he and his wife up . . .

When Eudora Welty said that beginning and professional writers have the same troubles—not being serious or truthful—she might have added that they both have the same troubles with grammar. Most editors find little that is grammatically weak about the writing they edit, and when they do, the weaknesses are usually confined to a few troubles to be expected in the writing of anyone using the American grammatical system. Frequently they involve (1) confusing word order, (2) lack of clear signal by pronouns, and (3) verbs that don't signal which nouns they belong to.

In reading over the first draft of your writing, look first for these possible weak spots.

Word order signals meaning:

Original. When green I love the woods most of all.

Is that when I am green (sick at the stomach) (young, like a green plant?), or when the woods are green? If the latter, the sentence should read:

Revision. I love the woods when green most of all.

or

Revision. I love the green woods most of all.

Thoreau opened Chapter Two of *Walden* with this sentence:

Original. At a certain season of our life we are accustomed to consider every spot as the possible site of a house.

His grammar would have been slightly confusing had he written:

Misrevision. We are accustomed to consider every spot at a certain season of our life as the possible site of a house.

Now *spot* and *season* are too close to each other. The phrase *at a certain season* should be close to *accustomed.*

In your writing, place next to each other those words which belong together in meaning. In the following sentence, the words in italics and in small capitals belong together in meaning but are separated from each other in position:

> This task, which George found highly agonizing, *grew* under the heat of the afternoon sun *soon* to be *unbearable,* and he QUIT working at it steadily EVENTUALLY.

When the words are rearranged (and a Whichery removed), the sentence is improved:

Revision. Under the heat of the afternoon sun, this agonizing task soon grew unbearable and George eventually quit working at it steadily.

The new order makes more sense, but it reveals the sloppy thought on the part of the writer. If the task "soon" grew unbearable, then why did George wait until "eventually" (whatever that means) to stop working at it? Either the "soon" or the "eventually" should be eliminated. Better yet, the writer might tell the reader what he means by "soon" or "eventually." How many hours or minutes?

Not every sentence changes its meaning with a change of word order. For example:

Original. Our minds thus grow in spots . . .

Revision. Thus our minds grow in spots . . .

Revision. Thus grow our minds in spots . . .

Revision. In spots thus grow our minds . . .

American-English grammar doesn't do all its signaling of meaning by word order.

REVISING TEN: Examine your last two long pieces of writing for blunders and weaknesses in word order. Write down on a separate sheet of paper your weak sentences and your revision of them. Reading aloud will help you in this task.

All writers and speakers occasionally let one of the segments of their sentence dangle out on a limb where it can fall off. The most distinguished example is probably a sentence in Thomas Jefferson's First Inaugural Address:

> About to enter, fellow citizens, on the exercise of duties which comprehend everything dear and valuable to you, it is proper that you should understand what I deem the essential principles of our government, and consequently those which ought to shape its administration.

What is "about to enter" is Jefferson, not "you," who are fellow citizens, or "it," which here is one of those vague words which can't enter anything. A dangling construction fails to make clear who is doing what.

> While walking back from my English class, a squirrel came up and stepped on my foot.

Squirrels returning from English classes upset anyone.

More examples of dangling constructions:

> Not finishing dinner until 8:30, another problem was in the making.

> By subtly mentioning to one set of parents that it would be nice if we could all be together, they usually take the hint and invite others.

But enough of these sinful errors. Good writers master grammar in order to control their words, and meaning is their target. In a given paragraph, they may use an expression that's technically a dangling construction but nevertheless communicates their meaning clearly. For example, here's the masterful English writer William Hazlitt beginning the third paragraph of his essay on Sir James Mackintosh:

> To consider him in the last point of view first. As a political partisan, he is rather the lecturer than the advocate.

The first sentence doesn't show clearly who is doing the considering, and the whole group of words is not really a sentence at all. But it works, and an editor would be a fool to change it.

The commonest word-order change made in manuscripts by editors is to bring together subjects and verbs which have been thoroughly separated.

Original. *Professor Rending,* in approaching his subject, stumbled in circles, like a drunk.

Revision. In approaching his subject, *Professor Rending* stumbled in circles, like a drunk.

The method here is to pull out the segment of a sentence which is properly introductory, such as

> When he was altogether prepared,

from the sentence in which it occurs:

> President Wilson, when he was altogether prepared, presented his plan to the League of Nations.

and put it at the beginning.

Revision. When he was altogether prepared, President Wilson presented his plan to the League of Nations.

Often, such rearrangement allows the writer to eliminate a wasted expression such as a Whooery:

Original. Queen Gertrude is a weak person, who is, in spite of her faults, held in high regard by the three men in her life.

Revised. In spite of her faults, Queen Gertrude is held in high regard by the three men in her life.

All writers slip occasionally in making clear the reference between pronouns and their antecedents and the agreement between subject and verb. Therefore editors routinely check for these slips and find them frequently:

> Sol and his buddy Georgie, who is his uncle's favorite baseball player, often *tries* to eat more than he can hold.

Revised. Sol and his buddy Georgie—his uncle's favorite baseball player—often *try* to eat more than they can hold.

> The haggling and the bickering and the many hours of long drawn-out close reading I had to do when I was tired—it was all too much for me.

Revised. The haggling and the bickering and the many hours of long drawn-out close reading I had to do when I was so tired were all too much for me.

Note that most slips in pronoun reference and noun-verb agreement occur in long sentences which interrupt themselves with qualifications and side-trips. Editors examine such sentences closely, expecting meaning may have slid into a ditch.

Commonly professional writers use *which* and *that* to refer to the word immediately preceding:

> I like HAMBURGERS *which* are well done but not dry.

But increasingly these days, they are using *which* or *that* to refer to a whole action described in a number of preceding words:

> Renny approves of making changes now, which is all right with me.

You will do well to stay with the conservative practice of including a clear referent word immediately preceding *which* or *that* as in HAMBURGERS *which*. If you ignore this practice and create a sentence that cannot be misunderstood by your reader, let it stand; but the odds are against you. Note that if the example contained three more words,

> Renny approves of making changes now in the plan, which is all right with me.

the reader couldn't be sure whether what is "all right with me" is the whole plan or the changes. The reader's understandable interpretation of the sentence is probably that *which* refers to *plan,* the word immediately preceding it.

These little matters of reference and agreement are the higgledy-piggledy of grammar. More crucial matters exist. When you think of word order—the way words come together in phrases and clauses (pieces, hunks, segments, absolutes, whatever you call them at the moment)—think of how you may control it to bring your writing alive.

Try telescoping three or four sentences into one, so that the first reaches out and grabs part of those that follow. Here are three sentences too closely related to stand separately:

Original. Immediately Juliet sees the only solution to her problem. That solution is suicide. This is a highly illogical choice.

You can tack on to the first sentence the essential elements of the second and third sentences:

Revision. Immediately Juliet sees the only solution to her problem—suicide, a highly illogical choice.

Such tacking-on must be done with care. If the sentences preceding those above have suggested that the author is judging Juliet's behavior, this revision may be clear. But if not, the reader might take the sentence to say that Juliet sees suicide as a highly illogical choice, a meaning which would jar against the notion embodied in "only solution."

Study the Tack-On sentences of good writers. You'll see that they frequently write down a subject and verb (and sometimes an object of the verb) and then simply add nouns or prepositional phrases, or phrases beginning with verb forms ending in *-ing* or *-ed:*

(a) *It would become a sorcery,*
a magic.

ARCHIBALD MAC LEISH

(b) *There is a pulpit at the head of the hall,*
occupied by a handsome gray-haired judge
with a faculty of appearing pleasant and impartial
to the disinterested spectator,
and
prejudiced and frosty
to the last degree
to the prisoner at the bar.

MARK TWAIN

(c) *Each of us lives and works on a small part of the earth's surface,*
moves in a small circle,
and
of these acquaintances
knows only a few intimately.

WALTER LIPPMANN

(d) *There were several ladies on board,*
quite remarkably beautiful or good-looking,
most of them, alas,
now dead.

IVAN TURGENEV

(e) *Let us arrange the contents of the heap into a line,* with
the works that convey pure information at one end, and
the works that create pure atmosphere at the other end, and
the works that do both in their intermediate positions,
the whole line being graded so that we pass from
one attitude to another.

E. M. FORSTER

Occasionally an author uses the Tack-On method at the beginning of his sentence:

(f) Approaching Concord, doing forty, doing forty-five, doing fifty,
the steering wheel held snug in my palms,
the highway held grimly in my vision,
the crown of the road now serving me (on the righthand curves),
now defeating me (on the lefthand curves),
I began to rouse myself from the stupefaction which
a day's motor journey induces.

E. B. WHITE

Most beginning writers need to nudge themselves into Tacking-On more often, but the habit comes naturally to many people. This statement was written by a high school student not coached to Tack-On:

While playing tennis I feel a sense
of freedom,
of being able to release the pent-up emotions from
hours, days.

Another way of exploiting the force of word-order in American-English is to place a word in an unusual or dominant position in the sentence.

> *[Ask] How many words out of their usual place, and whether this alteration makes the statement in any way more interesting or more energetic.*
>
> EZRA POUND

In many sentences the position of most weight for a word is the end. Frequently you can punch a word by putting it last in a sentence.

I went up to get a friend to go to class with. While waiting for her to get ready, I glanced around the dorm room. There were clothes, hairdryers, curlers, pressers, strewn all around the six-girl room. On the desk sat a book entitled *Social Disorganization*.

Note how the power of the statement would be lessened had the last sentence been written:

A book entitled *Social Disorganization* sat on the desk.

Of Sir Walter Scott, William Hazlitt wrote:

> The old world is to him a crowded map; the new one a dull, hateful blank.

Had he placed his words in normal order, he would have written less forcefully:

> The old world is a crowded map to him; the new one a dull, hateful blank.

Hazlitt's version forces the essential words to the end of each word group, where they gather power and achieve parallelism. To move a word out of normal position is to surprise the reader.

Normal Order. He was a lost man.
Unusual Order. He was a man lost.

Writers need to develop an ear for normal word order and respect that order. If they continually scramble it, they will confuse readers rather than surprise them. The principle involved here is the old one mentioned in Chapter 9: repeat and vary. Vary the normal pattern, but sparingly. And don't forget to create a pattern of expectation in the first place.

REVISING ELEVEN: Take two of your past writings, one free writing and one a planned longer work, and go over each word and sentence to see where you can change word order and improve the clarity or force of your statements. Write in the changes on the original so you and others can see what difference they make in the writing.

"He has got no good red blood in his body," said Sir James.

"No. Somebody put a drop under a magnifying-glass, and it was all semi-colons and parentheses," said Mrs. Cadwallader.

GEORGE ELIOT

chapter 23 observing conventions

FROM THE AGE OF FIVE onward most Americans know and practice the social conventions of their region and economic class. They say "thank you" and "you're welcome" and they eat with or without napkins or finger bowls or whatever is proper to the persons they associate with. Their ego is involved. They want to be liked, to feel right in the social circle they choose for themselves.

But most Americans don't know the publishing conventions of the educated world. They have been taught commas and semicolons as they have been taught "please" and "May I introduce my brother—" but each year in school they learn them for a test and forget them the following day. Why? Because they never expect to have their writing published, or even dittoed and passed around the class. Their ego is not involved.

But the torture of being required each year to learn again what they never learned and aren't going to remember once again this year is slow and unbearable. *Semicolon* becomes a dirty word. Like Mrs. Malaprop in Sheridan's play *The Rivals,* they confuse *apostrophe* with *parenthesis* and *hypothesis* with *apotheosis.*

What should they do if they're sixteen or sixty and haven't learned the American conventional system for aiding readers in understanding the meaning of printed rather than spoken sentences? About the only chance they have is to study sentences in print and deduce for themselves the system. If they look to a textbook for rules, they'll forget them again quickly and painfully.

If you're in this unhappy group of persons laden with guilt about commas and italics, begin observing. Construct generalizations which explain why certain mechanical conventions of print are used in the right-hand column of sentences below. For your convenience the left-hand column presents sentences naked and innocent of most punctuation or other signaling devices. Look at them first. Make your guess at what they need in the way of signals. Then study the signals printed in the right-hand column, which follow the normal conventions of writing published in most magazines or books. Note that they don't follow newspaper conventions, which are different from those of books.

DIALOGUE

Well, if we went to Raleigh we could get Mr. Isaacs Christmas candy. Before she could answer Mamas footsteps passed in the hall overhead so she said Don't you reckon we ought to stay closer-by than Raleigh? He turned to her. Look—are you sticking with me or not? She looked and said Yes. Let's go then. She scraped their dishes and left them in the sink and said I'll get my coat. Where from. My room. All right but come straight back

"Well, if we went to Raleigh, we could get Mr. Isaac's Christmas candy."

Before she could answer, Mama's footsteps passed in the hall overhead so she said, "Don't you reckon we ought to stay closer-by than Raleigh?"

He turned to her. "Look—are you sticking with me or not?"

She looked and said "Yes."

"Let's go then."

She scraped their dishes and left them in the sink and said, "I'll get my coat."

"Where from?"

"My room."

"All right, but come straight back."

REYNOLDS PRICE

SEMICOLONS, COMMAS, PERIODS, DASHES, COLONS

Learn these marks in this order if you want to master punctuation quickly. The semicolon has only four or five major uses, the comma dozens. If you know a semicolon is not called for, you can bet wisely that what you need is a comma.

UNPUNCTUATED	CONVENTIONALLY PUNCTUATED
1. Well I agree you could say the atom bomb doesn't go boom it just obliterates a few hundred thousand people.	Well, I agree. You could say the atom bomb doesn't go boom; it just obliterates a few hundred thousand people. (or): Well, I agree you could say the atom bomb doesn't go boom. It just obliterates a few hundred thousand people.
2. The world needs a little loosening of discipline and the schools need a little tightening of self-discipline.	The world needs a little loosening of discipline, and the schools need a little tightening of self-discipline.
3. He was no good for he had fallen apart at both the seams and the cuffs.	He was no good, for he had fallen apart at both the seams and the cuffs.
4. Renny a boy without guts was my enemy but Pedro a boy without guts was my friend.	Renny, a boy without guts, was my enemy; but Pedro, a boy without guts, was my friend.
5. I like Jackson Michigan Michigan City Indiana and Indianapolis Indiana.	I like Jackson, Michigan; Michigan City, Indiana; and Indianapolis, Indiana.
6. It was a large city however I walked its streets without fear.	It was a large city; however I walked its streets without fear. (or): It was a large city; however, I walked its streets without fear.
7. She was however a girl one could get along beautifully without.	She was, however, a girl one could get along beautifully without.
8. Those days when Grandpa was a boy are long gone now the snows are deep and my Jaguar won't start.	Those days when Grandpa was a boy are long gone; now the snows are deep and my Jaguar won't start.
9. In the last analysis Bertram doesn't measure up to the job.	In the last analysis, Bertram doesn't measure up to the job. (or): In the last analysis Bertram doesn't measure up to the job.

UNPUNCTUATED	CONVENTIONALLY PUNCTUATED
10. Although writers can lie about facts they should never lie about feelings.	Although writers can lie about facts, they should never lie about feelings.
11. When the moon comes over the woodshed behind the university library it feels out of place because Robert Frost is not there.	When the moon comes over the woodshed behind the university library, it feels out of place because Robert Frost is not there.

> *What a sight it is, to see Writers committed together by the eares, for* Ceremonies, Syllables, Points, Colons, Comma's, Hyphens, *and the like? fighting, as for their fires, and their Altars; and angry that none are frightened at their noyses, and loud brayings under their asses skins?*
>
> BEN JONSON

UNPUNCTUATED	CONVENTIONALLY PUNCTUATED
12. I liked working there in the city next to the subway with its rattle its earth jar its grimy dirt that settled in the whorls of the ear and transferred itself from my sweating neck to my white collar by nine each morning.	I liked working there in the city next to the subway with its rattle, its earth jar, its grimy dirt that settled in the whorls of the ear and transferred itself from my sweating neck to my white collar by nine each morning. (or): I like working there in the city next to the subway—with its rattle, its earth jar . . .
13. She is sweet notwithstanding her sour tongue and pretty as cottage cheese.	She is sweet, notwithstanding her sour tongue, and pretty as cottage cheese.
14. I always found Archie that sad bag of a man worth his weight in tin.	I always found Archie—that sad bag of a man—worth his weight in tin.
15. We walked across the square a place deserted by everyone but the familiar urchins who were dipping their feet in the fountain as if it were a cold day in February.	We walked across the square—a place deserted by everyone but the familiar urchins, who were dipping their feet in the fountain—as if it were a cold day in February.

UNPUNCTUATED	CONVENTIONALLY PUNCTUATED
16. She was a beautiful plump hen of a woman whose legs were properly pipe-stems ending with gigantic feet and I loved her clucking and pecking her squawking and fluttering.	She was a beautiful plump hen of a woman whose legs were properly pipe-stems ending with gigantic feet; and I loved her clucking and pecking, her squawking and fluttering.
17. The Alsatians were losing the Martian war quickly they had no missiles or orbiting vehicles.	The Alsatians were losing the Martian war quickly; they had no missiles or orbiting vehicles. (or): The Alsatians were losing the Martian war quickly: they had no missiles or orbiting vehicles.
18. The General Velocipedes car was a beauty stinking heater buckling back wheels and valves that needed regrinding after a turn around the block.	The General Velocipedes car was a beauty: stinking heater, buckling back wheels, and valves that needed regrinding after a turn around the block.

SIGNALS FOR EMPHASIS

Conventionally, book and magazine writers and editors emphasize words with italics and quotation marks. When they use a word as an example of a word rather than as a regular part of a sentence, they usually put it in italics, which are indicated in handwriting or typescript by a single underline. (A double underline indicates small capitals; triple underline, capitals.)

19. The use of and is more difficult than most beginning writers realize.	The use of *and* is more difficult than most beginning writers realize.
20. Phrases like in terms of and with respect to can kill off an otherwise good speech.	Phrases like "in terms of" and "with respect to" can kill off an otherwise good speech.

More often than not, the words *say, call, refer to as* are followed by quoted words.

21. Those are what Mr. Wick calls "critical elements."

Frightened by Mrs. Clutched, their old third-grade teacher, many beginning writers use quotation marks around any word that would seem unusual in the sterile air of Mrs. Clutched's classroom. They say:

> We had a "bunch" of good pitchers on our team and they used to "bug" each other constantly.

Nothing looks more square to an experienced editor or reader than this overuse of quotation marks. It implies either that the writer is a phony and won't admit that the words she's quoting belong in her vocabulary, or that the words *bunch* or *bug* are absolutely new to her readers in the use she has put them to. If they are slang, she should decide whether or not she wants to employ slang. If it's inappropriate to the subject and situation, she shouldn't use it. If it's customarily set in italics—and there you can see the principle behind italics and quotation marks: to help the reader when he needs help, to inform him of what he is not apt to see on his own when he is reading in a healthy state of perception—then she should use italics or quotation marks.

NUMERALS

Unless numerals are being used in an article or book constantly, the professional writer conventionally writes in words those numbers that can be written in two words or one, and all others in numerals. He never begins a sentence with a numeral; for without an opening capital letter, a sentence looks as if it is part of the preceding sentence.

> 22. We counted twenty-four eggs within one hundred feet but there were 142 in the whole area.

If a sentence requires a number like 136 (written in numerals because it cannot be written in two words) and several other numbers, they are all written in numerals, for the sake of consistency:

> 23. ALWAYS: Three thousand and eighty-four men were ready; they each had 136 ounces of food, 32 feet of rope, 2 cans of suppressed napalm, and 12 rounds of ammunition.
>
> NEVER: In the cages were rabbits in groups of 4, 3, and 6. 7 of them were kept in the barn in a larger enclosure, and 413 in all the buildings combined.

TITLES

Quotation marks are not used around words that appear above a piece of writing as its title. That would be like writing,

My name is "John."

Exception: When the title consists of, or in part of, words borrowed from another source, those borrowed words may be enclosed in quotation marks. Even then, if the borrowed word or phrase is well-known, it need not be quoted:

To Be or Not to Be a Ham

Writers citing names of other published works are careful to follow a consistent signaling system. Usually they *italicize* (or *underline*) names of whole works—a novel, history, encyclopedia, anthology, play, magazine, newspaper. They *put in quotation marks* smaller parts of those whole works: a chapter, article, poem, newspaper report (its title is its headline).

24. Jerry Kobrins Why Gleason Got the Headlines is another star-centered article in TV Guide but Up at Yale by Neil Hickey seriously looks at what college students are writing that could raise the level of television drama.

Jerry Kobrin's "Why Gleason Got the Headlines" is another star-centered article in *TV Guide,* but "Up at Yale" by Neil Hickey seriously looks at what college students are writing that could raise the level of television drama.

25. The Old which is the first chapter of Renfrew's latest book The Gnu and the Auld is a masterpiece of humor.

"The Old," which is the first chapter of Renfrew's latest book, *The Gnu and the Auld,* is a masterpiece of humor.

SIGNALING POSSESSION

The apostrophe to signal possession is the hardest conventional sign to remember because it is slowly fading away in use. In formal names printed in capital letters, it is no longer used:

VETERANS ADMINISTRATION

In the days before dictionaries began to establish conventions firmly (Dr. Samuel Johnson's *Dictionary* of 1755 solidified spelling and other writing conventions in England, and Noah Webster's *Dictionary* of 1828 did the same in America), writers often used the apostrophe to indicate plurals, as did Ben Jonson in 1640 in the line quoted in this chapter:

> . . . Points, Colons, Comma's

(Capital letters were conventionally used in England and America then for most major nouns in a sentence), and in Chaucer's day (1400), possession was signaled by an *-es* ending on words:

> As dide Demociones doghter deere . . .
> That lordes doughtres han in governaunce . . .

Chaucer used no apostrophes for possession, although here the daughters in both lines belong to the fathers mentioned. Writing about two hundred years later, Shakespeare commonly used an *-s* ending to signal possession, but still without an apostrophe:

> It was a Lordings daughter, the fairest one of three . . .
> A womans nay doth stand for nought . . .

Conventions in publishing change like conventions in ladies' dresses but not as fast. At the moment, most printed books and magazines in the United States are employing the apostrophe to signal possession, even though it is no more necessary in most instances than in Shakespeare's day.

26. I got my moneys worth when all the ladies cakes were left in my car.	I got my money's worth when all the ladies' cakes were left in my car.
27. A womans nay doth stand for nought.	A woman's nay doth stand for nought.
28. Jamess trouble was not the Worthingtons trouble.	James's trouble was not the Worthingtons' trouble.

SCHOLARLY WRITING

Two common miswritings in scholarly work are the abbreviation for *page* or *pages* and the signal for paragraph indention.

WRONG: pg (pgs)	RIGHT: p. (pp.)
WRONG: P	RIGHT: ¶

Pg. may be some lazy person's abbreviation for *pig,* but it isn't the conventional abbreviation for *page.* Understandably persons make the sign of a double-stemmed capital P to indicate *paragraph,* but the proper sign has nothing to do with the letter P. It is a sign used in illuminated manuscripts before 1440, then without such long stems, and still in use today.

Footnotes are a pain to writers, readers, editors, and printers; but some scholarly tasks require them so that scholar-readers may trace easily the steps through which a writer made his case. Like all conventions, footnotes are being constantly changed in form, usually in the direction of simplicity.

In footnotes, *Ibid.* means "the same as above." The following set of footnotes reveals a standard pattern. Why do some *Ibid.* entries include page numbers and some not?

[1] Fred M. Oliver, *Love Problems of High School* (New York, 1939), pp. 33–34.
[2] *Ibid.*
[3] *Ibid.*, p. 101.
[4] Karl Heimson, "The Courting Pattern," *New Ways in Education* (Englewood Cliffs, Texas, 1956), p. 555.
[5] Oliver, p. 101.
[6] Heimson, p. 420.
[7] *Ibid.*, pp. 419–425.
[8] William G. Looney and James Brass Smith, editors, *Thinking and Talking* (New York, 1965), p. 13.
[9] George Walker, "Sex," *The Teacher's Magazine,* vol. 14 (June 1967), pp. 13–14.

Text of paper employing above footnotes:

> Fred M. Oliver, psychologist at Nendy High School, Oak Pond, New York, cites the informal conversation of students. Jane, a senior, says "I'm mad for you, John," meaning in the new dialect of her group that she has decided to take John's part in his quarrel with his girl friend Susan.[1] This new game, played at several high schools in the area,[2] represents a clever playing with words—taking old slang or in-group expressions and giving them their literal rather than traditional meaning. "Cool it" to these students means to open the windows or turn down the thermostat.[3]
>
> Conventional students in a Kansas high school do just the opposite. They develop a new language for love and dating which consists of giving new double meanings to the commonest expressions, like "Wash the linoleum" or "Is it cold out?"[4]
>
> Oliver[5] and Heimson,[6] however, both state explicitly that they admire high school students' ability to invent new

> language. Heimson presents six pages of new expressions created by students in a high school of only one hundred students.[7] Thirteen out of the twenty-five articles in a recent anthology on language center on the speech of American teenagers.[8] Parallels with these American developments have been found in Hungary by George Walker.[9]

This passage is footnoted in conventional form, but it is ridiculously overfootnoted. The reader couldn't stand that many footnotes in that short a space. The writer of these paragraphs is so overwhelmed by his sources that he has lost command of his own expression and line of development. If you are required to use footnotes, reserve them for documenting ideas or facts either so unusual and controversial or so detailed that they need to be credited to a writer. Footnote what readers are likely to want to check further.

A list of books, which occurs at the end of a paper, an article, a chapter, or a book, usually contains fuller information about the books: the publisher, number of volumes in a set, etc. In footnotes, names of authors are arranged in normal order: first name first. In a bibliography, they are arranged last name first, so that the order of the books in the list will be useful, easy to consult because arranged by author's last names alphabetically:

BIBLIOGRAPHY

1. Heimson, Karl. "The Courting Pattern," *New Ways in Education* (Englewood Cliffs, Texas: Pinetree Press, 1956), 158 pp.

The "158 pp." indicates that the volume contains 158 numbered pages, a way to show the reader how extensive the book is.

2. Looney, William G. and James Brass Smith, editors. *Thinking and Talking* (New York: Mouth Press, 1965), 450 pp.

3. Oliver, Fred M. *Love Patterns of High School* (New York: Kissinger Co., 1939), 413 pp.

In short papers, documenting notes make more sense at the end of the paper than as footnotes at the foot of each page. Footnotes are hard to type at the bottom of the page—the writer can't gauge how much room she needs. And they're hard to set in type—the printer can't gauge the room either, and he must shift to smaller type as well. An intelligent alternative to footnotes used frequently in scientific publications employs parenthetical references: (2: 33–34), which means that the book referred to is number 2 in the bibliography and the references are to pages 33 and 34 in it. Part of the above text would then be written this way, referring to the piece of bibliography given above, which would be printed at the end of the paper or article. The paper would contain no footnotes:

> This new game, played at several high schools in the area (2: 33–34), represents a clever playing with words—taking old slang or in-group expressions and giving them their literal rather than traditional meaning . "Cool it" to these students means to open the window or turn down the thermostat (3: 101).

Wise writers and editors adopt a pattern of documentation of sources that fits the purposes of the writers and, as much as possible, of readers. If the place of publication and publisher are not apt to be significant to readers, they are omitted from footnotes and supplied only in a bibliography. Almost always page references and dates of publication are given because they are useful to readers in locating material and assessing the up-to-dateness of assertions and facts. All conventions need the help of common sense: the man who speaks outside in February with his head bare in order to observe a convention may find others soon observing his funeral.

Here are a few more models of conventional footnotes: For a book:

[1] George M. George. *The Georgeness of the World* (New York, George Book Company, 1918), pp. 33–34.

For a magazine:

[2] Margaret Mead, "Trends in Personal Life," *The New Republic* (September 23, 1946), 115: 348.

For a newspaper article:

[3] "College Dating Changes Pattern," *The New York Recorder,* June 2, 1952, p. 13.
[4] George Kriver, "Bronx Hospital Planned," *The Bronx Bomber,* June 3, 1967, p. 1.

For a government document:

[5] *Dating Problems in Urban High Schools,* United States Health Service Publication 1090 (Washington, 1953), p. 7.

For an encyclopedia:

[6] "Harvard University," *The Encyclopaedia Britannica,* 14th edition.

For an excerpt from a book not read in the original but seen reproduced in part in another book:

[7] Francis E. Merrill, *Courtship and Marriage* (New York, 1949), in Edwin R. Clapp and others, eds., *The College Quad* (New York, 1951), p. 74.

For a personal interview or conversation arranged by the author:

[8] Interview with John Rogers, Dean of Men, Northside High School, Chicago, Illinois, April 4, 1967.

BORROWING WORDS

Conventionally, professional writers command their words and those of others, but they never imply they own the words of others. They insert borrowed words naturally into their sentences.

Wasting Borrowed Words:	*Commanding Borrowed Words:*
His dearest relative described him as "He was a great guy, full of fun, but gentle."	His dearest relative described him as "a great guy, full of fun, but gentle."

Professional writers don't refer to statements they are quoting as *quotes,* for they are doing the quoting, not the authors. They call the statement a *statement,* an *assertion,* or an *argument,* etc. They remember that quotes don't speak, only persons.

For example, one quote states: "The Undersecretary rejected the budget proposals of the whole Council."	For example, an unidentified London *Times* reporter states that "The Undersecretary rejected the budget proposals of the whole Council."

Professional writers remember that in conversation they say "I quote" but in writing they indicate this act by quotation marks.

War Magazine says, and I quote, "Wretches strew the beaches in a lovely pattern."	*War Magazine* says, "Wretches strew the beaches in a lovely pattern."

If you respect your writing, learn the craft and learn the conventional systems of signaling meaning to the reader. But don't use these signals as a substitute for the order and clarity you must achieve with words. If you want the reader to become excited, you must write excitingly. You cannot force excitement by putting three exclamation marks at the end of your sentence!!! Three or four exclamation marks in a row are conventional in a comic strip, but comical elsewhere.

suggestions to teachers

Since I put together the first edition of this book in 1968, a great stirring has occurred in the field of teaching writing. Now it's possible to become an English teacher and do something different from marking errors in red ink and writing "awk" and "gr" in the margins—and still be considered respectable. The change has come about because teachers began to look closely at what they and their students were doing. They saw that most "composition" courses were artificial: they had little to do with the way people really produce good writing.

Anyone in this field today should be acquainted with the work of at least four of the major forces that have helped support teachers bringing about these changes:

1. The work of James Britton, Nancy Martin and many knowledgeable colleagues since the late '40s in the London Association for the Teaching of English, the University of London Institute of Education, and the Schools Council.

2. The more than a hundred sites of the National Writing Project around the country that grew out of the first summer program in 1974 of the Bay Area Writing Project at the University of California at Berkeley, headed by James Gray, Mary K. Healy, Miles Myers, and Keith Caldwell.

3. The Program in Teaching Writing for Rural and Small-Town teachers at Bread Loaf School of English, coordinated by Dixie Goswami, that has brought together on the same campus such writers and researchers as James Britton, Nancy Martin, Don Graves, Peter Elbow, Janet Emig, Shirley Brice Heath, Lee Odell, and James Moffett.

4. The books, including reprints of the work of British leaders, issued by Boynton/Cook Publishers, which since its inception has been the publisher for many of the teachers in this reform movement in research and teaching.

Without formally connecting themselves, these four centers of enlightenment have shared their discoveries, and many of the discoverers have become friends and co-workers. I call their informal, unorganized effort The Movement for Meaning.

• • •

I'd like to mention several helps for teaching I've stumbled on in the last ten years or so, or learned from colleagues in the Movement for Meaning.

—A great positive effect occurs when the directors or teachers of a writing group write in class alongside the others. I won't spell out arguments in favor of the practice. If you don't do it, try it. You'll see that it not only changes your view of writing, but your view of students—whoever they may be—and their view of you. It will improve your writing and responding in the Helping Circle as well as theirs.

—Over the years since 1968, other teacher friends and I (Peter Elbow and Donald Graves come to mind) have found to our surprise that often free, or timed, writing done in class by our students and ourselves has been better than that which we did outside class, when presumably we were working in more propitious circumstances, alone, with less chance of being interrupted. Writing is a performing art, as Dick Adler, the director of the Montana Writing Project, has said, and a group of people committed to writing more truthfully than usual often gain concentration, rather than lose it, as they sit together writing, hearing nothing but the sound of pens and pencils moving across a page. Exactly why this is so we don't know for sure. Possibly it's a supportive, encouraging feeling we get from sensing that others in the room are taking seriously a commitment to some kind of truth (factual or fantastic) alongside us. Possibly the sound that makes up that ceremony of meaning puts us into a kind of trance which allows us to tap our experience and feelings more fully than usual. We know that a concentration upon deep breathing can put people into that state of conscious/unconsciousness we all frequently experience when we are passing into or out of sleep—a twilight stage where our brain waves slow down and we're able to remember things more vividly and to put together ideas and experience in a rush of connections.

I'm not saying you should become self-conscious about trying to bring about such a state in free writing sessions in class, but merely that if you and your students experience such productivity sitting writing in a circle, you shouldn't be surprised.

—As I said in the Introduction, the practice of the teacher and students *reading aloud* the writing of professionals, their peers, and themselves charges up the activity of writing in ways we never dreamed of. But only if they read aloud *well*—that is, after rehearsing the writing first by a read-aloud that concentrates on meaning and takes advantage of the ability of human voices to register meaning with intonation, rhythm, emphasis, etc.

—In high school, where peer approval is so important to young people, many are unwilling to point out writing weaknesses, or even to state their reaction diplomatically by saying, "I liked the piece a great deal, but I think it could be improved here at this place. . . ." Criticism of peers in large groups is hard for any of us to engage in, unless we're especially down on ourselves and therefore anxious to attack others perversely. Strangely, but maybe not so strangely, students are often not reluctant to be frank about the weaknesses in a teacher's writing that is being read to a group.

—In directing writing seminars with people of all ages, I've found that the involuntary responses of people listening to a piece of writing read aloud to a group are often more trustworthy than their carefully phrased verbal comments. I'm talking about *involuntary* responses—grunts, oohs, aahs, laughter, changes in body posture, and such. The responder can't fake them in order to be nice to the writer. They just occur. What some of us have learned to do in the Helping Circle is to arrange for a meaningful reading of a paper while the author sits and observes the involuntary responses of the group. Even in break-out groups of three, four, or five, this practice has proved valuable. There may be a dozen different kinds of laughter that signify discrete things about the writing that is being read aloud. One tells the author that the listener is thinking, "Oh yeah, I know that's true! I've had an experience or feeling just like it." Another kind of laugh registers an engagement with a developing humorous point, and then breaks into another kind of laugh as that suspected point is validated. Still another is what I call the "har-har" response. It says that the listeners are too familiar with the experience or the point and are signifying that they find it stereotyped. Often this laugh occurs when an author has bragged about getting drunk or being sophisticated about performance with the other sex.

In the way of involuntary responses, the greatest compliment from the audience is the gasp or murmur that follows the laugh of recognition, and signifies that the author has taken the listeners into and beyond their former understanding of human experience.

• • •

Many teachers in the English-speaking world recently have broken loose and found a way of enabling students to write alive. By hit and miss they have constructed a whole enabling process. But what may work for them and their students may not be congenial to others.

Here's the process I've patched together. I don't say it is *the way,* but it has been tested. Every element in it contributes to three essentials:

—raising the level of truthtelling in a class

—inducing students in the first week to forget their English-teacher-inspired fears, and find authentic voices in writing

—creating a seminar in which students help each other learn the disciplines of the writing craft—partly unconsciously, as they constantly hear their writing and that of others read aloud and see it responded to.

These are notable accomplishments. I don't bring them about for every student, but usually for a majority of people in every class.

The following steps create a climate than encourages truthtelling and, in turn, live sentences:

1. I read aloud an example of *Engfish,* the stilted, word-wasting language of the schools. I point out its weaknesses, and read aloud a truthtelling student paper that speaks with authentic voice. In that first meeting, I point out some of the fine work done by students in past semesters of that class. It is posted on the walls of the room. I say, "This is the kind of writing that you will do." I don't say, "You might just possibly be able to do something as good as those papers on the wall there." The high expectation is part of the course, stated matter-of-factly.

2. I tell students: "No one speaks truth always. We all lie, consciously and unconsciously. I ask you to try for truths. I'm going to try for them in what I say and write here. You'll be astonished by the difference made by a constant effort to raise the level of truth in this room. In this class you will not try to sound like *a writer.* You will tell truths and be a writer."

NOTE: Every line in this litany is designed to help students feel like telling truths. To risk truths in front of the group, to write for every person in the room, not just for the teacher. In this program a steady effort to *protect feeling.*

3. I begin by asking for free, or timed, writing in class on the first day. I do that writing myself with the students. Before we begin, I read an example from a past class of strong free writing that has a core, and firm flesh, and is rounded. I no longer, as I once did, say, "Just write. If you can't think of anything to say, write, 'I can't think of anything to say.' " The models I give them are everything. Students will rise to their level.

At the next meeting, I have the best papers or passages read aloud to the group, after readers have practiced reading them aloud first in order to be sure of their meaning. If the class is large, I ask for two or three writings to be read to the whole group, and the rest to smaller, break-out groups. If it's small, the writings are read aloud to the whole class. I try to find at least a few sentences by everyone that are strong enough to elicit approval or praise.

4. For the first few meetings I prohibit negative comments on the writings. If listeners don't like writings, they are to say nothing. That's not lying, simply refraining from comment.

5. On opening day, I face the effects of grades upon truthtelling and upon performance in general. If the first grade is high, a student may not try to improve. If it's low, a student may sink into discouragement and never write honestly again. One expedient is to ask students to store their returned writing in a folder or envelope, and at the end of a grading period, or preferably at the end of the course, to present their best writings for a grade. Those having the greatest number of writings that have scored with students and the teacher in response sessions will receive the highest grades. But no grades early on unless students ask to know how they're doing. Then I look over the folder and grade it as of that moment. A request for such early grading is seldom made, because constant evaluation of everyone's writing has been occurring in the response sessions. Most students quickly find out how they're doing.

6. I ditto or xerox the best writings and pass them out to all members of the class before having them read aloud. I announce that those students who want a class response on a paper I've not chosen for distribution will be given that right.

Reproduction of papers is a burden, whether I retype them myself or ask students to write or type their best work on ditto masters. However the job is done, it's costly in time and money, but essential to the learning process. Funds for doing it should be provided in this laboratory just as they are provided for materials and equipment in the science lab. It's economical to type material for reproduction in two columns, single-spaced on a page. Saves 50 percent on paper.

7. Because comments on paper are made in class where they count, and can be judged by the writers as they compete for attention and belief, I don't need to waste time writing in their margins while reading them. Many studies have shown that written marginal comments have little effect. Late in the course I might write a note to a student I think is ripe for a certain suggestion.

8. After a paper has been read aloud, I ask the group, "Well, how does that strike you?" At that point my experience is to encounter silence. It seems to grow and spread through the room as I become more nervous, fearing the writer will take the silence as negative criticism. The students sit, eyes down, tongueless. For nine years I failed to real-

ize why the eyes were down. The students are on the spot. They're quickly reviewing the writing that's just been read, trying to sort out the reasons for their feelings. Sometimes unsure of their response, they're reading the work again to locate it.

I used to sit there thinking, "Come on, you dumb people. Are you incapable of responding to human experience recorded truthfully?" For nine years I forgot that *I* read the papers on initially receiving them, often type them on a ditto master, and then hear them read again in class. So the students are encountering the paper for the first time and I for the second or third. I have made my sortings, enjoyed the opportunity for revisions of judgment, and grown familiar with details.

Now I tell students that their reluctance to speak is intelligent and remind them of what they're doing during that silence. After a few moments for heads down—"Did anyone like anything in the paper?" If a number of positive responses are given, then later, "Now any suggestions for improvement?" Sometimes lively discussion erupts, sometimes continued reluctance; sometimes praise and help; occasionally confusion and pain.

The heads-down period is necessary: time to review first reactions, to collect thoughts and examples, to ponder a response that will be focused rather than fatuous, helpful rather than damaging.

9. I always ask students to comment on a piece of writing before I do. Teacher's comments later, or last, or never. Otherwise students step back into traditional school where the game is to find out what Teacher thinks and go along with it. Hour after hour, year after year, students have played that game. Even in this program they will revert to it unless the basepaths are obliterated.

10. I try to build the students' confidence and move the class forward on it. At first I reproduce good writing so students can advance from success to success. As the course proceeds with assignments, some students don't score. I ask them to do more free writing than the others are doing—outside class.

After they have received praise from the group, writers are usually strong enough to listen to others tell them that a subsequent work is weak in large ways.

11. When I give regular assignments (for example, "Tell an incident in your childhood that struck you hard"), I add that persons who find the assignment wrong for them at the moment can come to me and say they're writing on another topic of their choosing. I want to help people become powerful writers, not make them jump through identical hoops.

12. Sometimes I bring in a piece of my writing that has not been done for the class, in order to get help on it.

13. By subtle and direct means I let the class know I'm not asking for True Confessions. Truthtelling here doesn't imply, "I'm baring my soul, and I must tell you that once I—" This book demonstrates the power of telling facts, of objectifying experience so a reader can live it vicariously and a writer can re-experience it. Thus—objectivity, which is seldom the mark of True Confessions writing. This class is not designed to be therapeutic, but to produce strong writing. If it has a therapeutic effect, fine; but no psychiatrist works in this room.

14. If I sense a paper will be embarrassing or injurious when read aloud, I withhold the identity of the writer. Sometimes I ask writers about the wisdom of publishing their work to the class or outsiders. I'm reminded of a girl I'll call Mary in a college Shakespeare class who said she was afraid to write journal entries. Her sixth-grade teacher had once asked students to write honestly whatever came to their minds. "I won't reveal writers' names." Mary wrote of her attraction to a boy who sat two rows behind her. The next day the teacher identified her paper by name, read it aloud as an example of poor sentence structure, and chastised Mary before the class for "sloppiness." That was the end of Mary telling truths that counted for her in school.

Traditional school is the last place an outside observer should expect to encounter students speaking or writing truths that count for them. Unwittingly it's designed to nurture copycatting and phoniness. The Test-Grade System requires students to read a book or listen to teachers talk and give them back exactly what was said. The outcomes of doing exercises in the drillbook are expected to be exactly alike for every student. If instructors say, "Tell the truth," it is their truths they usually expect to hear; and if they receive a disappointing or offending truth, they're apt to say, "Sorry, but I'll have to give you a D for that."

What brings about truthtelling is a feeling that one is free to tell it, and that this act will occur in a group of seven or more persons (the response of a smaller number can be too easily dismissed as friendly or prejudiced) who are trying to respond honestly. And that the one expert—the teacher—will not be the sole responder and judge.

What brings about live voices in writing—the sound of individual human beings drawing upon all their powers—is a release through free writing at the beginning of a course and then a growing self-discipline in trying for truths.

In dozens of ways this program forces students to care for their writing. They have a real audience. They will become audience themselves. This double position is a responsible one.

15. If the class numbers more than twenty, I frequently break it

into smaller groups for reading of papers aloud. Students must perceive that the responses of their classmates carry weight. But I keep the whole group as the central testing ground, where I comment along with the students, where I can speak to the whole class for ten or fifteen minutes when I feel, like a teacher, that I have something for all of them. But I seldom sit in on the small groups solely as a listener. If I've done the same writing they have, I feel comfortable sitting in because my writing will be read also and will earn me the right to be there.

16. I promise publication of the best writing. The dittoed or xeroxed two-column handout is itself a kind of publication. My students have frequently said, "When I saw my paper *printed* [it was actually only dittoed or xeroxed] in the handout, I could spot faults immediately." I thumbtack good writing on bulletin boards in the halls. I try to find resources for publishing a magazine or handout to be distributed beyond the classroom. As writers, the wider our readership, the more we feel pressure and desire to tell truths that count.

Those sixteen points make up the core of a writing program. Not all teachers will find them essential. I caution readers against taking this book blindly, chapter by chapter, assignment by assignment. It provides more activities than most students can satisfactorily carry out in a semester or a year if, like professional writers, they are revising, rewriting, and abandoning some pieces. I wrote the book expansively, so that teachers could select those parts that will constitute a program fulfilling and comfortable for them.

All kinds of writing are presented here, not to furnish a hodgepodge, but from an inner necessity. All good writing—no matter what its type or form—has much in common with all other good writing. A precise statement of the parts of a vacuum cleaner and how to use it is more like Shakespeare's *Macbeth* than it is like a vague and lifeless description of a vacuum cleaner. Beginning writers would be mad to isolate a type of writing, like exposition, and concentrate on it as if the strategies of drama and story have nothing to do with their task. But that's what they're asked to do in many composition courses.

Instead of being required to follow all of the assignments in this book, students may be asked simply to write *in their own lives,* as they have real needs. A letter to a prospective employer—not the standard lifeless type but one that has powers that arise from experience. A biographical sketch required with an application to college or music camp. A journal of a student's plague year. The minutes of a meeting—this time human, not dehydrated, and terse as well as accurate. A letter to Father, who is in Europe on a sales tour, asking for help in buying a new motorcycle—but not in an imagined situation, only if the writer is thirsting for oil and gas and the opening road. Chapter 15, "Your Subject Choosing You," shows how students' experience can act as self-assignments that produce papers which eventually touch national issues. The suggestions given there for topics could take students through most of a semester.

In this approach to writing, instead of seeing their errors paraded before them and the class, students are forced to look at their best work and go on from there—frequently from success to success. Like professionals, they are thinking of producing a number of strong writings, not simply of periodically supplying a teacher with a paper to be graded. They write more than is presented to the group. They put aside writings that didn't go well after several tries. They take a short paragraph with good bones and put flesh on it. They add and cut drastically. They sharpen and polish.

They're advised to do these things by their classmates, the teacher, and the textbook. They feel the pressure of possible publication. Some teachers using this book have begun exchanging a group of student papers with a similar class in another part of the city or nation, and then exchanging student responses to the writings. A way toward more objective evaluation.

This program combines freedom and rigor. Students begin to learn the discipline of the craft, to control techniques and strategies. That's a creative discipline, in which there's a need to shape one's materials to an end that may surprise the writer—the very opposite of the need imposed by the major discipline of conventional school, supplying the expected answers in a test.

The most remarkable discovery of this approach has been that in free, or timed, writing persons who think they have no skills frequently find themselves exploiting major strategies of writing: alliteration, metaphor, rhythm, parallel structure, telling details, a building of suspense, words speaking to other words within the writing, dialogue, powerful endings. And before they have been instructed in them.

This book touches on punctuation and paragraphing and footnoting in a new way. Good writers utilize all the powers available to them. Some come free, and easy; others require study and discipline. This book furnishes training in both, but by its arrangement suggests that there is no use hammering away at mechanics before writers have moved real audiences with what they have to say.

Traditionally, without meaning to, school became a place where you and I were handed things—usually statements or combinations of numbers belonging to the experts or "authorities." We were to hand them back to teacher in the form of answers to tests or papers (usually collages of excerpted statements by authorities, or summaries of what they had said). That was learning. Teaching was asking people to do that.

This handing back and forth of the ideas and experience belonging to school left no room for students' experience, which must enter the transaction somewhere or there can be no relevance in learning. I have put the words *you* and *school* together—*Youschool*—to indicate that one should carry as much weight as the other. School shouldn't make you feel small. Ideally it involves the accumulated experience and wisdom of many you's, but it should exist for you, not you for it.

By *Youschool* I mean to specify not a place or method, but a relationship, in which the students' experience counts as much as the experience of the authorities, or "school." It's a relationship in which these two experiences are brought up against each other, and their strengths and weaknesses compared, so their knowings, feelings, and insights speak to each other.

Traditionally school has said to students, "This work is preparing you for college, or graduate school, or life." In fact it's often preparing them to say things that don't count for them, things they don't feel attached to. There's no life in that classroom, simply preparation; and so the student work counts solely for the teacher, and then only as something that can be graded.

Youschool turns all that around, but not easily, and not for everyone. In the past my writings have implied to some readers that a reform in education is simple to bring about. Nothing in this textbook is intended to oversimplify the difficulty of human beings working together. My book *A Vulnerable Teacher* documents how agonizing as well as joyful I've found the experience of trying to bring about *Youschool* for every one of my students.

list of sources

Page

9 Robert Morley, on the Jack Paar Show NBC–TV, February 12, 1965.

9 Quoted in Clara M. Siggins, "Then It Got Buggles," *College Composition and Communication* (February, 1962), p. 56.

12 Friedrich Nietzsche, *Beyond Good and Evil* (Chicago, Regnery, Gateway Edition, 1955), p. 77.

14 John Donne, "Satire III," *Poetry of the English Renaissance* (New York, F.S. Crofts, 1929), p. 482.

14 Eudora Welty, *Delta Wedding* (New York, New American Library, Signet Edition, 1963), p. 220.

14 Eudora Welty, quoted by Reynolds Price, "A Kind of Valedictory," *The Archive*, Duke University (April 1955), p. 2.

15 Peter Ernani, "What I'd Like to Be," *Portola Portals* (n.d.) submitted by Mrs. Nancy Wakefield.

17 Samuel Butler, Works (London, Jonathan Cape, 1923–26), XVIII, 210.

21 Wallace Stevens, "Adagia," *Opus Posthumous* (New York, Alfred A. Knopf, 1957), p. 158.

22 Alfred North Whitehead, quoted in *The Practical Cogitator,* edited by Charles P. Curtis, Jr., and Ferris Greenslet (Boston, Houghton Mifflin, 1953), p. 40.

23 E. M. Forster, *Aspects of the Novel* (New York, Harcourt, Brace, 1927), p. 197.

24 Henry Moore, "The Painter's Object," *The Creative Process,* edited by Brewster Ghiselin (New York, New American Library, Mentor Edition, 1955), p. 77.

25 Alfred Kazin, "The Language of Pundits," *Atlantic Monthly* (July, 1961), pp. 73–74.

26 Wallace Stevens, "Adagia," *Opus Posthumous* (New York, Alfred A. Knopf, 1957), p. 162.

28 Anne Haven Morgan, *The Field Book of Ponds and Streams* (New York, G.P. Putnam's Sons, 1930), p. 199.

29 John Ciardi, "Work Habits of Writers," *On Writing, by Writers,* edited by William W. West (Boston, Ginn, 1966), p. 153.

30 Irma S. Rombauer and Marion Rombauer Becker, *The Joy of Cooking* (Indianapolis, Bobbs-Merrill, 1953), p. 451.
30 Joyce Macrorie, Trip Directions.
31 *Draftee's Confidential Guide* (1966), pp. 9, 34–35.
33 Sidney Cox, *Indirections* (New York, Viking, Compass Books, 1962), p. 130.
34 William Hazlitt, "On the Familiar Style," *The Hazlitt Sampler* (New York, Fawcett World Library, 1961), p. 228.
34 Benjamin Franklin, quoted in Carl Becker, *The Declaration of Independence* (New York, Alfred A. Knopf, Vintage Books, 1953), pp. 208–209.
36 Wallace Stevens, "Adagia," *Opus Posthumous* (New York, Alfred A. Knopf, 1957), p. 169.
40 Samuel Butler, *The Note-Books* (London, Jonathan Cape, 1926), p. 97.
41 Sir William Osler, "Teacher and Student," *Aequanimitas* (New York, Blakiston, 1932), p. 38.
44 Ray Bradbury, "Seeds of Three Stories," *On Writing, by Writers,* edited by William W. West (Boston, Ginn, 1966), p. 48.
46 John Ciardi, "Manner of Speaking," *Saturday Review* (July 2, 1966), p. 6.
49 Eileen Crimmin, "Bernie Little and His Little Four-Seater," *Hot Boat* (Spring, 1966), p. 31.
52 Sidney Cox, *Indirections* (New York, Viking, 1962), p. 131.
55 Frank O'Connor interviewed by Anthony Whittier, *Writers at Work: The Paris Review Interviews,* First Series (New York, Viking, 1959), p. 169.
60 Henry David Thoreau, *Walden and Other Writings* (New York, The Modern Library, 1937), p. 86.
62 Bernard Shaw, *John Bull's Other Island* (New York, Harper & Brothers, 1942), p. 209.
62 Jack London, *People of the Abyss* (New York, Harcourt, Brace, 1946), p. 213.
63 Ralph Waldo Emerson, "Thoreau," *Lectures and Biographies* (Boston, Houghton Mifflin, 1893), p. 362.
67 Henry David Thoreau, *Walden and Other Writings* (New York, The Modern Library, 1937), p. 88.
67 Thomas Henry Huxley, To Charles Kingsley, September 23, 1860, in Leonard Huxley, *Life and Letters of Huxley* (New York, D. Appleton, 1901), I, 235.
68 Michihiko Hachiya, *Hiroshima Diary* (Chapel Hill, University of North Carolina Press, 1955), pp. 11, 91–92.
71 Wallace Stevens, "Adagia," *Opus Posthumous* (New York, Alfred A. Knopf, 1957), p. 179.
74 Stuart Chase, "Writing Nonfiction," *On Writing, by Writers,* edited by William W. West (Boston, Ginn, 1966), p. 327.
77 Dr. Seuss, *Horton Hatches the Egg* (New York, Random House, 1940), n.p.
77 Thomas Paine, "The American Crisis," *The Complete Writings,* edited by Philip S. Foner (New York, The Citadel Press, 1945), p. 55.
77 William Shakespeare, *Macbeth* (New York, New American Library, 1963), IV, iii., p. 105.

80 Lilian Moore, *A Pickle for a Nickle* (New York, The Golden Press, 1961), p. 22.

82 Longchamps advertisement, *New York Times,* May 25, 1966, p. 29.

83 Ralph Waldo Emerson, "The American Scholar," *The Complete Essays and Other Writings,* edited by Brooks Atkinson (New York, The Modern Library, 1950), p. 47.

83 James Baldwin, *The Fire Next Time* (New York, Dell, 1964), pp. 14–15.

83 N. H. and S. K. Mager, editors, *The Pocket Household Encyclopedia* (New York, Pocket Books, 1953), p. 168.

83 Irma S. Rombauer and Marion Rombauer Becker, *The Joy of Cooking* (Indianapolis, Bobbs-Merrill, 1953), p. 313.

84 Samuel Butler, *The Note-Books* (London, Jonathan Cape, 1926), p. 106.

85 Samuel Butler, *The Note-Books* (London, Jonathan Cape, 1926), p. 106.

88 T. S. Eliot interviewed by Donald Hall, *Writers at Work: The Paris Review Interviews,* Second Series (New York, Viking, 1965), p. 96.

91 Marianne Moore interviewed by Donald Hall, *Ibid.*, p. 82.

95 William Wordsworth, "The Prelude," *Complete Poetical Works* (Boston, Houghton Mifflin, 1904), p. 156.

95 Mark Twain, *Huckleberry Finn* (Boston, Houghton Mifflin, 1958), p. 42.

96 J. D. Salinger, *The Catcher in the Rye* (New York, New American Library, 1953), p. 144.

96 May Swenson, *To Mix with Time* (New York, Charles Scribner's Sons, 1963), pp. 86–87.

99 Sidney Cox, *Indirections* (New York, Viking, 1962), p. 6.

105 Truman Capote interviewed by Pati Hill, *Writers at Work: The Paris Review Interviews,* First Series (New York, Viking, 1964), pp. 294–295, 296–297.

106 Anton Chekhov, "My Life," and "In the Ravine," *Ward Six and Other Stories* (New York, New American Library, Signet Books, 1965), pp. 219, 339.

106 Reynolds Price, "The Warrior Princess Ozimba," in "A Story and Why," *Duke Alumni Register* (April, 1963), p. 33.

109 Bernard Shaw, in *Ellen Terry and Bernard Shaw: A Correspondence,* edited by Christopher St John (New York, The Fountain Press, 1931), pp. 113–114.

117 Ralph Waldo Emerson, "Self-Reliance," *The Complete Essays and Other Writings,* edited by Brooks Atkinson (New York, The Modern Library, 1950), p. 165.

119 Kenneth Clark, "The Value of Art in an Expanding World," *Hudson Review* (Spring, 1966), p. 23.

119 Samuel Butler, quoted in Henry Festing Jones, *Samuel Butler* (London, Macmillan, 1920), II, 294–295.

120 Ezra Pound, *ABC of Reading* (New York, New Directions, 1960), p. 62.

123 James Thurber interviewed by George Plimpton and Max Steele, *Writers at Work: The Paris Review Interviews* (New York, Viking, 1959), p. 87.

123 Eudora Welty, "Must the Novelist Crusade?" *Atlantic Monthly* (October, 1965), p. 106.

126 Wallace Stevens, "Adagia," *Opus Posthumous* (New York, Alfred A. Knopf, 1957), p. 170.
127 W. Nelson Francis, "Pressure from Below," *College Composition and Communication* (October, 1964), pp. 147–148.
129 Henry David Thoreau, *Walden and Other Writings* (New York, The Modern Library, 1937), p. 288.
129 William Hazlitt, *The Spirit of the Age* (London, Oxford University Press, 1935), p. 13.
130 Anne Haven Morgan, *The Field Book of Ponds and Streams* (New York, G.P. Putnam's Sons, 1930), p. 388.
130 Sharon Butler, in "The Bicycle Spoke," *The Western Review,* Western Michigan University (January 24, 1966), p. 2.
131 E. E. Cummings, "XIV," *Poems, 1923–1954* (New York, Harcourt, Brace and World, 1954), p. 397.
131 Joseph Conrad, preface to *The Nigger of the "Narcissus"* in *Three Great Tales* (New York, Alfred A. Knopf, Vintage Books, n.d.), p. ix.
132 Lewis Carroll, *Through the Looking Glass* (New York, Random House, 1946), pp. 92–93.
133 *Ibid.,* p. 18.
133 Samuel Butler, *The Way of All Flesh* (New York, The Modern Library, 1950), p. 200.
134 Lewis Carroll, *Through the Looking Glass* (New York, Random House, 1946), pp. 64–65.
135 Ring Lardner, source unknown.
135 Henry Vaughan, "The World," *Poetry of the English Renaissance,* 1509–1660, edited by J. William Hebel and Hoyt H. Hudson (New York, F.S. Crofts, 1938), p. 799.
135 William Shakespeare, *Macbeth,* edited by Maynard Mack and Robert W. Boynton (Rochelle Park, New Jersey, Hayden Book Co., Inc., 1973), V, ii.
135 Reynolds Price, *A Long and Happy Life* (New York, Avon Books, 1963), p. 120.
136 William Shakespeare, *Henry IV, Part I,* edited by Maynard Mack and Robert W. Boynton (Rochelle Park, New Jersey, Hayden Book Co., Inc., 1973), II, ii.
137 *Ibid.,* I, ii.
138 Henry David Thoreau, *Walden and Other Writings* (New York, The Modern Library, 1937), p. 123.
139 Lewis Carroll, *Through the Looking Glass* (New York, Random House, 1946), p. 29.
140 Samuel Butler, *The Note-Books* (London, Jonathan Cape, 1926), p. 102.
155 *The Heart of Emerson's Journals,* edited by Bliss Perry (Boston, Houghton Mifflin, 1926), p. 333.
156 Henry David Thoreau, *Journals* (Boston, Houghton Mifflin, 1906), IX, 158–160.
157 Samuel Butler, *The Note-Books* (London, Jonathan Cape, 1926), p. 97.
158 Dorothy Lambert, "What Is A Journal?" see p. v.

161 Samuel Butler, *The Note-Books* (London, Jonathan Cape, 1926), pp. 231–232.

165 *Benjamin Franklin,* edited by Chester E. Jorgenson and Frank Luther Mott (New York, Hill and Wang, 1962), p. 14.

165 Henry David Thoreau, *A Week on the Concord and Merrimack Rivers,* edited by Walter Harding (New York, Holt, Rinehart and Winston, 1963), p. 106.

165 Henry David Thoreau, "Walking," *Walden and Other Writings* (New York, The Modern Library, 1937), p. 622.

168 Ben Jonson, *Timber, or Discoveries,* in *English Prose, 1600–1660,* edited by Victor Harris and Itrat Husain (New York, Holt, Rinehart and Winston, 1965), p. 330.

168 Anatole Broyard, "The Obstetrics of the Soul" in *The New York Times* (Jan uary 25, 1973).

178 A. A. Milne, *The House at Pooh Corner* (New York, E. P. Dutton, 1928), p. 96.

181 Lewis Carroll, *Alice in Wonderland* (New York, Random House, 1946), pp. 140–141.

185 Sidney Cox, *Indirections* (New York, Viking, 1962), p. 132.

187 Oscar Wilde, *A Woman of No Importance,* quoted in *The Wit and Humor of Oscar Wilde,* edited by Alvin Redman (New York, Dover, 1952), p. 33.

188 James Agee, *A Death in the Family* (New York, McDowell Obolensky, 1957), p. 3.

189 Karl Shapiro and Robert Beum, *A Prosody Handbook* (New York, Harper & Row, 1965), pp. 14–15.

190 John Donne, "Devotion No. 17," *English Prose, 1600–1660,* edited by Victor Harris and Itrat Husain (New York, Holt, Rinehart and Winston, 1965), p. 274.

191 Ralph Waldo Emerson, "Self-Reliance," *The Complete Essays and Other Writings,* edited by Brooks Atkinson (New York, The Modern Library, 1950), p. 165.

194 Mark Twain, *Huckleberry Finn* (New York, Houghton Mifflin, 1958), p. 4.

195 Sidney Cox, *Indirections* (New York, Viking, 1962), p. 31.

197 Gerhart Wiebe, "Mass Communications," in Eugene and Ruth Hartley, *Fundamentals of Social Psychology* (New York, Alfred A. Knopf, 1952), p. 179.

197 Ernest Hemingway interviewed by George Plimpton, *Writers at Work: The Paris Review Interviews* (New York, Viking, 1965), p. 235.

199 Robert Lipsyte, "Mets Beat Giants 8–6," in *The New York Times,* August 5, 1966.

203 Mike Recht, "Mets Shock Giants," Associated Press story in *The Kalamazoo Gazette,* August 5, 1966.

213 Sidney Cox, *Indirections* (New York, Viking, 1962), p. 131.

212 Lois Berg, "Old Creepy Death," *Western Review,* Western Michigan University (November 22, 1965), p. 2.

214 Wallace Stevens, "Adagia," *Opus Posthumous* (New York, Alfred A. Knopf, 1957), p. 176.

222 Issa, in *To Walk in Seasons,* edited by W. H. Cohen (Tokyo, Charles E. Tuttle Publishing Co., Inc.), p. 64.

222 Oemaru, in *To Walk in Seasons,* edited by W. H. Cohen (Tokyo, Charles E. Tuttle Publishing Co., Inc.), p. 86.

226 William Carlos Williams, "The Dance," *The Collected Later Poems* (New York, New Dimensions, 1950), p. 11.

226 William Carlos Williams, "Poem," *The Collected Earlier Poems* (New York, New Directions, 1951), p. 340.

244 Gabor Peterdi, *Printmaking* (New York, Macmillan, 1959), p. xxii.

245 J. D. Salinger, *Catcher in the Rye* (New York, New American Library, 1953), p. 157.

247 William Hazlitt, *The Spirit of the Age* (London, Oxford University Press, 1904), pp. 130–131.

250 Archibald MacLeish, "Poetry and the Press," in *Thought and Statement,* edited by William G. Leary and James Steel Smith (New York, Harcourt, Brace, 1960), p. 481.

250 Mark Twain, "The Evidence in the Case," *Ibid.,* p. 373.

250 Walter Lippmann, "Stereotypes," *Ibid.,* p. 221.

250 Ivan Turgenev, "A Fire at Sea," *Ibid.,* p. 25.

250 E. M. Forster, "Anonymity, An Inquiry," *Ibid.,* pp. 440–441.

251 E. B. White, "Walden," *Ibid.,* p. 39.

251 Ezra Pound, *The ABC of Reading* (New York, New Directions, 1960), p. 64.

252 William Hazlitt, *The Spirit of the Age* (London, Oxford University Press, 1904), p. 76.

253 George Eliot, *Middlemarch* (New York, Houghton Mifflin, 1956), p. 52.

254 Reynolds Price, *A Long and Happy Life* (New York, Avon Books, 1960), p. 121.

256 Ben Jonson, *Timber, or Discoveries,* in *English Prose, 1600–1660,* edited by Victor Harris and Itrat Husain (New York, Holt, Rinehart, and Winston, 1965), p. 330.

index

Adjectives, 27, 116
Adverbs, 115
All, use of, 36
Alliteration, 186–187
Alternating current, 207–213
Ambiguity, 47
And, use of, 49
Apologies, 48
Apostrophe, 259–260
Assignments
COLLECTING
(1) children's statements, 12
(2) Engfish, 12
(3) five fabulous realities, 62
(4) more fabulous realities, 62
(5) clichés, 93
REVISING
(1) tightening, 36
(2) Whooery, Whichery, Thatery, Namery, 39
(3) verbosity, 39
(4) revising case history, 74
(5) repetitions in case history, 80
(6) Is-ness, 112
(7) Is-ness, 112
(8) It-ache, There-ache, 113
(9) weak verbs, adjectives, adverbs, 118
(10) word order, 246
(11) word order, 252
WRITING
(1) free, unfocused, 17
(2) more free unfocused, 20
(3) free, focused, 21–24
(4) free, 20–30 minutes, 24
(5) dialogues, 58
(6) long fabulous reality, 63
(7) case history, 71–74
(8) free repeating, 80
(9) playing with comparisons, 83
(10) childhood experience, 104
(11) shaping a free writing, 126
(12) shaping case history and childhood story, 126
(13) twisting clichés, 129
(14) word play with titles, 131
(15) word play, 113
(16) notes for metaphors, 137
(17) free metaphors, 139
(18) central issue of the day, 154
(19) keeping a journal, 155
(20) working up a journal entry, 166
(21) repeated entries on one subject, 166
(22) why a writing affects you, 172
(23) differences and likenesses, 182
(24) recording sounds, 193
(25) a report, 211
(26) an editorial or column, 211
(27) a short poem, 222

(28) three haiku poems, 223
(29) forging a poem, 228
(30) interviewing classmates, 239
(31) interviewing an outsider, 243

Baldwin, James, 83
Before and After, 124
Beginnings, 49, 104–105
Beum, Robert, 189
Bias, 197
Bibliography entries, 262
"Big Smile," 142
"Big Swallows," 149
"Bird," 99
"Birth of a Lamb, The," 69
Boatwright, James, 98
"Bookstore," 224
Borrowing words, 264
Bradbury, Ray, 44
Broyard, Anatole, 168–172
"Bumps," 216
Butler, Samuel, 17, 84, 85, 119, 133, 135, 140, 157, 181

Capote, Truman, 105, 173
Car and Driver, 27
Carroll, Lewis, 132, 139
Case histories, 67–74
Categorizing words, 37
"Centaur, The," 96
Chase, Stuart, 74
Chaucer, 260
Chekhov, Anton, 106
Childhood, writing about, 95–108
Ciardi, John, 29, 46
Clark, Kenneth, 119
Clichés, 94, 129, 220
Colons, 254–257
Commas, 254–257
Comparing, 124, 136, 182–183
Compression, in poems, 223
Conrad, Joseph, 131
Conventions of writing, 253–265
Conversations, 52–59
Cox, Sidney, 33, 52, 98, 131, 185, 195, 213
Crockett, Davy, 195–197, 209, 213
Cummings, E. E., 130–131, 165

"Dance, The," 226
Dangling constructions, 247
Dashes, 254–257
David and Goliath, as plot, 124
Death as a Fact of Life, 168
Deceiving Oneself, 41–51
Declaration of Independence, The, 1, 208
Delta Wedding, 14
Dialogue, 52–59
  punctuating and indenting of, 254
Did, use of, 51
Distance, in writing, 95
Donne, John, 14
"Don't Feel Bad," 152
Draftee's Confidential Guide, 30
Durso, Joseph, 27

Elegant variation, 76
Elevated language, 191, 207–213
Eliot, George, 253
Eliot, T. S., 88, 132
Emerson, Ralph, 63, 83, 117, 155
Endings, 108, 122
Engfish, 12
Exclamation mark, 265

Fabulous realities, 60–66
Falstaff, 136, 137
Footnotes, 261–262
Form, 119–126
Forster, E. M., 23
Francis, W. Nelson, 127
Franklin, Benjamin, 34, 165
Free writing, 14–24

Gag-humor, 134
Go, use of, 114

Grammar, 227, 244–252
Graves, Donald, 2

Hachiya, Michihiko, 68–69
Haiku poems, 222
Hamlet, 29, 165
Hart, James D., 195
Have, use of, 114
Hazlitt, William, 34, 129, 247
Helping circle, 80–94
Hemingway, Ernest, 197
Hendin, David, 168–171
Hiroshima Diary, 68–69
Hook, the, 125
Huckleberry Finn, 95–96
Huxley, Thomas Henry, 67

Ibid., 261
Iceberg principle, 197
Important, use of, 178, 181
In Cold Blood, 172–173
Indirections, 131
In fact, use of, 180
Interviewing, 230–243
Introductions, irrelevant, 48
Irony, 56–57
Is-ness, 111–112
It-ache, 113
Italics, 257

"Jabberwocky," 133
Jefferson, Thomas, 34, 247
Johnson, Samuel, 15, 259
Jonson, Ben, 168, 256, 260
Journals, 155–167
Journey, as plot, 124
Joy of Cooking, The, 30
Just, use of, 221

Kazin, Alfred, 25
Kind of, use of, 178
Kitchen language, 207–213

Lambert, Dorothy, 158
Lardner, Ring, 135
Lenin, 205–206
Libel, 74
Lightness, 30
Lipsyte, Robert, 199
"Little Spot, A," 205–206
London, Jack, 62–63
Lu Po Hua, 230, 233

Macbeth, 77
Make, use of, 114, 118
Malaprop, Mrs., 253
Metaphor, 127–139
Milton, John, 218–221
Moore, Henry, 24
Moore, Lilian, 80
Moore, Marianne, 91
Morgan, Anne Haven, 28, 130, 191
Morley, Robert, 9
"My Sorceress," 43

Namery, 37–39
"Neat," 141
New, use of, 77
Nietzsche, Friedrich, 12
Nugent, Elliott, 123
Numerals, 258

Objectivity, 172
O'Connor, Frank, 55
Of course, use of, 180
"Old Creepy Death," 212
On the Beach, 166
Once, Secret of, 18–20
Order of words, 244–252
Osler, Sir William, 41
Owen, Wilfred, 131
Oxford Companion to American Literature, 195

Page, abbreviation for, 260–261
Paine, Thomas, 77

Paragraph, sign for, 260
Parallel construction, 80–83, 189
Periods, 254–256
Peterdi, Gabor, 244
Pickle for a Nickle, A, 80
"Pirate Ship, The," 102–103
Plagiarism, 165–166
Playing with words, 127–139
Plot, 123
"Poem," 226–227
"Poems," 214–215
Poems, writing of, 214–229
Point, in writing, 121
Pound, Ezra, 88, 121
Price, Reynolds, 106, 135
Pronoun signaling, 245, 249
Pseudonyms, 150
Punctuating dialogue, 254
Puns, 127

Questions, false, 47–48
Quindlen, Anna, 1–2
Quotation marks, 257–258
Quote, use of, 264

Rather, use of, 50
Recht, Mike, 203
Reading aloud, 2–8
"Reed," 72
Repeat-and-vary, 35
Repeating, 75–79
Reports, 195–213
Rhyme, 80, 214
Rhythm, 189–193
Roget, *Thesaurus,* 41
Rombauer, Irma S. and Marion B., 30, 83

Salinger, J. D., 96
Saroyan, William, 174
Scholarly writing, 260–264
Sears catalog, 26
Semicolons, 254–256
Seuss, Dr., 77
Shakespeare, 77, 135, 136, 137, 165, 202, 260
Shapiro, Karl, 189
Sharpening, 109–118
Shaw, Bernard, 62, 109
Shepherd, Jean, 28–29
Skid Row, U.S.A., 176
Something, use of, 181
"Sorrow, My True Story," 44
Sort of, use of, 178
Sound, 185–194
Sound effects, 194
Sounds
  of consonants, 185–188
  interior, 221
  of vowels, 188
Spender, Stephen, 48
Stafford, William, 18–19
Stevens, Wallace, 21, 71, 126, 214
Subject choosing you, 140–154
Subjectivity, 172
Suspense, 46–47
Swenson, May, 96

Tack-on sentences, 249–251
"Taps," 223
Tempest, The, 202
Thatery, 36
There-ache, 114–115
Thing, use of, 37
Thoreau, Henry, 60, 67, 129, 138, 155–157, 165
"Three Deaths," 225
Through the Looking Glass, 132
Thurber, James, 123
Tightening, 34–40
Titles, 131, 259
Truthtelling, 14–17
Twain, Mark (Clemens), 95–96
Tweedledum and Tweedledee, 132

Van Doren, Mark, 29
Vaughan, Henry, 135
Verbs, metaphorical, 112
Voice, in writing, 1–8, 49, 192

Walden, 138
Way of All Flesh, The, 133
Weasel words, 178–179, 182
Welty, Eudora, 14, 41, 123, 245
What, use of, 36
Which, reference of, 246
Whichery, 36
Whitehead, Alfred North, 22
Whooery, 36
Wiebe, Gerhart, 197
Williams, William Carlos, 226–227
Word order, 244
Word play, 78, 127–139
Wordsworth, William, 95, 215, 219